Jean-Baptiste Morin

Astrologia Gallica

Book Thirteen
The Proper Natures and Strengths of the Individual Planets and the Fixed Stars

Book Fourteen
The Primum Caelum and its Division into Twelve Parts

Book Fifteen
The Essential Dignities of the Planets

Book Nineteen
The Elements of Astrology or the Principles of Judgments

Translated from the Latin
By
James Herschel Holden, M.A.
Fellow of the American Federation of Astrologers

First Printing 2006

ISBN-10: 0-86690-571-5
ISBN-13: 978-0-86690-571-8

Published by:
American Federation of Astrologers, Inc.
6535 S. Rural Road
Tempe, AZ 85283

Printed in the United States of America.

Table of Contents

This is an omnibus edition of the translations of Books 13-15 & 19. Each book is complete with its own Title Page, Table of Contents, Translator's Preface, Text, and Index of Persons.

Jean-Baptiste Morin

Astrologia Gallica

Book Thirteen

The Proper Natures and Strengths of the Individual Planets and the Fixed Stars

Translated from the Latin

By

James Herschel Holden, M.A.
Fellow of the American Federation of Astrologers

TABLE OF CONTENTS

Translator's Preface

In *Astrologia Gallica*, Book 13, Morin discusses some of the fundamental technical terms used in astrology and also sets forth the influences of the seven planets in great detail in a very nicely designed tabular format. Due to the smaller size of the pages of this translation and my inherent dislike of text printed sideways, I have not attempted to reproduce the tables in their original format, but instead I have listed their contents sequentially.

As I have done in my translations of other books of the *Astrologia Gallica*, I have tried to turn Morin's scholarly Latin into readable English as literally as possible. But he had a large vocabulary, and rather than attempting to match him by studding the English sentences with uncommon words, I have used more common renderings of seldom encountered Latin words. I have also tried to keep paraphrase to a minimum.

Also, as previously, I have retained the Latin word *Caelum* 'sky' as a technical term; it refers to the zodiac and the placement of the Sun, Moon, planets, and fixed stars in it at a particular moment. I have also retained *Primum Caelum* 'first sky', which refers to the supposed outer sphere of the universe more commonly called *Primum Mobile*, which contains the signs of the zodiac And the reader will find that in this book (from p. 62 on) Morin frequently uses the word "space" as a synonym for "house."

As a writer, Morin resembles a college professor teaching a course in astrology. He talks extensively about each topic that he introduces, explaining the background and the justifications of the rules that he introduces. From time to time he even raises objections to the rules and refutes them. And he cites the rules that some of his predecessors have stated and discusses them. Thus, the reader not only learns what Morin believed to be true, but he is also introduced to some alternative theories that were current in the 17th century. Some of this may seem excessive, but Morin took great pains to discuss all aspects of his topics.

If this is the first book of the *Astrologia Gallica* that the reader has taken up, he will be immediately struck by the length of some of the sentences. Morin sometimes extends a sentence into half of a page. His idea of the proper length of a paragraph also differs considerably from ours. I have occasionally broken up some of his long sentences into two or more shorter ones, but more often I have kept them together with commas, semi-colons, and dashes. I have occasionally used italics to emphasize a word where Morin did not, and I have added some words in brackets where I thought they were needed.

Also, the reader may find that after having read one of Morin's extra long sentences, he is uncertain whether he has understood it. In such a case, my advice is to read it again and think about how the several clauses fit together. Morin is not an especially easy author. He should not be skimmed. To derive the maximum benefit from what he has to say, it may be necessary to re-read some parts of it and think about them. Unlike most astrological writers, Morin does not simply state a rule, but as mentioned above he also discusses the reasons for the rule.

One feature of Morin's discussion that is seldom encountered in modern astrological texts is his quotations from the Bible and his not infrequent digressions into religious or philosophical justifications of the rules and explanations that he sets forth. Morin was a devout Catholic, and he was at pains to try to show that nothing in his book was contrary to Catholic dogma. This was partly due to the sincerity of his personal religious beliefs and partly due to a desire to avoid giving religious opponents of astrology obvious targets to attack. But he also tried to find Biblical justification for some of his explanations or procedures.

The reader will also find frequent references to Claudius Ptolemy's *Tetrabiblos* (or *Quadripartite*, as the Latin translation was called). Morin seems to have generally cited the Latin version printed by Jerome Cardan in his voluminous *Commentary on the Quadripartite*. Since the numbering of the chapters in that text does not agree exactly with those in F.E. Robbins's edition and translation of the *Tetrabiblos* in the Loeb Classical Library, I have generally changed the chapter numbers cited by Morin to agree with the chapter numbers in the LCL version. And I have sometimes expanded Morin's citations of passages in Cardan's book to agree with the numbering in the Lyons omnibus edition of Cardan's works published in 1663. (Morin of course used an earlier edition, which I have not seen.) I do not have access to all of the books by the other authors that Morin mentions from time to time, so I am unable to augment his references to those. I have, however, supplied references to their place and date of publication.

It will soon become obvious to the reader that Morin usually cites Ptolemy or Cardan merely in order to disagree with their statements. In the 17th century they were considered to be the two leading authorities on astrology. And, since Morin had devised a system of astrology that differed in important respects from the tradition set forth by his two eminent predecessors, he felt obliged to point out the differences and explain why he thought that his system was preferable. He particularly cites numerous passages from Cardan and delivers what he believed to be logical arguments against them. And he also cites passages from Jofrancus Offusius (16th century) in order to show that from his point of view they too were erroneous. Offusius, like Morin, had discarded a good bit of traditional astrology and substituted a system of his own devising. But not surprisingly, Morin thought that his own system was better than Offusius's, and he goes into detail to explain why. I think the reader will agree with him. However, we must remember that Ptolemy, Cardan, and Offusius all lived before the invention of the telescope. Consequently, some of their statements relating to the structure of the solar system, while generally believed to be correct as late as the end of the 16th century, were found to be incorrect in the early 17th century.

In Section 1, Chapters 2 & 3, of the present book, Morin goes on at great length about the strengths of the planets, even assigning numerical values to them and criticizing the methods that Offusius had used and the numerical values that he had assigned. This could perhaps be called an excursion into *physical* astrology—that is, an attempt to quantify the actual strength of the astrological influences. It is a topic that has not attracted many astrologers, and the 21st century reader who is mainly interested in learning how to interpret horoscopes may not find it especially helpful, but it was Morin's attempt to apply scientific measurement procedures to astrology.

From time to time in the *Astrologia Gallica*, Morin mentions some of the brighter fixed stars, and in Section 3, Chapter 5, of the present book he lists the ones that he thinks are of the most importance. For the benefit of the reader, I have added two tables of those fixed stars in Appendix 1 and Appendix 2. The longitudes and latitudes are given for 1 January 1600 (I chose that date because it is approximately in the middle of the dates of the example charts that Morin cites in the later books) and for 1 January 2000. If the reader requires their positions for some other year not too far removed from either of those dates, he need only change the longitudes by adding (or, for earlier dates, by subtracting) 50 seconds of arc for each year removed from 1600 or 2000. The latitudes will remain very nearly unchanged.

Finally, I might mention that I previously published a translation of the "Table of Universal Rulerships of the Planets" in an addendum to my translation of *Astrologia Gallica*, Book 22.[1] It is reprinted here without any essential change. I would like to thank Mr. Sriram Ponoda, who, at the suggestion of my friend Robert Corre, prepared a CD-ROM containing the entire text of my translation of Book 22. I no longer had a computer version of that text, so I was able to copy the needed text of the Table from the CD-ROM, thereby saving me the trouble of re-typing the previous translation or scanning the individual pages.

And I also want to thank my friend Kris Brandt Riske for converting my word-processor files to publishing files and seeing the present book through the publishing process.

James Herschel Holden, January 2005

[1] Jean-Baptiste Morin, *Astrologica Gallica/Book Twenty-two/Directions* (Tempe, Az.: A.F.A., Inc., 1994). This book is still available from the publisher.

ASTROLOGIA GALLICA

BOOK THIRTEEN

PREFACE

In Book 9, the Planets were shown to be mixed from elements of the Ether and the Caelum. *And in Books 11 and 12, the celestial bodies' various powers of acting were only set forth in general terms. Now it seems appropriate to scrutinize the proper natures of the Planets more thoroughly, to the extent that we have been able to do this by logic and experience. In truth, the proper nature of each Planet is twofold—namely, substantial and accidental. The substantial form of the Planet is unique in number. But the accidental is found to be threefold—that is, elemental, ethereal, and celestial—for a Planet is composed of a threefold kind of mixture of these, as was stated in Book 9. For having thus mixed the sublunars, the natures, accidentals, and strengths are diverse, from the diverse mixture of which they are composed; as is plain in vinegar, the rose, opium, etc.; in which a nature that is hot and cold, or watery and fiery is perceived at the same time, each of which works by itself. Moreover, the elemental nature of the Planets is not unique and simple, because not all of them consist of one and the same element, but rather of manifold elements; and all are contained in them formally, on account of the mixture of elements, and also eminently on account of the adjoined celestial material, to which the strengths of the elements belong. And all of them are apparent from the production of heat and cold in these inferior things—the formal to be sure, because the Sun sensibly heats, and Saturn, as well as the Moon in new Moons or eclipses, cools; but [it is] also eminent because when the Sun is subterranean, if it is the ruler of the ASC, it impresses a hot temperament upon the native, which cannot be from the formal or actual heat of the Sun, which cannot penetrate the entire Earth; but it is [also] found to be especially ethereal from the diverse motion in men of the humors, spirits & corporeal faculties; and finally, it is celestial from the various accidents of good fortune or misfortune that affect during life the body, the mental makeup, and external good events, as will be explained in its own place. These natures must now be discussed individually, and first the elementals.*

SECTION I
The Elemental, Etheric, and Celestial Nature of the Planets.

Chapter 1.

That Ptolemy, Cardan, and the other Old Astrologers made Many Errors in Handing down the Elemental Nature of the Planets.

This, moreover, must be begun with that prince of astrologers, Ptolemy,[1] who indeed in assigning the individual qualities of the individual planets, did not deviate much from the truth, but with regard to their causes he lapsed into the absurd and contradictory, namely since he expounds the arrangement of the planets and their distance from the Earth, the Sun, and from each other for causes in Book I, Chapter 4 of the *Quadripartite*. For if (as he will have it), Saturn is cold and dry because it is very greatly distant from the heat of the Sun and the vapors of the Earth; therefore, by that same reasoning Mars will be colder than Venus, because it is indeed more distant from the Sun. Moreover, Jupiter will be drier than Mars, because it is further from the Earth. Besides, if Jupiter is consequently of a temperate nature because it moves in the middle between the chilling Saturn and the burning Mars, therefore Mars, which is in the middle between Jupiter and Venus, will be the most temperate of all the planets. And yet all these things in Ptolemy are absurd and contradictory. Besides, when he says that the Moon is humid because it is closest to the Earth and adjacent to its humid vapors, he is very much mistaken if he thinks that the humid vapors of the Earth extend to the Moon, so that it is thereby

[1] Claudius Ptolemy (2nd century). The references are to his *Tetrabiblos* (or *Quadripartite)*. Morin usually cites that work from Cardan's *Commentary,* but I have altered Morin's numbering of the chapters to agree with the Loeb Classical Library edition and translation by F. E. Robbins (London and Cambridge, Mass., 1940), which is a convenient source for the modern reader. Morin often disagrees with Ptolemy.

made humid; and it must not be sought here what sort [of body] the Moon is from [those] vapors, but what sort it is inherently; for the sort that it is inherently should produce effects of that kind, as is plain from the Sun, which consequently heats because it is inherently hot and fiery. Ptolemy is also mistaken when he says similarly that the Moon does heat a little, and that is because it receives the light of the Sun. For the *light* of the Sun does not heat, as we have shown in Book 11, but rather its *heat*, which heats up the Earth and the waters from their inherent coldness. And the very nature of the Moon is not hot, but cold, as the sympathy of the Moon with the waters testifies, and also as the Moon herself [does] in eclipses. Finally, he wrongly asserts that Jupiter is humid, since a moderate dryness agrees with it better, as will be shown in its own place, and as has already been stated in Book 9, Section 3, Chapter 8.

Therefore, it was preferable to Ptolemy and more appropriate to the science to hunt down the intrinsic natures of the planets from their own characteristic effects, namely because these are assimilated to their own causes, and consequently they can detect them at least *a posteriori*; whence, Proclus[1] rightly says "the effective forces of the stars and the planets must be taken from that which they exercise upon us," which nevertheless you should understand as it is, and not from the vapors or prime qualities diffused through the ambient, since it is certain that the stars affect us through the medium of their own strength; and in the rigid winter [cold], men are born who are hot-blooded and peevish; just as in the fiery summer, cold-natured and phlegmatic ones are born, as is proved by daily experience.

But Cardan[2] erred to begin with in his *Commentary on the*

[1] Proclus the Philosopher (412-485) was the last important classical philosopher. *A Paraphrase of Ptolemy's Tetrabiblos* is attributed to him. The Latin translation by Leo Allatius (1586-1669) of the Greek text was published by Elsevir at Leiden in 1635. It is probably that book to which Morin refers.

[2] Jerome Cardan (1501-1576), Italian physician, mathematician, astrologer, and prolific miscellaneous writer. His extensive *Commentary on the Quadripartite* (in Latin) was first published at Basel by M. Petri in 1554 and subsequently re-

Quadripartite of Ptolemy, because he held him to be an Evangelist, from whose teaching down to the least detail he had received out of reverence [not wanting] to depart [from it]; and he has delivered himself up to defend Ptolemy in everything, [while] here and there asserting that some particular thing had become known to no one before himself. Then, in expounding those things he lapsed into many errors, and frequently he proposes things that are the more absurd, the more true, and the greater mysteries that he offers. Therefore, I—the slave of no author—but free in my intellect to philosophize, and intent on nature alone; I shall also comment on Cardan's errors about the natures of the planets, because that is a matter of great moment, as something that relates to the [fundamental] principles of astrology; and Cardan's authority has led many persons astray who were too credulous or less perspicacious, to the great harm of astrology and philosophy, although it may frankly be confessed that many things have also been set forth accurately and skillfully by him, so that among all the other astrologers who have philosophized on this most abstruse science, he deserves the first place. But we are men living here in a darkness, which to penetrate and dissipate by the force of the intellect is troublesome and very difficult; and I do not profess that I myself among the other recent [authorities] am immune from criticism; and also it is not required that I should rebut [all] the individual errors of it, for that would be too lengthy, too tedious—indeed superfluous—and would require a special book even more extensive than his *Commentary on Ptolemy's Tetrabiblos* is; but instead I shall only rebut his principal errors, where it seems to be necessary, for [the rebuttal of] the rest will be evident from the true principles of astrology propounded by me.

And so, Cardan in Book 1, Chapter 4, Text XIX, of his *Com-*

---

printed. It contains a Latin translation of Ptolemy's *Tetrabiblos* and Cardan's *Commentary*. I have used the omnibus edition of Cardan's books (Lyons: Huguetan & Ravaud, 1663. 10 vols; New York and London: Johnson Reprint, 1967. 10 vols. repr. in facs.). The *Commentary* is in vol. 5, and all references hereafter are to the numbering and pages of that edition. Morin usually cites Cardan in order to disagree with him.

mentary supposes in the first place that "there are only two qualities in nature, one acting *celestially*, and it is called heat, and the other, which is moisture, called *elemental*,"[1] but he says that cold and dryness are only deprivations, the latter of moisture and the former of heat. Which plainly erroneous opinion has already been sufficiently refuted by us in Book 3, Section 1, Chapter 3. Moreover, from that false foundation he deduces that "all the stars are hot, because they act,"[2] as if only heat could be capable of acting; and from that, would it not also follow that ice is hot, which to be sure at least drives heat from the subject, which heat it would be foolish to deny cannot be expelled except by some acting force. Moreover, he is out of his wits when he says, "heat is not simply a quality, but a substance in light;"[3] first, because he will have it that heat is a substance, and then because he will have it that light is a subject of that sort of substance. As for that, when he says that heat is not a quality, and when he confirms that same [statement] further on, saying that neither the Sun nor any other star is endowed with any quality, he contradicts himself, since he asserted earlier that there are only two qualities in nature, namely celestial heat and elemental moisture. But he contradicts himself again when he says that heat is twofold and moisture is also twofold; once indeed by substance by which, he says, the Sun is very hot and very moist;[4] and again according to an impressed quality, by which the

[1] Cardan (p. 120, col. 2) actually says this: *declarauimus . . . non esse nisi duas qualitates, unam quidem agentem coelestemque, & vocatur calor cui opponitur priuatio quae est frigiditas, alteram quae est humidum elementale, cui siccitas, tanquam priuatio opposita est* . . . 'we have declared . . .that there are only two qualities, one indeed acting and celestial, and it is called heat, to which is opposed its deprivation which is cold, the other which is elemental moisture, to which dryness, as its deprivation, is opposed'.

[2] Cardan, loc. cit, *Omnia igitur astro calida sunt, quia omnia aliqud operantur* 'All the stars are hot, because they all do something'.

[3] Cardan, Text XXX (p. 122, col. 2), *Sednec simpliciter calor qualitasest . . . sed substantiam in lumine, vt icon dixi* 'But heat is not simply a quality . . . but a substance in light, as I have already said'.

[4] Cardan, Text XXIX (p. 121, col. 2). He says that the Sun must be very hot and very humid because, of all the planets, it promotes the longest life among men,

Sun is moderately hot and a little bit dry; for when he makes the Sun to be very moist by substance, he admits some moisture other than elemental; which he only calls "according to the impressed quality;" consequently, there will be many more qualities than the two mentioned by him above. Well then, [you can see] how badly Cardan's doctrine on the qualities of the stars hangs together!

But all the same, he tries to assert that Saturn is the author of cold, and since it is colder than any other star, it always chills. And he explains that in two ways: first, "because Saturn has less of any kind of heat than any other star, and therefore joined to the Moon it is said to chill, because it heats less than the Moon;" "for less heat," he says, "mixed with more heat is moderated, as is plain from lukewarm and hot water mixed together."[1] Truly here Cardan is mistaken. For in the case of water, the temperature is not made by the reduced heat of the lukewarm [portion], but by cold allied to it; and that is proved from this: because never does less heating reduce the effect of more heating by its own heat; even so, moreover, less light by its own light does not reduce the light of a brighter object; otherwise, it would be action from a proportion of a lesser inequality, which in nature is absurd. Since if heat can act upon heat, it is agreeable to reason that a greater thing can increase a lesser thing as much as the latter can reduce the former, or adulterate its quantity. Secondly, "because Saturn impedes the work of the other hotter stars," but by what strength does it impede? Certainly, not by a greater heat, hypothetically, nor even a lesser heat; for, since it is entirely certain that a united strength is stronger than a separated one, as experience proves, it is necessary that by many heats

---

and that would require much heat and much moisture. But then he tries to reconcile that statement with Ptolemy's dictum that the Sun is very hot and a little dry (for Ptolemy does not say that the Sun is moist). Morin seized upon this disagreement and derides it at some length.

[1] Cardan, Text XXX (p. 123, col. 1), . . . *quia iunctus Lunae frigiditatem auget, maxime hyemis tempore, sed id etiamfit, quia cum Saturni color minor sit quam Lunae, vt tepida aquaferuenti mixta, minus calidam efficit seruente* ' . . .because joined to the Moon it increases the cold, especially in the time of winter, but this is also done because since Saturn's heat is less than the Moon's, as lukewarm water mixed with boiling water makes it less hot'.

occurring together, a more intense effect is produced from all of them than from any one of them as individuals; and it is ridiculous to suppose that the light and heat of the Sun are impeded by the light and heat of a candle; therefore, it is necessary that Saturn chills by some other quality than heat, which cannot be anything other than the actual cold of Saturn.

Besides, since Cardan has explained his own ideas in a rather confused and outlandish way, intermixed too with many contradictions, so that they can hardly be understood anywhere, I shall explain them briefly here. And so, he would have it that no star is affected formally by any elemental quality, as for example those of heat and humidity, which he supposes to be alone in nature, but they only contain them by strength, or especially when he says that "a star is hot and humid by substance;" and yet he will have it that those stars are effectively hot and humid—that is, such qualities are impressed on sublunar bodies—when he says "a star is hot and humid according to the impressed quality;" and this is the common doctrine of Ptolemy, Aristotle, and the other old philosophers who deny all generation or corruptive alteration in the *Caelum*;[1] which, since that is erroneous, as was made plain in this century from the generation of new stars, comets, and sunspots, it only remains to be said here that Cardan also erred along with the old authorities. Moreover, he erred more seriously in other things when he allows [only] a unique active quality, i.e. heat, in the stars, since light is another active quality arising from heat; besides, not only did many of the older authorities[2] think that there are influences that are greatly active qualities, both in method and heat and light; but we have most plainly proved that in Book 12, Chapter 27.

And so, having rejected his opinion on the qualities of the

[1] Here and elsewhere below I have chosen to keep the Latin word *Caelum* as a technical term rather than translate it as 'sky'. It of course designates the outer space beyond the Earth and all the things in it.

[2] Here Morin notes the contrast between the ancient views and the modern ones. The ancients held that the *Caelum* was inalterable. The invention of the telescope in the early 17th century disproved this by showing various changes in the *Caelum*.

stars in general, it must now be seen what he thinks about the individual planets. And first, he says about the Sun that it is very hot and very humid according to its substance, but according to its impressed quality, it is moderately hot and a little dry; that is, not so formally or by its action, but only by its strength is it very hot and very humid; for in fact by its impression or action, it is moderately hot and a little dry. But in Book 9, Section 3, Chapter 6, we have proved that it is formally hot. And since according to Cardan every star has the same sort of strength as it has (that is to say, *makes*) an impression, how can he call it very moist according to its substance, if according to its impression it is a little dry? Here again he contradicts himself. Besides, surely it will not dry up [things] because it is very moist? Indeed Cardan says—again contradicting himself—that on the Island of St. Thomas on the equator,[1] when winter occurs with the Sun standing vertically [overhead], with many vapors having been attracted into the air; therefore, the Sun, according to its impressed quality, will not be hot and dry there, but cold and moist; and for that reason it will also be that way according to its substance. Therefore, it is plain from Cardan [speaking] against himself that fiery qualities ought to be admitted to be in the Sun—in fact, the greatest heat with a reduced dryness—which is compatible with the airy or ethereal moisture mixed in the body of the Sun itself, as is plain in a flame in our country, which is nothing other than burning oil; for from those two qualities all the superior effects of the Sun are produced, either by itself or by accident.

But for the other celestial bodies, Cardan supposes that they shine in two different ways like the Moon—namely by their own light and by that of the Sun—but that is also erroneous in the case of the fixed stars and the planets; for the fixed stars shine only by their own light, and the light of the Sun does not reach them; but the planets, not excepting the Earth, are lacking in light of their own, and only their own opaque bodies receive their light on their surface from outside, [namely] from the Sun, and that [light] re-

[1] The Portugese Island São Tomé off the coast of West Africa at 0N41 6E01.

flects upon these lower places,[1] as is plain from the horned shape of the Moon and Venus;[2] and we have already proved all of these things in their own place. Consequently therefore, Cardan errs when he says that the Moon moistens by its own light and by attracting vapors by the Sun's light, but it heats only by the reflected light of the Sun. As for this, if it acts by both lights, then it heats by both lights, and it cannot attract vapors by both unless it heats by both, or it will have to be said that vapors are not made by heat, and not raised up, which Cardan himself does not allow.

After that, expounding the natures of the other planets, he says "Saturn receives the rays of the Sun only weakly because it withdraws very much from it, and therefore it heats very little" (and, with respect to us, it chills very much), but it dries a little because it is far distant from the moist Earth, from which it cannot raise up many vapors." And this is Ptolemy's doctrine that was already rejected above as being plainly absurd, since the planets themselves take their proper natures not more from themselves and from their distance from the Sun or the Earth, than the Sun or the Earth take from their own distance, or from the mutual distance between them and the others; and those planets have proper natures before they raise vapors. And about the rest of the planets, Cardan agrees with Ptolemy, already refuted above, but about the Moon (which he makes to be equally moist and hot with the Sun) he disagrees, because he attributes its own heat to it, very similarly to the heat of Saturn; and from that it follows that like Saturn it chills, against Ptolemy's opinion. But the Moon according to Ptolemy himself and Cardan ought to be hotter too than Mars, namely because it is nearer the Sun. And if someone says that Cardan is to be understood here [as speaking] about the *proper* heat of the Moon, not about its coming forth from rays and its distance from the Sun, Why, I say, is the [amount of] heat determined in the case of the other planets by that distance, and not in the case of the

---

[1] By "these lower places,' Morin means the Earth.

[2] It was observed in the telescope that Venus could assume a crescent shape like the Moon.

Moon? Indeed, why does he admit a proper heat in the case of the Moon, and not in the case of the other planets, since all of them act by their proper strength, and whatever they do, they do by means of heat according to Cardan [as mentioned] above? But if he admits it in all of them, why does he determine their natures from that which is extrinsic and alien to them, but not proper to them? It is, therefore, most evidently plain how badly Ptolemy and Cardan have philosophized about the natures of the planets; that is why, having repudiated their doctrine, we believe that we must stand on those things that were said by us in Book 9, Section 3, about such elementary natures of the planets, since they agree with effects and experiences.

And Marsilio Ficino[1] must also not be listened to in Book 2, Chapter 6, of his [translation of the] *Enneads* of Plotinus,[2] where having followed the opinion of Averroes[3] and Abraham Avenezra,[4] he asserts, "In the *Caelum* there is nothing of cold or dryness, but only heat and humor; and the planets that abound more in humor, such as Saturn, heat things less, and because of that they are said to be cold; but those that abound more in heat, such as the Sun and Mars, are said to be hotter and dry, because they are less moist." For except that Plotinus and the other Platonists scarcely ever prove any of those things that they offer; if moisture would predominate in Saturn, it would moisten [things] by itself, but on the contrary it dries [them], as is plain from the temperaments of the natives over whom it rules, especially from [a position in] fire or earth signs, by which its proper dryness is not moderated.

---

[1] Marsilio Ficino (1433-1499), famous Italian Greek scholar and Platonist. Translator (into Latin) of works by Plato and Plotinus (the *Enneads)*.

[2] First printed at Florence in 1492, and reprinted at Basel in 1580 with the Greek text edited by Petrus Perna.

[3] Abû-l-Walîd ibn Rushd (1126-1198), Arabian philosopher, known for his commentaries on Aristotle and the neo-Platonists.

[4] Abraham ibn Ezra (1092-1167), famous Jewish scholar, known to astrologers for his books *The Beginning of Wisdom* and *Nativities* that were translated into Latin in the 12th century.

But it does not seem that the inexperience of those common astrologers ought to be omitted, who never seem to acknowledge either formally or eminently the quality of heat, cold, moisture, or dryness in any planet, while in thinking about the temperament of natives, they settle the nature of a planet by the nature of the sign in which it is posited; as, if Saturn and Venus were in air signs, they make them both and equally hot and moist; if in earth signs, both and equally cold and dry, without having taken into consideration the proper nature of the planets, as if they would take their force of acting from the signs alone, and that force would be varied immediately by a change of sign, both of which [assertions] are rejected by us in Book 20. But while we are contemplating removing the above said errors, it seems that it ought to be stated and warning given that the intellect of man is too weak to define the elemental qualities precisely; and yet, although this determination, if not exact, is at least reasonable and concordant with experience, it is of the utmost necessity in astrological [considerations], and for that reason we shall expound it here in what follows below, having taken into account only the qualities predominating in the individual planets or the qualities that are contrary to that predomination.

Chapter 2.

In which the Elemental Strengths of the Individual Planets are Determined from the Experiences of Astrologers with Respect to the Terrestrial Globe.

It is absurd that astrologers generally want to be very exact in calculating the places of the planets, and [yet] they have not thought out any accurately defined reason for the strength of a planet, since they nevertheless investigate houses with regard to their strengths, and that from the kinds that they are, they produce the same effects; but so that we may remedy this defect in their strengths, it will be necessary for us to proceed thus.

It was prescribed by Ptolemy, and the more skilled of the astrologers taught by experience, that Venus is naturally hot and moist, but that moisture predominates in it; therefore, let it be ½ degree hot and 4 degrees moist. Besides, even if Cardan in his *Commentary on the Quadripartite*, Book 1, chapter 4, states that Venus is hotter than Jupiter, because it is closer to the Sun, and brighter by its own light (as he badly opines) than Jupiter itself; nevertheless, Ptolemy and all the rest make Jupiter to be hotter than Venus, but less moist, but in the truth of the matter it is a little dry; therefore, let its heat be put at 1½ and its dryness at 1. But now no one will deny that the Sun is hotter and dryer than Jupiter. Therefore, let its heat be at 5½ and its dryness at 2, seeing that by its own heat it overcomes the cold of both the Moon and Saturn. And finally then, everyone agrees that Mars is hotter and dryer than the Sun, not indeed in quantity but in quality; that is, of the planets it pours forth the highest heat, but a smaller amount, for if it were more abundant, it would be too much corruptive and lethal. But the Sun on the other hand pours out a more copious amount, but a milder form, which is generative and also vital. Let us, therefore, put the heat of Mars at 2½ and its dryness at 3. But to Saturn, which is cold and dry, let there be given 3½ [degrees] of cold and 3 of dryness. But to the Moon, which we experience to be the moistest of all, even though its moistness is of somewhat dulled strength in acting, let there be given 6 degrees of moistness. And because it is cold, but less cold than the Sun is hot, let us suppose that its cold is at 5 degrees; moreover, that I have attributed so much cold to the Moon, and more than [the amount] to Saturn, hardly any astrologer will contest, who will contemplate with an attentive mind, that the Moon rules Cancer, the coldest of the signs, and that both in her own [eclipses] and in total eclipses of the Sun she noticeably cools these sublunar [regions].

Now the one [planet] remaining to us will be Mercury, which astrologers want to be of no personal nature, but [rather] to be like Proteus,[1] convertible to whatever nature, either of the sign in which it is placed, or of the planet to which it is joined, either by body or by aspect. But it is a very great error in astrology to deny

[1] In Greek mythology, a shape-shifting demi-god.

that Mercury has a proper nature, without which it would not exist. And the proper natures of the planets are not changed into others; namely, Mercury receives something from the Moon or Saturn—not the light, or the heat that they lack, nor their cold, on account of its closeness to the Sun, which defends Mercury from their cold; and much less does it receive the influence by which it acts on these inferior things; but the individual planets and the signs act individually with their own natures; and there is a mixture of their strengths in their concourse, as we have shown elsewhere. And although it can receive light and heat from the Sun, and like the Moon, reflect it upon these lower things according to its own measure; this is extrinsic to its own nature, in accordance with which it acts by itself, and which we are here inquiring into; moreover, some say that it is dry, and, among others, Ptolemy, in Book 1, Chapter 17, in which he discusses the exaltations of the planets, and then Pontanus at the end of Book 2 of his *De Rebus Coelestibus*,[1] and also Jofrancus Offusius, in his book *De Divina Astrorum Facultate*,[2] in which he discusses these elemental qualities of the stars most precisely. But I say in addition that Mercury itself is somewhat inherently cold, namely because it emulates the nature of Saturn before all the others, and they help each other mutually in acting, as experience proves; and this is confirmed by that text of Ptolemy in Book 3, chapter 12,[3] where he states that "Mer-

[1] Giovanni Gioviano Pontano (1426-1503), *De Rebus Coelestibus* (Naples: Sigismund Mayr, 1512).

[2] Offusius (16th century) was a German physician, astronomer, and astrologer who lived in France for many years. Like Morin, he rejected much of traditional astrology and devised his own system. His book *De divina astrorum facultate in larvatam astrologiam* [The Divine Power of the Stars against a Decadent Astrology] was published at Paris in 1570. Morin cites passages from Offusius's book mainly to disagree with them. It should be noted that, like Cardan, he lived and wrote before the revised view of the solar system and the cosmos was ushered in by the discoveries made by Galileo and others with the newly invented telescope in the early 1600s.

[3] Morin has Book 3, Chapter 17, which corresponds to Book 3, Chapter 16, Text LXI (p. 292 col. 2) in Cardan's *Commetary,* and to Book 3, Chapter 12 (p. 329), of Robbins's edition of the *Tetrabiblos*.

cury joined to Saturn inclines to cold, and joined to Mars to dryness." for indeed that "inclination to cold" cannot be perceived except in the greater cold [resulting] from Saturn and Mercury together, rather than from Saturn alone; whence it can be conjectured that each of these planets is inherently cold, for a united strength is stronger than a separated one. And the reasoning is the same for the dryness of Mercury conjoined with Mars; consequently 1½ degrees of cold are attributed by me to Mercury and 1 of dryness. And there are the above said qualities in the individual planets [arising] from their action and formally, or extrinsically; moreover, for the planets Saturn, Jupiter, Mars, Venus, and Mercury, opposite ones coincide with them intrinsically and eminently by an equal degree for the reason set forth elsewhere; and they coincide with these in their medium distance from the Earth, and in the horizon, also in the medium circle between both hemispheres, where those powers of theirs on the temperament of natives is apprehended to be most powerful; for, in accordance with their greater and lesser distance from the Earth, and not with respect to their altitude or depression from the horizon—those qualities in which they are varied to us—as we shall cite below from Jofrancus Offusius. For the moment, let this table be noted [see p. 24], in which is put just as much in the planets' essence of heat as of cold, and as much of moistness as of dryness, not otherwise than in those elements. And from which it is plain that the Sun and the Moon, arranged around the Earth,[1] are among the planets masculine and feminine of sublunar effects; and indeed the Sun is male, hot and dry, but the Moon is female, cold and moist.

Moreover, this table is more conformable to the natures and effects of the planets, and also to things that are pleasing to astrologers, than those [numbers] of Offusius, in which the Sun is supposed to be nearly twice as dry as it is hot, and four times dryer

[1] Morin had adopted Tycho Brahe's concept of the solar system, in which the Earth was at the center and both the Sun and the Moon revolved about it. This avoided censure by the Catholic Church that insisted upon the Earth's being the center of the universe.

	Heat	Cold	Wetness	Dryness
Sun	5½			2
Moon		5	6	
Saturn		3½		3
Jupiter	1½			1
Mars	2½			3
Venus	½		4	
Mercury		1½		1
Sum	10	10	10	10

than Mars, and that one is twelve times dryer than it is hot. Besides, Saturn is made to be four times colder than the Sun is made to be hot; Jupiter and Venus of about the same nature hot and moist, but each of these one hundred and twenty-eight times more moist than hot. Mercury, moreover, is equally as dry as Mars or Saturn. All of which deviates very much from the common opinion of astrologers, especially since he attributes four times more cold than heat to all the planets taken together, when, having added up the forces of the individual [planets], there is reported for their sum 28 degrees of heat, 114 of cold, 133 of moistness, and 85 of dryness. This table[1] will be fundamental for these things and a basis for the judgment of temperaments in nativities, not only for the planets, but also for the signs, aspects, and positions with respect to the Sun. For all of these things are referred to this table, as can be inferred from Section 2, Chapter 5 of the *Practice of Astrology*.[2]

[1] Morin means "my table as shown above."

[2] This sounds like the book that Morin mentions occasionally in other chapters of the *Astrologia Gallica* that he intended to write if God granted him longer life. But the fact that he here mentions Section and Chapter numbers would seem to imply that he had already written part of the book or else that he had at least constructed an outline of it. If so, it seems to have perished after his death.

Chapter 3.

In how many Ways a Superior Planet by its own Nature with Respect to us is Increased or Decreased.

Offusius rightly judges it firstly to be increased or decreased [in strength] according to the greater or lesser distance of the planets from the Earth; for because the strength of the agent is weaker the more it distances itself, [and] the longer that it departs from its own source, as is plain on Earth from the light of the fixed stars, it follows that a subject is more weakly affected when it is being influenced by a more distant agent than by a nearer one. Therefore, since the superior nature of each planet is attributed to it when it is in its middle distance from the Earth, so at least the approximate quantity of the strength of individual [planets] will be found when they are in perigee or apogee or in intermediate places.

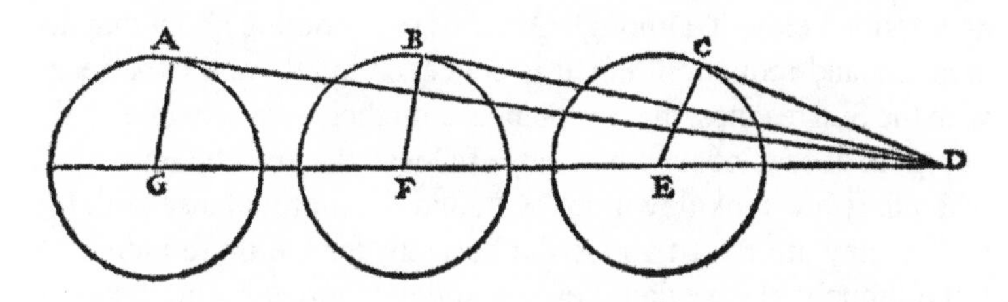

Let it be supposed [in the figure above] that Jupiter is in apogee at G, at its middle [distance] at F, and in its perigee at E, of which the semi diameters are GA, FB, or EC. And let the Earth be at D, and let a straight line DG be drawn through the centers of Jupiter. Then DA, DB, and DC touching its body at A, B, and C; the straight lines DE, DF, and DG are given by the tables, and the diameter of Jupiter with the right angles at A, B, and C; and consequently the greatest angle to the Earth will be given as EDC for Jupiter in perigee, the middle angle as FDB for the middle distance, and the least angle GDA for [its distance] in apogee; and so the sines of these angles are taken from the tables; and finally let it be done that the sine of the angle FDB at 1½ degrees of Jupiter's heat, so the sine of the angle EDC to the other, and that is made to be the degree of Jupiter's heat in perigee; and the same thing is done for the apogee. Then [we will have] 1 degree of dryness in the perigee, and in the apogee, and in the intermediate places.[1]

Offusius offers another method with a table erected with the distances of the planets from the Earth; but because those distances are not recognized by modern astronomers, and because he will have it that if the Sun is above its own mean distance from the Earth, it would recede from us by two fourths of its medium distance, i.e. by 188 diameters of the Earth, its heat would not be felt on these inferior [regions], even if the Sun were located far below the mean distance of Mars; consequently, in this matter we do not stick with him.

Secondly, its [strength] is increased with the greater elevation of the planet above the horizon, but it is reduced with the greater depression below it, although Offusius says nothing about that depression and reduction. For it is conceded by all, and experience with the Sun teaches, that the planets emit their own sensible qualities more efficaciously when they are located above the Earth than when they are sunk down below it, and the more intense still, the higher they are raised above the horizon; for the more their rays fall obliquely, the weaker they act, and the more upright, the more powerfully. Therefore, since the Sun, for example, is given 5½ degrees of heat and 2 of dryness on the horizon, it must be understood that that quantity of strength coincides with it from its own nature, and it affects us according to it when the Sun itself is located at its mean distance from the Earth and from the horizon. Whence, if the Sun is in its apogee, its perigee, or in an intermediate [place], that quantity is corrected previously by its distance, as above. And the quantity of the solar strength on the horizon is made in accordance with its distance at the apogee, the perigee, or an intermediate [place], which quantity is again increased with re-

[1] This is not clear. If the dryness is set at 1½ degrees in the middle, then it should be more at one extreme of the diagram and less at the other. Perhaps some numbers have dropped out of the printed text.

spect to us by the Sun's ascent from the horizon to the zenith, as conversely it is diminished by its descent from the horizon to the nadir, where it leaves off altogether with respect to us, on account of the Earth's being diametrically interposed. Whence it is conjectured that nights in the torrid zone are very frigid,[1] but especially under the equator when the Sun is located in it, namely because it then descends down to the nadir. From this, moreover, it follows that the Sun from the nadir to the ASC increases with respect to us by 5 ½ degrees of heat and 2 of dryness when it stands at its mean distance from the Earth; whereby, from the ASC to the zenith, it increases as many times more as the Sun itself acts more efficaciously above than below the horizon; and the same thing must be concluded about the amount of strength of the Sun when it is in apogee or perigee. But it seems to be very difficult to define the [exact] amount of the increment, the necessary experience being lacking in this matter; indeed, those [experiments] would have to be done in very calm air, and entirely free from winds, especially in the right sphere,[2] in which the Sun on the equator is raised up in equal times and equal arcs.

Offusius will have the heat of the Sun to be increased cubically both by its approach to the Earth and by its altitude above the horizon, but the other qualities squared; by which rule he constructed the tables that he used. For example, having put the Sun on the horizon, he multiplies the qualities due to it by reason of its distance by 1, which is the same cubed and raised to the square, and those qualities remain the same horizontally. But having put the Sun at an altitude of 3¾ degrees, he multiplies its horizontal heat by the cube 1 and 217/512 and its dryness by the square 1 and 17/64, and these are the qualities corresponding to that altitude. And with the Sun posited in an altitude of 30°, he multiplies the horizontal heat by the cube 8 and the dryness by the square 4; at an altitude of 60° he uses the cube 27 and the square 9; and at an alti-

[1] But this conjecture is not true, except in desert regions. Elsewhere, it is generally cooler at night, but not excessively so.

[2] The celestial sphere.

tude of 90°, the cube 64 and the square 16, as is seen in his table, for which he offers no [explanatory] reason.[1]

But finally, since the longer the Sun stays above the horizon in the same altitude, the more it heats, having found the quantity of heat from the altitude, he again multiplies it by the augment corresponding to the diurnal stay[2] of the Sun above the horizon, for which thing he also has a table for the individual times from 1 hour to 24. For example, (as we may use Offusius's own example), for the Moon let it be given to be in perigee and elevated 65° above the horizon; since in perigee it moistens by 121 degrees; and since elevated by 65° (which from the table should be 10), it moistens by 10 times 121, that is by 1,210 degrees; and since it stays 16 hours above the horizon (which from the table should be 9), it moistens by 9 times 1,210, that is by 10,890 degrees.

Besides, the following considerations prove that no faith can be had in these tables: first, because if the heat is augmented cubically, why is the cold only augmented by the square, since the cold, especially in the winter and in northern places, is attended by so much violence and is so intolerable that it kills plants, animals, and sometimes men themselves, which the heat of the Sun even on the equator does not do? Second, the increase of the quality by its elevation above the horizon and by its stay cannot be observed separately, because the elevation is never without a stay, and vice versa. Third, it is absurd to multiply the qualities of the Moon found in a given altitude by the whole diurnal stay of the Moon, since that contains not only the elapsed time from the rising of the Moon to its given altitude, but also the future time from its given

---

[1] Offusius seems to have equated the number series 1, 2, 3, 4 with the angles 0°, 30°, 60°, and 90°. The cubes and squares of those numbers give the figures cited by Morin from Offusius's table. If then we divide the angle 3.75° by 30° and add 1, we get 1.125; and if we cube and square that number, we get 1.4238 and 1.2656, which can be expressed fractionally as 1 and 217/512 and 1 and 17/64, which are the numbers Morin cites for that elevation.

[2] By "stay" Morin evidently means here the entire diurnal arc, i.e. twice the diurnal semi-arc; but below he more often seems to refer to its actual arc above the horizon in a given instance.

altitude to the Moon's setting, which time, because it has not yet occurred, cannot increase its quality; and it will be an even more serious an error if the altitude was in the east. On which account, having [already] rejected these tables and methods of Offusius, it seems that we must also make the same judgment about these [theories].

First, since with the Thermoscope (a most ingenious instrument for measuring the heat and cold of the air)[1] a most exact observation of the increase of the Sun's heat can be made through [a period of] 4 or 5 hours, having noted the increases at each individual hour, and that on some sphere, especially on the right sphere, on the day of the equinox; for that observation will stand as a foundation and measurement for the oblique or parallel sphere,[2] as will be said below.

Then, since the altitude of the Sun above the horizon, and the length of time of its rising up to that altitude and its diurnal time always concur, having made two observations, either in the same location or in others, it should be noted that if the altitudes and the times are the same in both observations, the diurnal will be the same; [but] if the altitudes are the same and the times different, or vice versa, the altitudes will be different. And indeed from these 3 [considerations], namely two of the times, two of the altitudes, and two of the diurnal [times], if two of them agree in being equal, the third should also agree, for otherwise the individual [numbers] will be unequal.

Having established these principles, let the Sun be observed on the equator on the day of the equinox and from two altitudes taken of it, from the first and the third hour after its rising. The first

[1] That is, a device for measuring temperature differences. Originally, it was a thermometer without a standard scale. It was devised by Italian scientists in the late 1500s, and thermometers with graduated scales began to be made in the 1650s, but the Fahrenheit and Celsius scales with which we are familiar were not invented until the early 18th century. Morin probably refers to an earlier device with arbitrary scale markings.

[2] The apparent sphere at a particular place.

altitude will be 15°, and the second 45°. And because the diurnal [time] of the Sun is the same for both observations, the difference of heat produced at both times can only arise from the difference of stay and the difference of altitudes of the Sun above the horizon; namely because the heat at each time is composed of the stay and of the altitude of the Sun at that very time; consequently, it results that the product from the altitude and the stay of the first time, i.e. from 15° to 1, is namely 15 to the product of the altitude, and the stay of the second time, i.e. 45° to 3, is namely 35.[1] So, the increase in heat from one hour from the rising (which is, for the sake of an example, observed at 2/3 of a degree or 40') to another 3 will make 6 degrees of heat for the increase of heat at 3 hours from the rising of the Sun; and such ought to be found by an observation with the Thermoscope; therefore, if to this are added 3 degrees of heat consistent with the Sun on the horizon and at about its mean distance, 9 degrees of heat are made, with which the Sun itself heats at the second time. By the same reasoning, if the product of 15 to 1 is made to 2/3, and the product from 90 to 6 to another; they will produce 24 degrees of heat for the increase when the Sun is in the zenith itself of the right sphere.[2] And thus with the others at the same place on the same day, whatever the latitude of the place is, because the diurnal [time] is also given to be the same, provided that the observation of the increase of the heat is made for one or two hours at the same place on the same day by the use of the Thermoscope, as was done above for the right sphere, or taken at the same altitude in the right and the oblique sphere; and the increment having been found in the right sphere, the increment should be found proportionally in the oblique sphere, as we have already shown above.

Therefore, [if] in different spheres the same altitudes of the Sun are given at the same time, it is certain that the stay and the diurnal times will be different, and moreover the proportion of the heat will be found thus. So that the ratio of the stay of the Sun at its

[1] We should presumably read 135 instead of 35.

[2] I do not understand these numbers.

semidiurnal time in one sphere may be at the ratio of the stay of the Sun at its semidiurnal time in another sphere, so the increment of the heat from the rising of the Sun in the first sphere may be the increment of the heat in the second sphere. And with this in mind, let the Sun be put in the right sphere and the parallel sphere elevated 15 degrees above the horizon, its stay in the right sphere will be 1 hour and the semidiurnal time 6 hours; consequently by dividing the stay by the semidiurnal time, the ratio of the stay to the semidiurnal time will be 1/6; but its stay in the parallel sphere will be 41 days, and the semidiurnal time is 93 days. Therefore, the ratio of the stay to the semidiurnal time is 41/93, therefore the increment of heat from the rising of the Sun in the right sphere is 2/3 or 40?. And let there be made [the ratios] 1/6 to 41/93, so 2/3 to another; they will make 164/93 for the increment of the heat from the rising of the Sun in the parallel sphere; that is, 1 degree and 71/93.[1]

Again, let the Sun be put in those same spheres, elevated 23°30', which is the maximum altitude of the Sun in the parallel sphere. The stay of the Sun in the right sphere will be 1 hour and 34 minutes or 94/60 hours, and the semidiurnal time is about 6 hours; and therefore the ratio of the stay to the semidiurnal time will be 47/180; but the stay in the parallel sphere will be 93 days;[2] and consequently, the ratio of the stay to the semidiurnal time will be 1. Since if the increment of the heat at the selected altitude in the right sphere is 122/75 and it is made 74/780 to 1; so 122/75 to another will make 6 162/805 for the maximum increment of heat in the parallel sphere or under the pole,[3] which is certainly much more than in the right sphere, not however beyond reason, having seen the diversity of the stays, nor from experience, since from Olaus

[1] The ratios are like this: 2/3 is 4 times 1/6, so 4 times 41/93 is 164/93, which is 1 and 71/93.

[2] That is the number of days required for the Sun to advance from the vernal equinox to the summer solstice.

[3] Some of these fractions are blurred in the Latin text, and I may not have read them correctly. But if I have read them correctly, I do not understand them.

Magnus,[1] [we read that] also among the Vestergoths[2] in some fields the barley gathered together at the end of June is collected around the middle of August.

But if it would be as a product of the altitude and the stay in the right sphere to a product of the altitude and the stay in the parallel sphere, then the increment of the heat in the right sphere or 122/75 at the other, would produce more than 2,000 degrees of heat for the increment in the parallel sphere, which cannot be, for such an increment would be intolerable to every living thing, since in the zenith itself of the right sphere the increment is only 24 degrees, as was made plain above.

In short, it must be concluded in the same manner, the Sun's altitude having been given in the same place with different stays, if in fact these can only happen on different days; consequently, having previously found the semidiurnal times of the Sun for those same days, the calculation by stays and semidiurnal times would be as above; moreover, what we are saying here about the Sun and its heat should also be understood to have been said about the cold of the Moon and Saturn. For about moisture and dryness, in fact I would not have dared to assert the same thing freely; and after all, even if the things said above may seem to square sufficiently with reason and experience, nevertheless, because in this matter we are devoid of suitable observations, these matters must be entrusted to the experiences of our successors, and it must suffice for us that we have not wished to leave untouched this matter, which is not unpleasing, and not useless.

Next, two things must be noted here. First, the superior portions of heat and cold are frequently perturbed by accidents of the air, especially by winds, vapors, and exhalations. Second, this only serves to determine how much of their own elemental strength the planets pour forth into the air at any particular moment in time,

[1] Olaus Magnus (1490-1558), Swedish ecclesiastic and author of *Historia de Gentibus Septentrionalibus* 'History of the Northern Peoples' (Rome, 1555).

[2] Probably the inhabitants of the old region of Västergötland in Western Sweden, not far below the Arctic Circle.

which certainly should by no means be scorned; not, moreover, so that the temperament of the child being born and then of the man may be known (which must be carefully noted), for this is not determined solely by the qualities of the ambient, otherwise in the harsh winter no one would be born of a hot disposition, which goes against experience, but with other causes unknown to Offusius, as will be said in its own place. For the Sun does not act solely by its own heat and dryness, which Offusius supposed, writing against a decadent (as he calls it) astrology; otherwise, from a hot coal or a glowing iron globe of the same magnitude as the Sun there could be done whatever is accomplished by the Sun, but besides and especially it acts through the influences and its own substantial form, the noblest of all material things, if you except the unique form of the *Primum Caelum*;[1] the same thing must be said about the Moon, which would only be taken for a globe of ice, then Saturn, which would be taken for a globe of earth. And what we are saying here about the particular celestial constitutions of men being born, we also want to be said about universal [charts] erected at the moments of eclipses, lunations, and the annual revolutions of the world; for in all of these the planets operate influentially in accordance with their own position in the zodiac, their position with respect to the Sun and to the astrological houses, as will be shown in its own place.

Therefore, having abandoned the [exact] manner of the increment, let us return to Ptolemy. In Book 1, chapter 6, he and the other astrologers after him think that the elemental qualities of the planets are increased and decreased by reason of their location with respect to the Sun. And first about the Moon, Ptolemy wants it to be moister from the conjunction to the first quarter; then to the full Moon to heat more; thence to the second quarter to dry more; and finally, to the new Moon to chill more. But the others make the Moon in the first location to be hot but more moist; in the second,

[1] The *Primum Caelum,* Latin for 'first sky', designates what the early astronomers and astrologers considered to be the outermost sphere of the universe that contained the signs of the zodiac. I have retained it as a technical term.

dry but hotter; in the third, cold but dryer; and in the fourth, moist but colder.

Next, it can be doubted whether the Moon from the first square to the full Moon is truly hot and dry; for if it were, the property of its elementary nature put down above will be altogether changed, which it would be absurd to suppose; and this was not Ptolemy's opinion, for he would have used the words *increased* and *decreased* in vain. Therefore, it must be judged from his [account] that the proper qualities of the Moon, cold and moist, are increased or decreased by similar things, or they are relaxed or impeded by contrary things, but not absolutely destroyed or weakened. Whether and how that can be done, we shall look into below.

Therefore, let it be supposed that the Moon is full; then as much of its cold can be released from that location if not formally, at least effectively; it is not nevertheless entirely destroyed; whereby, if we were to give to this location of the Moon 2 degrees of heat, 2 degrees will seem to be a suitable measure of the principal or more intense quality of this location or quadrant of the Moon; and half of that, namely 1 degree, will be the measure of the other ones; consequently, such will be the qualities of the individual quadrants for the Moon, in accordance with which her proper strengths are increased or decreased, at least effectively.

	Hot	Cold	Moist	Dry
From ☌ to 1st □	1		2	
From 1st □ to ☍	2			1
From ☍ to 2nd □		1		2
From 2nd □ to ☌		2	1	

But for the superior planets Saturn, Jupiter, and Mars, he also considers 4 locations or statuses with respect to the Sun; namely, from the conjunction to the first station;[1] then from the opposition to the Sun; then, at the second station;[2] and finally at occultation; to which he attributes the same qualities as those of the Moon.

Therefore, let it be supposed that Jupiter is [going] from its 2nd station to its occultation, where its heat and dryness are discarded. And if at this location, which principally chills, it is given 1 degree of cold (lest the entire heat of Jupiter be destroyed), there will be a 1 degree measure of intensified quality at this location, and 30' will be the measure of the next one; consequently, such will be the qualities of the individual locations.

	Hot	Cold	Moist	Dry
From ☌ to 1st Sta.	30'		60'	
From 1st Sta. to ☍	60'			30'
From ☍ to 2nd Sta.		30'		60'
From 2nd Sta. to ☌		60'	30'	

Others think that oriental planets increase their active strengths and decrease their passive ones; but the occidental planets decrease their active strengths and increase their passive strengths. But it would be better to say that in those locations those qualities are increased and decreased, not indeed formally or in themselves, but in their sublunar effects. But nevertheless, the way that it is made difficult is to define it, as will be made plain below.

Moreover, what this location of the planets is will be made plain here thus: if one of them is direct and preceding the Sun, that one is [going] from conjunction to its first station; if it is retrograde and preceding or dexter to the Sun, it is going from its first station

[1] The *first station* is what we would call static retrograde or SRx.

[2] The *second station* is what we would call static direct or SD.

to opposition; if it is retrograde and following the Sun, it is going from opposition to its second station; if it is direct and following the Sun or is sinister to it, it is going from its second station to conjunction [with the Sun].

Next, Ptolemy made no mention of Venus and Mercury, and Proclus and Haly[1] want to exclude them, because with respect to us they can never come to an opposition of the Sun; and consequently they cannot accurately receive the moderation—which reason seems to be incongruous, since Mercury and Venus experience the same phases as the Moon with respect to us; and, like Saturn, Jupiter, and Mars they are arranged about the Sun, [and are] direct, stationary, and retrograde; whence, it seems agreeable [to suppose] that they are subject to the laws of those [planets] rather than to the laws of the Moon; having taken them in conjunction with the Sun in the highest part of its own eccentric for the opposition, because with full light they are turned towards us, even though being combust they are not then seen. But from the apogee going on[2] to the first station they arise in their vespertine rising; and they are said to be *oriental vespertine*. From the first station or being *vespertine*, where they are greatly elongated from the Sun, they go on to perigee, and they fall into their *vespertine setting*. After their perigee, they arise in their *matutine rising*, extending to the second station, which is called *matutine*. After which, repeating their apogee, they are hidden again, or they set in a *matutine setting*. Consequently, from opposition to the Sun to conjunction with the Sun, or from apogee to perigee, they rise and set *vespertine*; but from conjunction to opposition, they rise and set *matutine*; and in the latter case they are said to be *oriental* to the Sun, and in the former case *occidental* to the Sun. Moreover, the oriental [planets] increase their own elemental qualities, but the occidental [planets] decrease them; and the same with the influen-

[1] Probably Haly Abenragel or 'Alî ibn abi al-Rijâl (llth century), *Liber complete de iudiciis astrorum* 'The Complete Book on the Judgments of the Stars' (Venice: J. B. Sessa, 1503 et al).

[2] Reading *pergentes* 'going on' rather than *per gentes* 'by the peoples'. A simple typographical error.

tial [qualities]. And it should be judged in the same way about them by their stations, just as with Saturn, Jupiter, and Mars, Moreover, Venus is retrograde oriental from the conjunction to the first station; direct and oriental from the first station to the opposition; direct occidental from the opposition to the second station; and retrograde occidental from the second station to the conjunction.

Besides, in addition to the four superior stations of the planets, Cardan adds a fifth; namely, when the Moon and the other planets are hidden under the Sun; in which status Cardan takes all their force away from them, so that, if I may use his words, "they can do absolutely nothing." But from this a significant error is preserved in astrology—that *combust planets* (as they call them) are of no strength at all; and they do nothing with respect to these lower things while they are in that state; but they only begin to act, when first emerging from under the Sun's beams, they begin to shine on us in the morning or in the evening, which error, from another one by Cardan and others, has led to a more serious one, because (as they will have it) all the force of the stars depends upon their light; and consequently, they do not affect us if they don't shine upon us. But besides that in Book 11, Chapter 13, it was shown by us that there is no force in the light of the stars except for illuminating, the planets under the Sun are at least hardly at all deprived of their own strengths of acting, and we shall prove for them that they also act then, when the discussion will be about eclipses and combust planets; and especially in the case of Mercury, which is nearly always combust, and yet they always attribute effects to it, plainly asserting with a ridiculous exception that it is "accustomed to combustion or occultation." For the moment, it must be stated here that Cardan is deceived on his fifth status that he tried to deduce from Ptolemy, contrary to the latter's words and opinion. For Ptolemy will plainly have the first status of the Moon to begin from its conjunction with the Sun, and the first status of Saturn, Jupiter, and Mars from the moment when they become matutine, i.e. when the Sun departs from their conjunction; but also the last status of the Moon and Saturn will end at their occultation—that must be understood as the mean occultation, or the mean moment of time of the whole occultation, which occurs in their conjunction with the Sun. And consequently there will be only four status positions, [which is] also according to the opinion of the rest of the astrologers. But if Ptolemy thought otherwise, then certainly in this too, as in many other things he was wrong.

Ptolemy's doctrine thus expounded, must now it seems be subjected to the examination of reason, and that more courageously, because to confirm it by evident experiences, I know is very much more difficult. First, therefore, if the elemental natures of the planets are increased or decreased according to their diverse location with respect to the Sun, either formally as Ptolemy and the old astrologers seem to have thought; or only effectively as it seems to us, it is necessary that that effect is either from the Sun itself or from the quantity of light apparent to us that is received by those planets from the Sun or from the status itself; but already the cold of Saturn is increased by the Sun, or the heat of Mars is decreased, as it is supposed in the third status, but especially in the fourth status, in which both planets are nearer to the Sun; [but] this is absolutely alien to the nature of the Sun itself, which is also said by Cardan to be hot according to its substance and according to its impressed (as he calls it) quality. But it cannot be from the quantity of its light [that is] apparent to us, both because the light only illuminates and does not do anything else, as has been proved by us; and then, because it is absurd that by that light, [that is] the same in nature and quantity (as it is in the first and fourth status), heat and cold [which are] contrary qualities are also produced. Therefore, since this diversity of effect from the Sun or from its light cannot be sought from the same amount of determination, it seems to remain that it must be sought from the location, which is indeed different in the statuses of the individual planets. But that it cannot be from the location is proved thus: for the dexter site nearer to the Sun would be cold for the Moon and hot for Saturn—consequently hot and cold at the same time; indeed that site coincides with the first site of Saturn, which heats, and the fourth of the Moon, which chills. But the same site cannot be cold and hot at the same time.

Someone might argue that this is indeed true with respect to heat, but not of diverse [bodies] such as Saturn and the Moon; but first the nature of the site must be inquired into, viewed [solely] in itself, and not with respect to different [bodies], for whatever that nature is will be participated in by the planets. Then Saturn and Mars, even though diverse in nature, are nevertheless affected in the same manner by the same site above; consequently, the argument is not valid; and he will not come forward again to argue it. Consequently, the cold of Saturn is decreased in the first status because not much after its rising above the horizon there follows the rising of the Sun pouring out a huge amount of heat, by which the cold of Saturn itself is reduced; whence, that status can be said to be hot; for it would follow that at least in the second status, especially around the opposition, the cold of Saturn is reduced less because between its rising and that of the Sun there is a greater distance of time, but on the contrary it must be reduced more, because the second status is assigned to be hotter than the first. Whence, therefore, it is plain that neither the Sun, nor its light, nor the site itself is inherently the cause of those contrary qualities.

Only one thing [then] is left that can at least probably be offered for the defense of those four statuses—namely, their analogy with the four parts of the year and the day; for as the Sun revolves around the Earth in its annual and diurnal motion, and each revolution is divided into four parts or quadrants that are diverse in temperature, so all the planets with respect to the Sun exhibit to us the appearance of a certain revolution, when they arise from [beneath] its rays, they set in them, and they are allotted intermediate statuses. Consequently, so many effects are produced by the planets, which can only be referred to an analogy, e.g. that the ruler of the MC swift and direct signifies swiftness and continuation of actions; but on the contrary, slow and retrograde it indicates slowness and interruption; so the first status of the Moon and the rest of the planets in temperature or in nature, corresponds by analogy with Spring or with the first part of the day from the rising of the Sun towards noon, which corresponds to more intensity of moisture and less intensity of heat; the second status corresponds with

Summer or the second part of the day from noon to the setting of the Sun, corresponding to more intense heat and less dryness. The third [corresponds] with Autumn or the third part of the day—more intense dryness and less intense cold; and finally the fourth status corresponds with Winter or the fourth part of the day from midnight to the rising of the Sun, corresponding to more intense cold and less intense dryness.

And so, therefore, the cold of the Moon from new Moon to the opposition will be tempered by a twofold cause; namely, from the first and second statuses of the Moon, which are hot; then from the heat of the Sun, which is received both on its own surface and on its very vast craters,[1] with its light reflecting upon these lower [regions], especially at [the time of] full Moon, when those craters are filled by a fuller and denser light, appearing like glowing furnaces. Moreover, from full Moon to new Moon, the Moon returns to her cold, which is also in the fourth status increased in its effect. And the same thing must be judged about the rest of the planets reflecting in their own measure the light and heat of the Sun on these lower [regions], although that heat even like the proper heat of Mars is absolutely imperceptible to us by our senses alone.

Finally, the qualities assigned above to each status must be understood to agree with it, not in the beginning but in the end or the completion of its status, e.g. the Moon there after the conjunction is not hot as a [degree] 1 and moist as a [degree] 2, but only at that instant when she reaches the square, gradually acquiring those qualities in the intermediate time; and when two statuses adjacent to each other are opposite in any quality, there is only a successive change to the following quality before having gradually lost the previous opposite one; therefore, as the qualities and the times of the statuses are proportional to each other, so there must be a ratio for that proportion, since the forces of the planets will be exactly

---

[1] Morin is referring to the craters (he calls them in Latin *cavitates* 'hollows') on the surface of the Moon, some of which have "rays" emanating from them. At full Moon some of the craters appear brighter than their surroundings. They would appear especially bright to an observer using a telescope.

defined. Where, nevertheless, it must be noted that when we say here that the Moon is made hot by 1 [degree] and moist by 2 [degrees], it must be understood that the cold is reduced by 1 degree but the moisture increased by 2 degrees, not formally or intrinsically, but only accidentally and extrinsically by reason of the sublunar effects. And so it is with the rest [of the planets]. And nevertheless, we judge that much less certainty and efficacy ought to be assigned to that cause than to the signs under which they are seen and with which the planets themselves act with their elemental strength.

Besides, since it was said above that the four statuses preserve an analogy with the four parts of the year and the day, here it must be noted in addition that the elemental forces of the planets seem not to be increased or decreased obscurely in those same parts of the year and the day according to their nature. For Mars in the Summer above the Earth at the hour around noon heats and dries more intensely; and Saturn in the Winter above the Earth during nocturnal hours chills more intensely; therefore, if Mars is in the first status with regard to the Sun, above the Earth by day, at an hour around noon in the summertime, still much more intensely will it heat and dry; and the same reasoning applies to the rest [of the planets]. But because the parts of the year and the day are caused by the Sun and the Earth, the former of which is hot, but the latter cold; both of them, moreover, pour out their own force into the air, as was said about the Earth in Book 3, Section 1, Chapter 10. Consequently, it must rather be asserted that from the mutual concourse of qualities, of the Sun, the Earth and any other planet, there arises in the air a mixed constitution, in which each one acts differently in accordance with its strengths; so it must be thought to increase its strength by the nature of a similar companion and to decrease it with a dissimilar one; and consequently the previous notion of the constitution of the air can be allowed and must not be rejected; and it is plain that the above said increase and decrease of the proper elemental nature of the planets is not formally or intrinsically theirs, but only accidentally from the cause mentioned above, and extrinsic by reason of the increased or decreased effect on these lower things, which must indeed be noted. Therefore, Jupiter will be better in its rising; Mars at the MC lower for heat and dryness; Saturn in its setting lower for cold and dryness; and the Moon in the IMC lower for cold and moistness.

Chapter 4.

The Ethereal Nature of the Planets in General.

This has hitherto become known to very few, or rather I should say to no one, and less to astrologers than to the rest of the philosophers; for the former, addicted to the elemental and influential nature as being the better known, omitted the less known ethereal nature, especially because the planets are mixed bodies, and they did not think that the ethereal nature predominates in them. But now, since we have proved this to be so in Book 9, Chapters 4 & 5, it may rightly be inferred that just as they strengthen the elemental nature by an elemental mixture, so do they strengthen the ethereal nature by an ethereal mixture; and since Plato, Aristotle, and the Princes of Medicine also discovered this in sublunar mixtures, indeed in the seed of an animal, and consequently in the humors from which the seed is made, how much more will it be necessary to give precedence to the ethereal mixtures? Moreover, its strength in man is detected most powerfully in those same spirits and humors, then in those parts that the faculties of the humors and spirits productive of them occupy; for in these, besides the elemental qualities, the force that is in the forces of the elements is superior according to Aristotle and corresponds to the element of the stars, and by reason of its similitude for the various status and motion of the planets, those humors, spirits, and faculties experience various motions and dispositions, as especially from seed and lust; then from the diverse status of Venus and the motion over the vital places of Venus in the nativity of a man, it is permitted to observe [them], and so also about the bile and the irascible appetite; then about Mars in [the nativity of] a bilious man; and so on with the rest [of the planets].

Next, this ethereal nature is simple and unique and the same in all the planets because the ether is unique in all of them; and yet it is not of the same strength in all of them, because the ether is inherently duplex, as was said in Book 2, Section 2, Chapter 2. And compared with the rest of the principal materials by which a planet is made of its associated form; it also receives its formal strength very readily before the rest; and consequently there is in Saturn [strength] of the Saturnine nature, only acting in accordance with the Saturnine nature; in Jupiter [strength] in accordance with the Jupiterean [nature], and so on with the rest of them; which cannot be said of the elemental qualities of the planets, which act according to their own strengths, not, moreover, in accordance with the formal [strengths] that are in the planets, as is shown by our sensation from the heat of the Sun, which burns like a sublunar fire.

Chapter 5.

The Celestial Nature of the Planets in General.

By whatever ratio the elemental and ethereal nature is in the planets, the same celestial nature is in them—namely, by reason of a mixture; moreover, the latter nature, since it is more divine than the others, also produces more divine effects. For since the planets have a participation in the prime physical cause (that is, in the *Primum Caelum*), which eminently contains all the forms of things, and is all powerful in nature, so the individual planets have from it, that which can do something in any generation and can evoke the corporeal forms of things on the worldly stage; and in any mutable physical body they can do whatever is naturally possible, as will be proved in its own place. Moreover, there is also in these planets, arising from that same celestial nature, that marvelous faculty that they say is universally influential, from which so many stupendous things happen, especially of their own kind—good fortune, misfortune, and other various accidents that unskilled philosophers think occur beyond reason and [merely] by chance, not because this faculty of the planets themselves is not greatly appropriate to the forms, for their formal strength is different in the individual things for which they are specifically distinguished among themselves, but because this combines with these same forms by reason of the mixture of the celestial material; for the forms of the individual mixtures and their formal strengths are only given to mixtures, and to those in keeping with their proportions.

Chapter 6.

What the Planets Do with their Individual Natures.

Therefore, from what was said above, it is plain that the planets by their own elemental strength alter the alterable bodies elementarily, of course by heating, cooling, humidifying, desiccating, and other things that follow from those, such as by causing open texture, lightness, etc.

But the ethereal nature causes the spirits and faculties to change, to arouse, and to direct themselves to the performance of their proper duties. For the spirits and the faculties are not inherently subject to the action of the elements, since they are such as are not suited to be heated or chilled, to be moistened or dried; which are the proper effects of the elements; therefore, the spirits and the faculties ought to be subject to another higher cause, to which they are more comparable, and by which they can experience their own alterations, since it is necessary that they be subjected to an alteration and to motions proper to themselves, because GOD alone is immutable. Whence it is deduced that if indeed the force of acting directly upon the mental faculties is inherent in the elements, [then] much less do they act upon the substantial forms—those, namely of generating and corrupting—so that those [writers] are [merely] chattering, who contend that everything is done by contrary qualities, since of the forms it is far more noble, sublime, and remote from the elementary nature than from the faculties, and the latter depend upon the former.

Finally, by the celestial nature the forms of things are led out of the darkness into the light; consequently, they generate and corrupt individual things; and they perform marvelous effects of influences. So that consequently in mixed sublunar things, the material is from the elements; moreover, its sensible alteration results from them and from the elemental nature of the planets, but the spirits and the faculties of the body and their motions result from the ether and from the ethereal nature of the planets; but their forms are from the *Caelum* and the celestial nature of the stars, since they release those lying latent or bound up in seeds, and they compel them to come forth onto the worldly scene. So, nevertheless, anything a planet does will be related to the specific nature of the planet, as much as it can be. Consequently, it may be said that Saturn acts in a Saturnian manner, Jupiter in a Jovian manner, and so on with the rest [of the planets]. Consequently, moreover, it was necessary for the planets to be able to act in an elementary manner, so that they could supply the forces of the elements in the meantime—one of which is when a storm, which per se is destructive of all living things, as is plain from the coldest winter, by which crops on Earth and under snowstorms, then the fish under glacial waters, especially around the poles, for this reason live, because the elemental ethereal nature of the planets supplies the deficit of the elements, and thus fosters and preserves living things.

But besides the superior natures, the elementary, ethereal, and celestial ones, which are only the qualities of the planets coming to them from the mixture, there is also a proper substantial form for each one of them, by which the individuals differ specifically among themselves, to which the above said natures are subordinated in acting—indeed, to be the principal cause of all the effects—at least of those that exceed the proper effectiveness of the elementary qualities—and from which substantial form there flows forth the primary or formal strength of each planet, concerning which, what it is was stated in Book 12, Section 3, Chapters 1 & 2.

SECTION II
The Various Divisions of the Planets.

Chapter 1.

Masculine and Feminine Planets.

The planets are formally said to be masculine or feminine from their more effective or weaker proper force of acting, or from their masculine or feminine effects, which in accordance with the diversity of their own nature and status they produce on these sublunar things, although by reason of the celestial material, of which they are composed, they are eminently masculine and at the same time feminine.

Firstly, therefore, a planet is formally said to be masculine or feminine from its own self or from its proper nature; and so the masculine ones are those in which the active qualities predominate over the passive qualities, according to our Table in Section I, Chapter 2. For action particularly pertains to males. And the Sun, Saturn, Jupiter, and Mars are of that sort, for in the Sun, Jupiter, and Mars heat is dominant, and in Saturn cold is dominant; and consequently, it is especially from these planets that the major changes are made in the world, as is known to astrologers. But the feminine planets are those in which the passive qualities prevail over the active ones; and the Moon and Venus, in which wetness exceeds, are of that sort. But Mercury is commonly believed to be twofold both in its nature and also in its sex, nevertheless easily convertible into either sex by [the action of] some other source. Truly, since dryness prevails in it—a passive quality—it seems that it must rather be referred to the feminine sex than to the masculine sex; and its color does not hinder this, since it is sometimes red, and therefore appears to be masculine, since that redness is from the denser vapors and exhalations near the horizon, where Mercury is commonly only seen, and in which when all the other planets are located there, they are seen to be more reddish, especially if an exhalation of vapor prevails. Next, it is plain here that we are departing from the opinion of Ptolemy; both because he makes Mercury to be of a duplex nature, which it is plain here is feminine; and then because he has not distinguished the masculine sex from the feminine one in general by active and passive qualities, but only by the heat that he attributes to the masculine sex and the humor that he attributes to the feminine sex, although Saturn is nevertheless masculine to him, even though it is the coldest of all.

Second. The planets are said to be or to be made masculine or feminine by an accidental formality, due to extrinsic causes, for instance from their own location with respect to the Sun and the Moon. Since those that are oriental to the Sun and occidental to the Moon are said to be masculine, but those that are occidental to the Sun and oriental to the moon are feminine—namely, because of the greater strength of the planets in the former status and the lesser strength in the latter. Moreover, those are oriental to the Sun who are not distant from the Sun itself by 6 signs or 180, and it is their strongest status, since first they emerge from [under] the Sun's rays, and they are seen to rise before it in the morning in about a semi-sextile aspect. But those are occidental from which the Sun is distant in the order of the signs by less than 180o. And it is their worse and weaker status, since they go under the rays of the Sun, by which, but especially in [orb of] conjunction of the Sun, their force is greatly weakened by the super eminent strength and heat of the Sun, by which the forces of the other planets seem to be absorbed as it were and devoured, but not by the light, as has been believed hitherto, since no effect besides illumination coincides with the light; consequently, Cardan [says] badly in his *Commentary*, Book 1, Chapter 6, Text 33, and after him Origanus[1] and many others, that the planets are oriental by day, therefore they think that they are weaker, and all the stars lose their forces because they are obscured by the presence of the

[1] David Origanus (1558-1628), German mathematics professor and astrologer. His book *Astrologia naturalis* . . . 'Natural Astrology . . .' was published at Marseilles in 1645 and was thus one of the most recent books cited by Morin in the Astrologia Gallica.

Sun's light. For granted this, a diurnal planet above the Earth by day would be weaker than at night—indeed, all the planets would be stronger by day under the Earth than above it, which is by experience and reason absolutely alien to the opinion of all astrologers. And so, the planets are weakened by their approach, at least their near approach, to the Sun, but they are said to increase their strengths by their departure [from the Sun], because they are restored to their former [strengths]. But the rest of the planets are [also] made oriental and occidental to the Moon, just as to the Sun; but they are affected otherwise by those positions. For they are said to be strengthened by their approach to the Moon and weakened by their departure [from it]—namely, from the two lights arranged around the Earth,[1] that is the Sun and the Moon, the latter, by the forces of the Earth and the Sun and of nature, is more affected than the Sun, since both the Moon and the Earth are opaque bodies illuminated solely by the Sun; consequently, when they come together to act upon the Earth, those planets are helped by the Moon, but not hindered; whence, they are rightly said to be strengthened by its approach and weakened by its separation.

Third. Planets are [made] masculine or feminine by their own location with respect to the horizon and the meridian, which circles, since they divide the circumference of the whole *Caelum* into 4 quadrants, and the one of these that from the rising on the horizon comes to the summit of the *Caelum,* predominates in heat; the one following, from the summit of the *Caelum* down to the setting, in dryness; then from the setting to the IMC, in cold; and thence to the rising, in moistness; just as they manifest these things to our sense by the time of day and night. From this it is [plain] that the planets, in the quadrants which the active qualities heat and cold preside over, may be said to be masculine; and those [in the quadrants] which the passive qualities preside over may be said to be

[1] Remember that Morin had adopted Tycho's hypothesis of the solar system, in which the Earth was fixed in the center of the universe, and both the Sun and the Moon revolved around it.

feminine. If indeed from the predominating quality the sex of each quarter is in accordance with the reason mentioned above, which Cardan, Origanus, and others are not perceiving, [for] they have thought up absurd reasons from right, and from oblique ascensions, which it is known do not have any place in the right sphere; and Cardan much more absurdly makes the stars to ascend from the 7th house to the 4th, and to descend from the 4th to the ASC, which is repugnant to sense.

Fourth. Finally, the planets are [made] masculine or feminine by their position in the signs of the zodiac, which neither Ptolemy nor the rest of the astrologers after him remarked; and in this they erred no little; for if these planets, by reason of their position in the houses of the celestial figure become masculine or feminine, how much more and more effectively [is this done] by reason of their location in the signs of the zodiac, which along with the planets act upon these lower things, and they are formally determined to the natures of the planets – indeed, some of those are masculine and some are feminine, as Ptolemy himself declared in Book 1, Chapter 12, along with all the rest of the astrologers. Therefore, any planet in a masculine sign, Aries, Gemini, Leo, Libra, Sagittarius, or Aquarius may be said to be made masculine, but in the rest of the signs [that are] feminine, [they are made] feminine.

Next, it must be known about the planets, that [if they are] by nature masculine in a wholly masculine status, they will give forth illustrious effects of a masculine nature, and similarly [those] with a feminine nature in a wholly feminine status, will produce illustrious effects of a feminine nature; but masculine planets in a feminine status, or feminine planets in a masculine status, produce mixed effects, that more or less share a masculine or feminine nature by reason of the predominance of one or the other sex in that case; and so from Saturn or Mars made feminine, or Venus made masculine, badly afflicted anywhere, monsters are often generated.

Chapter 2.

Diurnal and Nocturnal Planets.

After Ptolemy, in Book I, Chapter 6, divided the planets into masculine and feminine [categories] from an intrinsic cause, namely from their proper nature; then from an extrinsic cause, namely from their position with respect to the Sun and the quadrants of the celestial figure; in the following Chapter 7,[1] he divided them again into diurnal and nocturnal [planets] but by a very confused logic. For not intrinsically and by their own nature, since they agree more on the qualities of day and night; and not extrinsically as they happen to be by day or night; but when they are posited above the horizon [by] day or night, do they make their effects more temperate with respect to man. And thus Saturn affects the day and Mars the night, so that the immoderate dryness of the latter is tempered by the moistness of the night, but the excessive cold of the former is tempered by the heat of the day.

But that Ptolemy, Cardan, and their followers erred in this, is made plain by this: that just as in the division of the planets by sex, Ptolemy considered the intrinsic and extrinsic causes of that sex. So it must also be done here; consequently, for dividing the planets into the categories of a diurnal and nocturnal sect; they must [for example] be termed diurnal from an intrinsic cause, or from their own nature in which the active qualities predominate—of this sort are the Sun, Saturn, Jupiter, and Mars, and so they are rendered masculine and diurnal. For [if this was] not being determined by the proper natures of the planets, it must be considered how that departure in them would be regulated—that since it is [something] extrinsic to them, and he supposes that it is intrinsic, but such [sexes] are inherent in them; otherwise, it would have to have been

[1] I have added the Book number, and I have corrected the Chapter numbers from 4 and 5 to 6 and 7 to agree with F.E. Robbins's edition and translation of the *Tetrabiblos* (Cardan uses a Latin version that numbers them differently). Hereafter I will correct Morin's chapter references to agree with the numbering in Robbins's edition. The other reference is to Cardan's *Commentary*, Book I, Chapter 4, Text XXXI (p. 126, col, 2).

said for the sex of Mars that it is masculine when it is occidental to the Sun and in the fourth [quadrant] of the figure from the IMC to the ASC. Indeed Cardan himself, who frequently wavers in his own opinions, in Book 1, Text 42, says that Mars is truly diurnal inherently. And the same logic applies to the Moon, Venus, and Mercury [as being] nocturnal planets.

Furthermore, this doctrine is truer and more in accord with the dogmas of astrology, because in Genesis, Chapter 1, (in which the principal fundamentals of astrology are contained in very few words) it is said, "GOD made the two great lights, the greater light that it might rule over the day, and the lesser light that it might rule over the night, and the stars that they might rule over the day and the night."[1] By the stars, in Hebrew *chochavvim*,[2] are understood to be the five lesser planets, for *chocha* among the Hebrews signifies a wandering and dominating star; and that name is attributed by many rabbis in particular to Mercury, although in many places in the sacred scriptures *chochavvim* also signifies fixed stars or all the stars, except the Sun and the Moon, indiscriminately.

But although it is common to all the planets to shine upon the Earth, and so to divide the light from the darkness according to the property of each of them, or with their borrowed light, as it is held in that same chapter; nevertheless, it is not therefore principally said that the Sun is to rule the day because it does that; for why would the Moon be said to rule the night, and the rest of the planets

[1] Genesis 1:16, but Morin has added some words at the end! Jerome's version actually reads "...and the lesser light that it might rule over the night, and [he also made] the stars." In the Latin, the words are *nocti* 'night' and *stellas* 'stars', but *nocti* is in the dative case as the object of *praeesset* 'might rule', while *stellas* is in the accusative case and is not the object *of praeesset,* but rather the object *of Fecitque Deus* 'And God made' at the beginning of the sentence. The modern translations from the Hebrew agree with that construction, and the *Septuagint,* the Greek translation from the early Hebrew made in the second century B.C. reads . . . *kai tous asteras* 'and [also] the stars', again in the accusative case. So the Biblical text *does not say* that the stars rule over the day and night. However, having adopted the extended reading, Morin discusses the stellar rulership at length in the succeeding paragraphs.

[2] In the modem transcription, *ko-khav* and *ko-khavvim,* 'star' and 'stars'.

the day and the night, since neither the Moon nor the rest of the planets make the day or the night, but the day and the night are only due to [the presence or] the absence of the Sun, the day indeed from its presence above the horizon? And similarly, it is not because the Sun illuminates the Earth by day, and the Moon illuminates it by night; for the rest of the planets are said to rule over the day and they do not illuminate the Earth by day. It only remains therefore to be understood that the Sun must consequently be said to rule the day principally because it rules its diurnal effects, and the Moon the night because it rules the nocturnal ones; but the rest of the planets [rule] the day and the night because they rule both. Moreover, to rule the diurnal effects is nothing else than to rule those that principally depend upon that planet that is said to rule them, as far as that is done or it is, or the planet itself concurs with them primarily. Whence, according to astrological doctrine, the *Septuagint* has rightly interpreted [the Hebrew text to read] "GOD made the Sun to rule the day, the Moon to rule the night, and the stars to rule the day and night;"[1] that is, the diurnal and nocturnal effects, namely those that happen by day or night.

Nevertheless, it must not be thought that the Sun itself rules alone over the diurnal effects, and that they are therefore all ruled by the Sun, and the nocturnal effects only by the Moon; for [otherwise] it would be said in vain that the day and night are ruled by the rest of the planets, by each of which many things are done both by day and by night, as experience proves; but between these and the lights there is this difference; that by the lights and the rest of the planets that are above the Earth, the former generally rule primar-

---

[1] Morin refers to the *Septuagint* as *Version 70.* But as mentioned in a previous note, the *Septuagint does not* agree with the text that Morin gives. It reads *Kai epoiêsen 'o Theos tous duo phôstêras tous megalous, ton phôstêra ton megan eis archas tês hêmeras, kai ton phôstêra ton elassô eis archas tês nyktos, kai tous asteras* 'And God made the two great lights, the great light for rulership of the day, and the lesser light for the rulership of the night, and [he also made] the stars', which is virtually the same as Jerome's Latin version. And neither one of them says anything about the stars ruling the day and night. We may wonder whether Morin either accidentally or deliberately misread the biblical text.

ily, and the rest only secondarily. Which is the reason why in celestial figures astrologers always want to consider the way in which a lesser planet that is the significator of any particular thing is related to the Light of the Time, i.e. to the Sun by day and to the Moon by night, if that was above the horizon (for below, the Light of the Time will be looked for in vain[1]). Namely, whether it is oriental or occidental to that Light. Indeed, Ptolemy, in Book 2, Chapter 8, will have it "that the Sun and the Moon are the governors of the other stars and the principal causes of events, and they manage the rulerships of the stars, and the powers of the ruling [planets] either strengthen or weaken them," where "by the stars" he means also the lesser planets that rule the effects.

Again, it must not be thought that the Sun only rules diurnal effects, but in no way the nocturnal ones, and the Moon only the nocturnal ones, but not at all the diurnal ones, because that is inconsistent with the truest aphorisms of the Sun's [influence when] it is under the Earth, from which, nevertheless, experience proves that it does have an influence upon the native, as well as does the Moon posited by day above the Earth. But since a planet can rule three ways—namely, by presence, by aspect, and by particular rulership; and moreover, the Sun can rule by the latter two both by day and by night, but by its own presence only by day; therefore, from the rule [given] for the Sun and all the planets, it is manifest that in the sacred writings, and among the old astrologers, it rules the day, the Moon rules the night, but in fact the rest of the planets are said to rule day and night only by reason of their presence, as it is felt that the Sun by day and the Moon by night primarily rule by their own presence, or that they rule generally, but the rest rule by day and by night only secondarily, unless both lights should be under the Earth; for then anyone of the rest of the planets can rule primarily by its own presence above the horizon at night. And each planet can by its own presence rule by its light, either its own as in the case of the Sun, or only its shared light, as in the case of the

[1] This is an additional restriction that Morin has placed upon the *Light of Time,* since other authors merely state that it is the Sun by day and the Moon by night.

Moon and the rest of the planets; then, by their elemental qualities and by their influence; and the same planet can also rule by means of some particular effect, at the same time as it rules by its presence, its aspect, and some particular rulership.

But, having explained these things, it must now be sought why by its presence the Sun only rules the day, and the Moon only rules the night, [but] Saturn, Jupiter, Mars, Venus, and Mercury rule the day and the night? For if it was according to Ptolemy's opinion that the Sun is of a masculine nature, and the Moon is of a feminine one; and the day, moreover, agrees more with the masculine nature, or with active qualities, and the night with feminine or passive qualities; therefore, Saturn, Jupiter, Mars, Venus, and Mercury will consequently rule the day and the night, because some of them are of a masculine nature, and likewise of a feminine nature; although in Chapter 1 we have said that only Saturn, Jupiter, and Mars are masculine, but Venus and Mercury are feminine. But for what reason will he have it that the Sun is only masculine, and the Moon only feminine, but the rest of them are masculine and feminine at the same time? And how will this apparent contradiction be reconciled?

It should be remembered from Book 9, Section 2, Chapter 5, that all the planets are bodies mixed together from the elements, the ether, and celestial material; and from Chapter 6 that the forces or natures of these miscible characteristics remain in the mixed action; and finally from Book 3, Section 3, Chapter 3, that the celestial material is eminently hot, cold, moist, or dry. Which having supposed, it seems that it must now be stated from the substantial forms of the Sun and the Moon what are most powerful in the rest of the forms of the planets, whose celestial material, by reason of being eminently hot, cold, moist, or dry, is totally impelled and determined to an actual or formal elementary nature that is conformable to their bodies. And so the Sun in all of its own intrinsic nature is only of the nature of fire, the masculine sex, and the diurnal sect, but the Moon is only of the nature of water, the feminine sex, and the nocturnal sect; but in the case of the other planets, Saturn, Jupiter, Mars, Venus, and Mercury, whose substantial forms are inferior in strength and dignity, or in which by approaching more to the *Caelum* than do the Sun and the Moon, there is proportionately more of the celestial material; this was, indeed, determined by their forms to an actual elemental nature conformable to their forms, but not totally impelled to it; and consequently, each one of them in its own total intrinsic is not of only a single elemental nature, but of a twofold and contrary one; of which one is formally within them, or by the action of a predominating elemental mingling, but the other only eminently from the celestial material not impelled within. Or it can also be said that in the case of the Sun its nature is formally fiery, and in the case of the Moon it is formally watery (especially when they are conjoined with similars), in fact strong and predominating, so that the contraries in them are eminently of no strength or efficacy. But in the lesser planets the formally dominant elemental natures, are not so strong that the contrary ones are not eminently effective.

So, therefore, Mars from its celestial material is eminently hot, cold, moist, and dry, but since from the predomination of the elemental mixture it is formally hot, dry, or fiery (to which nature its celestial material was determined by its substantial form, but not thoroughly impelled), this will, therefore, be its principal or predominating nature—namely, the one that it contains eminently and formally; and consequently the rest, namely cold and moist or watery, will be less important for it, namely for that which it contains only eminently; for Mars does not have more than these two natures on account of its eminent heat and dryness, which were determined to a fiery nature by Mars's form; whence, the airy and earthy [natures] are suppressed in it. And by a similar reasoning, Saturn will be formally cold, dry, and eminently hot and moist; Jupiter hot and dry formally, but cold and moist eminently; Venus formally hot and moist, but eminently cold and dry; and finally Mercury, formally cold and dry, but eminently hot and moist.

Therefore, since having agreed that a duplex elemental nature, one of which is masculine, and the other feminine, is found in the individual lesser planets, it follows that each one of them is also intrinsically masculine and feminine, and also diurnal and nocturnal. Moreover, this duplex sex and duplex sect was from an intrinsic cause, hitherto unknown to any astrologer, but only the sex and the sect from the elemental nature formally existing in the planets themselves, and consequently more effective and more evident. Besides, Ptolemy only looked at the sect of the planets from an intrinsic cause, but not from an extrinsic one; by which he erred, as was already stated above, seeing that the cause must especially be looked at in that place after the investigation of the sex from a similarly extrinsic cause.

Therefore, the sect is from an extrinsic or accidental cause, which happens to the planets themselves from the day or the night. Whence, those are only said to be diurnal or nocturnal extrinsically that occur in the day or the night. And since the day and night are only made above [and below] the horizon; those, therefore, are said to be diurnal extrinsically that are [above the horizon] by day; and those are nocturnal that are located above the horizon by night. And that is confirmed to be sure by those things that were said about sex. For as a planet is said to be extrinsically or accidentally masculine, when it is in fact oriental to the Sun, or in an oriental quadrant, or in a masculine sign, that same planet must [also] be said to be diurnal, which actually happens by day, that is [when] it is above the horizon by day. Otherwise, Ptolemy's doctrine on sect will be contrary to his doctrine on sex; whence, it is not surprising if he only refers to that doctrine accepted by the ancients with these words,[1] "Therefore, they relate that nocturnal stars, etc."

Moreover, because this is said about the planets, the same

---

[1] *Tetrabiblos* i. 7, . . . *nykterinous men akolouthôs paradedôkasi tên te Selênên kai to tês Aphroditês* '. . . accordingly they have handed down that the Moon and the [star] of Venus are nocturnal'. Curiously, Morin's phrase *Tradunt igitur nocturnas stellas* 'Therefore, they relate that the nocturnal stars . . .' does not occur in the translation of this chapter *(Quadripartite* i. 6, *Commentary,* p. 128, col. 1) published by Cardan, which has only *Stellarum quoque consimili ratione nocturnam esse docuere Venerem & Lunam* 'They have taught of the stars that by a similar reasoning, Venus and Mercury are nocturnal . . .'

thing must also be judged about the signs—namely, that they have a sect from the intrinsic reason of their own nature or their own sex; and then, from the extrinsic reason of day and night; and so it is plain that the planets are not allotted an extrinsic sect either from their own position under the earth or from the signs of the zodiac, but only from their own position above the horizon.

And so, it will be sufficient to say about Saturn, Jupiter, Mars, Venus, or Mercury that without any regard to the sign, the planet is extrinsically diurnal, as that is understood to be above the Earth by day, and extrinsically nocturnal, as that is known to be above the Earth by night. And consequently, when it is commonly said that a planet is diurnal by day above the Earth; it is the same thing as if it is said that a planet is diurnal intrinsically and extrinsically, because that is partly the maximum strength of a planet; but when it is commonly said that a diurnal planet is by night above the Earth, it is the same as if it is said that a planet that is intrinsically diurnal is extrinsically nocturnal, which is a debility of a planet; and the same logic applies to planets that are intrinsically nocturnal.

But these ancient forms of saying diurnal by day, and nocturnal by night below the Earth, will be rejected; because every planet below the Earth is lacking in an extrinsic sect with respect to us, which is one of the principal causes of the debility that is commonly attributed to planets posited below the Earth.

But this can be objected to; because if Mars was intrinsically diurnal and nocturnal, then if it was above the Earth by day, that will not be a more powerful reason why it is said to be [diurnal] above the Earth by day, than nocturnal above the Earth by day; and so, its intrinsic sect will be either null or else ordinary, which is seen to be absurd.

But I reply. It is more in keeping with reason that the nomenclature of a planet, as far as its intrinsic sect, should be made from the sect predominating in it. And consequently, since Mars is formally, and at the same time eminently, fiery, masculine, and diurnal, and only eminently watery, feminine, and nocturnal, it will, therefore, be called diurnal rather than nocturnal. And so with the rest [of the planets]; and having agreed on this, the above said error of Ptolemy is again quashed.

But the consequence is denied. For if Mars is at night above the Earth in a feminine sign, and especially a water sign—especially indeed, in Scorpio its own domicile—and with all these accidental causes entirely favoring the extrinsic nocturnal sect, its nocturnal intrinsic is very much strengthened; and as a result it will preponderate as much as it can be made to do so toward the feminine sex and the nocturnal sect; and yet this would not happen if it were lacking a nocturnal intrinsic. Nevertheless, with Mars posited thus, it will always have less strength for the feminine sex and the nocturnal sect, than for the masculine sex and the diurnal sect, if it is posited by day above the horizon in a masculine domicile—especially a fiery one, and especially in its own domicile Aries.

Furthermore, it must be known about the planets that by their intrinsic sect, especially formally, along with their conformable extrinsics, the planets produce greater and more evident effects in accordance with the nature of the sect, or the sex that is conformable to it; but if they are not conformable, they produce lesser or more obscure effects and those that are mixed and not pure, or different in some way. Planets formally masculine and diurnal act more effectively above the Earth by day than by night. And consequently, since Saturn is already harmfully cold inherently, it will be better for it to be above the Earth by day than by night; just as Mars will be more temperate by night above the Earth, especially in Pisces, than by day, especially in Aries or Leo, as this is also proved by experience. And let those things that have been said about the sex and the sect of the planets be sufficient; how truthful and important they are will be more evident in what follows.

Chapter 3.

Benefic and Malefic Planets.

About this division of the planets of great importance among the others, [if it is] not at least the ultimate fundamental of astrology, the principals of this science agree very little among themselves. Indeed, in this matter they all agree that Jupiter and Venus are benefic planets, and Saturn and Mars are malefic; and then Mercury is of a wavering nature—since with the benefics it is benefic, and with the malefics it is malefic; but they disagree with each other about the lights.

For Ptolemy, in Book 1, Chapter 5 of the *Quadripartite*,[1] along with the older [authorities] will have it that the Moon is benefic, but the Sun is of a common nature, which Cardan, nevertheless, in his *Commentary* says "is of the greatest good fortune, and that no planet is more benefic." But Origanus on the other hand judges the Sun to be malefic, since joined to the planets it burns them and impedites them with its light, extinguishing their own light as it were; and thus it frustrates the powers of the benefics, but it encourages and increases the powers of the malefics. In which there is a contradiction or an absurdity, since the Sun extinguishes the light of the malefics no less than it extinguishes the light of the benefics. But Schöner[2] and Dorotheus[3] make the Sun, Moon, and Mercury to be of a common nature. Moreover, Hermes[4] says in general that a planet is neither fortunate nor unfortunate inherently, but that it has whatever strength

---

[1] Morin does not give the Book number and says the Chapter number is 3. In the translation I have corrected the reference.

[2] Johann Schöner (1477-1547), *De Judiciis Nativitatum libri tres* 'Three Books on the Judgments of Nativities' (Nürnberg: J. Montani et Ulrici, 1545).

[3] Dorotheus lived in the first century and was the author of five books on astrology called *Pentateuch,* but Morin has cited his opinion from the book of some later astrologer.

[4] A number of treatises are attributed to Hermes Trismegistus. Morin was possibly referring to the *De revolutionibus nativitatum* 'The Revolutions of Nativities' (Basel, 1559), now known to be by Albumasar.

and individual power over those things that it rules, such as Saturn over agriculture, Jupiter over judgments, etc.

Besides, Ptolemy, Cardan, and all the other astrologers judge only by elemental qualities whether a planet is benefic or malefic, and they do not offer reasons about this in which they agree among themselves. For Ptolemy says that Jupiter, Venus, and the Moon are benefic planets, because heat and moisture abound in them; and yet moisture does not abound in Jupiter since it is moderately dry, nor does heat abound in the Moon, since it is inherently cold. Why then will the Sun not be inherently benefic for Ptolemy, since in fact a pleasant and vital heat exceeds in it, and it does not have a noxious dryness like Mars or Saturn?

Finally, Ptolemy, and the others, who make the Sun and Mercury to be of a dual nature, say that they are made benefic with the benefics Jupiter or Venus, but malefics with the malefics Saturn or Mars. Others, like Alchabitius,[1] say that the Sun will be benefic in trine or sextile aspect, but malefic in conjunction or opposition. And yet must it not be asked and determined, not what sort [of nature] they have from extrinsic causes or from the aspects of other [planets], but what sort [of nature] they have from their own selves and from their own nature?

Therefore, from these things it is plain how many are the difficulties that present themselves to us on the very threshold of astrology; and which we shall elucidate individually:

First it must be said that all the planets are innately or unqualifiedly good; both because being and good are interchangeable; and because in Genesis, Chapter 1, it is said about the creation of the Sun, the Moon, and the Stars, *And God saw that it was good*, and again at the end of the Chapter, *And God saw all the things that he had made, and they were very good.*[2]

---

[1] Abû al-Saqr al-Qabîsî (d.c. 967). His book was very popular and often reprinted. Morin perhaps had this edition: *Alcabitii ad magisterium iudiciorum astrorum* 'Alchabitius's Book on the Art of the Judgments of the Stars' (Paris: Simon de Colines, 1521).

[2] Genesis 1:18 & 31.

Second. Not everything that is innately or unqualifiedly good is good with respect to something else; [that is], not everything that is good in itself is good to some other thing. This is plain from the wolf, which is very bad for a sheep; and from poisons, which are lethal for men and animals, even though they are innately good.

Third. Just as among the minerals, vegetables, and animals, some are beneficial to man if they are applied, and some are harmful; and so among the planets this same thing is not found to be alien to reason. For even though in Deuteronomy, Chapter 4, it is said that "God created these things for the service of all the people that are under the sky;"[1] consequently, no star should be said to be harmful to man; and likewise, it is certain that the same thing can also be said about the sublunar mixtures harmful to man—namely about those that were created for the use and service of man. But as in any sublunar mixture that is said to be harmful to man, there is also something in it beneficial to him if it is carefully prepared and applied; and so it must be judged about the stars that are harmful to man; namely, that they are not in themselves absolutely harmful to man, but in some way they are also beneficial; indeed, because just as poison itself and caustic applied to some particular use are useful to man, so that malignant nature of the stars duly applied can be beneficial to man.

Fourth. With respect to man, the planets must properly be said to be neither good nor evil, but benefic or malefic.[2] For goodness and evil are properly only referred to an entity or to morals; but a planet is not inherently or morally evil, since all of them are inherently good; but evil morals are only possessed by free creatures, which the planets are not; but beneficence or maleficence are properly referred to an efficient and affecting cause; therefore, since all the planets are efficient causes with respect to man, and causes af-

[1] Deuteronomy 4:19 (Jerome's Latin version) ". . . *solem et lunam, et omnia astra caeli . . . quae creavit Dominus Deus tuus in ministerium cunctis gentibus quae sub caelo sunt.* 'the Sun and the Moon, and all the stars of the sky . . . that your Lord God has created for the service of all the people that are under the sky'.

[2] That is "doing good" or "doing evil," as distinguished from "being good" or "being evil."

fecting him; therefore, just as they are affecting well or evilly, they will properly be said to be benefic or malefic, or at least effective of good or evil.

Fifth. The planets must be defined benefic or malefic not only because of their elemental qualities, but especially because of their own influential ones. For they affect men much more effectively by their own influences rather than by their elemental qualities, of which the only property is to heat, to chill, etc.; also, to rarefy, to make more dense, etc.; but not to produce those stupendous effects that happen to men in connection with their life, mental abilities, character, riches, honors, actions, marriages, lawsuits, violent death, etc., all of which are produced by influences; and it is certain that they exceed the effectiveness of the elemental qualities. But nothing keeps the same planet from being malefic by its elemental qualities and benefic by its influential ones, or vice versa, just as that same planet is not in both ways benefic or malefic.

Sixth. As for the benefic or malefic nature, this must not be determined about any planet, [only by] what kind it is from extrinsic causes, e.g. from a conjunction or an aspect with other planets, but from what kind it is inherently. For if the planet itself, for example the Sun, is not connected by body or by aspect with another planet (which often happens), and it is in the first space or the first house of the figure, it cannot be said that it has no power or efficacy in the native's figure, but it will be the significator of life and behavior, and more purely according to its own nature than if it were configured with another planet. But also it cannot be said that its effect will be indifferent, both because its effect differs from the effect of some other planet that might be put similarly in the same space—even in the same degree of the zodiac; and also, because from such an indifference of effect, it would follow that the native is either going to be successful or not be successful, which implies that either if he does not live as a result of that, it will therefore be malefic; if he does live, but is badly afflicted in his health or his behavior, again therefore it is malefic; but if he lives well affected in both categories, it is therefore benefic. And it will not be useful to say that determination about the life and behavior of the native must be made in accordance with the state of the Sun's ruler; for if the Sun is put in Leo,[1] it will submit to the rulership of no other planet; and yet it will act more purely according to its own nature. Therefore, the nature of a planet must be defined solely from its own nature, whether it is benefic or malefic.

Seventh. No planet is indifferent to man from its own nature, that is, it is neither benefic nor malefic. For if from its own nature it was indifferent, and it is put in the first space, as was said above of the Sun, it will, therefore, produce an indifferent effect on life, character, mental abilities, etc.; this is neither good for man, nor evil, contrary to the reasoning above. But if it does not produce an indifferent effect, but either a good or an evil one (as is certainly necessary), that planet will, therefore, not be indifferent due to its own nature, but [rather] determined both toward the kind and toward the quality of the effect. I say "toward the kind," for the Sun by its own nature produces only solar effects in whatever space of the figure it falls, Saturn produces Saturnine effects, etc. "Toward the quality of the effect," for either no effect is produced by the Sun, or to the question "what kind" is it with respect to the man who is affected, one will have to reply, "good or evil," but not "indifferent," because indifference is neither a quality, nor does it affect any subject. Add to these, that about any planet whatsoever, whatever its status in the natal figure was, any astrologer at all would have always said that it was indifferent to doing good or doing evil, even if it should rarely happen that the planet is in its own domicile, configured with no other planet.

Eighth. That planet with elemental qualities must be said to be malefic to man, in which the contrary qualities exceed by too much the two foundations of life, namely the native heat and the radical moisture. And consequently, since Saturn is a planet that is very cold and dry, it is plain, that from its nature also it will be greatly

[1] Reading the symbol for Leo rather than the symbol for the North Node, a simple typographical error.

and totally contrary to the foundations of life. Similarly, Mars, even though it is hot and must therefore be thought to be a friend of life; nevertheless, because its heat is too greatly fierce and fiery, and not[1] mild and ethereal; therefore the heat of Mars is very inimical to life, especially since having the added maximum dryness, it very strongly destroys and dissolves the radical moisture. And so, concerning these two, Saturn and Mars, it is established that from their elemental nature they are malefic, and also as such they have hitherto been perceived and so called by all astrologers. But as for what pertains to the rest of the planets, it is certain that Jupiter and Venus are not malefic, for mild and vital heat prevails in both of them—in Jupiter with a very reduced dryness, but in Venus with an abundant and benign moisture; and consequently, since they are friends of life, by the ancients—taught by experience—they are rightly held to be benefics.

There remain the Sun, the Moon, and Mercury, which many make to be of a dual nature; but it is proved by No. 7 [above] that no planet is by it own nature indifferent; by their own nature they will therefore be malefic or benefic.

And it is proved about the Sun that it is benefic; both because it abounds in mild and vital heat more than all the other planets, by which it also excites a native feminine heat for life and the duties of life, and it nourishes living things; then, because by its annual entrance[2] as the author of life it enlivens the universal nature of vegetation, animals, and men; but they are saddened by its retreat, because the rulership of earthly cold that follows in the air is inimical to life.

But the Moon, even though by reason of its cold, it may seem to be opposed to life; nevertheless, because its elemental nature is watery, and water is the principle of generation and fecundity, since that time when the spirit of the Lord was brooding over the waters. Indeed, water is necessary for the nutrition of all living

[1] Reading *neque vero* 'and not' rather than *nativus vero* 'native in fact'.

[2] Morin refers to the entrance of the Sun into Aries.

things, and it is especially necessary for animals to drink; for that reason, there is no one who can say that the Moon is malefic because it is of a watery nature. But if the Sun and the Moon were malefic because of their own elemental natures, without doubt from their own magnitude and conspicuous activity as compared with the rest of the planets, all these lower things would be destroyed, and those men capable of reason would fear and shrink from their sight—the contrary of which we experience.

Finally, Mercury, since its elemental nature emulates that of Saturn, but is somewhat relaxed in intensity, and also inherently, deserves to be said to be somewhat malefic rather than benefic due to its elemental qualities.

Furthermore, it seems to be very probable, indeed it is certain, that the ethereal nature which is very friendly to life is innate in all the planets; it checks the noxious elemental nature of the malefics and sharpens and strengthens the auspicious nature of the benefics,.

Ninth. That planet must be said to be benefic in its influences, which in its own domicile where it acts more purely in accordance with its own nature, and posited in good spaces of the figure, from itself produces good in conformity with those spaces without any evil or difficulty. But posited in evil spaces of the figure, it either removes an evil conformable to those spaces, or it at least diminishes it, or it frees [the native] from it. Moreover [a planet] must be called malefic if even in its own domicile and posited in good spaces of the figure, a good thing conformable to those spaces neither occurs nor at least it does not occur without malice and difficulty. But in evil spaces of the figure, evil that is worse and more certain occurs, and it increases it. This is said of its own self, because benefic or malefic must here be considered to be in accordance with itself and insofar as it is abstracted from the mixture with others.

Tenth. Jupiter, Venus, the Sun, Mercury, and the Moon are planets benefic from their own influences. About Jupiter and Venus there is no controversy, but about the Sun, the Moon, and Mercury[1] it is [also] proved, because for these, no less than for Jupiter and Venus, the description above suits a benefic planet, as will be plain for anyone of them both from our own experience, and from the experience of all the old astrologers, [that is] if the Sun, Moon, or Mercury are in good spaces of the figure and in their own domiciles, free from a bad connection with Saturn or Mars. And in fact, wherever they are said by the old [astrologers] to be malefics, there is always detected either that connection or some other conspicuous accident to have arisen as the cause; and since no planet can be said to be inherently indifferent between a benefic and malefic [nature], then from No. 7 [above], if the Sun and the Moon were not benefics from their own proper influences, then they would be malefics. But it was not proper for the planets that are primary by their strength and dignity to be malefics because of their own nature, on account of the reason already explained in No. 8; therefore, by nature they are both benefics.

Eleventh. Saturn and Mars are planets that are malefics because of their own influences. And this is proved, both by the common consensus of astrologers, and because of these [planets] alone[2] the previous description of malefics is appropriate, as is witnessed by daily experience. Because, if it should happen otherwise, there will be discovered to be either a mingling [of influences] with the benefics, or some other conspicuous occurrence to have been involved in the cause. Besides it is certainly established by experience that if Saturn and Mars from any house of the figure, in any sign of the zodiac and configuration with others are in square or opposition to the ASC or the MC, they make the significations unfortunate. Therefore, they do not have that malefic force from the house, the sign, or the configuration, but from their own selves; consequently, they are rightly said by Ptolemy to be inherently *anaeretas* or cutters-off of life, honors, etc.

Twelfth. Planets that are by their own nature benefics some-

[1] The text says Venus, but that must be a typographical error.

[2] Reading *his solis* 'to these alone' rather than *his Solis* 'to these of the Sun'—a typographical error.

times degenerate into malefics in their effect, and malefics into benefics. As, if Jupiter or the Sun, ruler of the eighth space, which is [the house] of death is by body in the first space, which is [the house] of life, and also by many other ways that will be explained in its own place.

Moreover, someone will speak in favor of the old opinion; consequently, to state that the Sun and the Moon in their own influences are of both natures and not absolutely of a benefic nature, because in fact in good spaces they produce good things, but in evil spaces they at least neither take away the evils nor reduce them, as Jupiter and Venus do, but they make them greater and more notable. For the Sun or the Moon in the 12th arouses great enemies and great illnesses. And in the 8th,[1] a public death or the likelihood of a public disaster, or something notable in another way, such as in a shipwreck, or a common brawl.

But I reply that it is common to all the planets to have an influence derived from their own nature on the signification of the house in which they are posited, or which they rule, or which they aspect. But the benefics influence well; and therefore they further the good things conformable to those spaces, but they take away or diminish the evil things, or at least they influence them to be few and light with [the possibility of] remedy and evasion. And that works more powerfully, the better the status in which they are located.

But already the Sun and the Moon, on account of their very great strength and outstanding dignity that is greater than that of the rest of the planets, also act or influence more powerfully than they do—both for good things and for evil ones, and they produce more notable effects. But they seem to differ altogether from the malefics, both because they do not make evil influences, and because in evil spaces they do not increase the malign quality of the evils; of which things the contraries are effected by the malefics. They therefore agree more with the benefics, because like them

[1] Reading the figure 8 rather than ♉ the sign of Taurus, a typographical error.

they always make good influences in the good spaces, and they do not increase the quality of the evils in evil spaces, but only as they influence more notable good things in the good spaces; so in the evil spaces they influence more notable or more public evils—namely, because they only act in accordance with their own nature, which rules only those things of both the macrocosm and the microcosm that are more notable, more universal, and primary.

You will object against what was just said that it is abominable to assert that Mars influences a disposition to perpetrate murder, or that Saturn subjects a man to an ignominious death. And that that is injurious to the Author of Nature, who "saw those things that he had made and that they were very good," Genesis 1. Therefore, Saturn and Mars are not malefics in their influences, nor any other planet; and consequently it is also false that Venus calls out [people] to sexual indulgence, etc.

But I respond in similar fashion that it will [then] be necessary to deny the force of arsenic, of the viper, the scorpion, or hemlock to kill men, of cantharides[1] to excite [them] to an almost insane sexual state, of hyoscyamine to disturb the imagination, and then pestilential constitutions of the air that wherever and whenever they come are cutting off a third part of the men in any region or city in a plainly horrendous spectacle; moreover, since these things cannot be denied, and [likewise] the goodness of GOD towards men should not be denied, but His wisdom should be greatly praised.

It must be said first that we have not asserted above that Saturn and Mars in their own influxes are altogether malefic—namely, because there is in them something of an intrinsically beneficent nature, by which they are sometimes observed to do good, especially when they are fortunately posited in the *Caelum*; but their nature is such that if they are mingled in a sign by conjunction or by aspect in a manner incongruous to the natures

[1] Spanish Fly, used as an aphrodisiac.

of the other planets, and thus by a bad site with respect to the horizon they act upon sublunar things, far more frequently they do evil rather than doing good; consequently, these two planets are rightly said to be malefics as compared with the others that are commingled harmlessly and more frequently do good.

I say second. Those words of Genesis must be understood in this way—namely, that whatever GOD has made, those things were very much perfected in their own kind, or if you prefer (and which seems to me to be the truer sense) they were very good for the purpose for which they were created by GOD. So, arsenic, the viper, monkshood,[1] and such like things on Earth; then, Saturn, Mars, the Head of Medusa, Cor Scorpii,[2] and such like things in the *Caelum*, are very good.

I say third. GOD created such malefic stars, so that man, exposed to their bad influences, might be afraid and beware of them no less than from thunder and lightning threatening destruction on his own head, and so that in these as well as in those he would be mindful of his own subjection and weakness and moreover of the justice and omnipotence of GOD, and he would return with prayers to His pity, strength, and grace. For GOD [made] those stars—both the malefic ones as well as the benefic ones—and the whole *Caelum*, and also displayed their motion to the eyes of men, so that they may foresee the evils to which they are exposed, and prudently beware of things acting exterior to them, namely those things illuminated by the celestial lights, but that they may be internally converted to GOD, so that his rulership over all Heaven and Earth, and as the most powerful governor, who, according as he wishes, tightens and loosens the reins of the secondary causes; for everything that, what in itself is, he has made, and man will call upon GOD with a humble and contrite heart, equally certain that he will be freed from the threatening tempest of malign influxes, just as the Ninevites were converted by the

[1] Monkshood is the poisonous herb Aconitum napellus.

[2] The Head of Medusa is the star Algol; and Cor Scorpii is the star Antares; both of which stars are generally accounted to be malefic.

prognostication of Jonah.[1] Of course it is greatly characteristic of GOD to pity even those not invoking [his name]; how much more then is it characteristic to pity those who are invoking [his name]? And this is plain in the case of criminals who perish at last by the hand of the executioner. Such persons, if indeed they are indulging in bad inclinations, which they have derived from bad influxes, GOD pityingly ends their understanding [of them], so that at least in the last hour of this life, inspired by Him, they come to their senses; and the grace of future life is bestowed on them by their own ministers.

SECTION III
The Proper Celestial Nature of the Individual Planets. And also about the Fixed Stars.

Chapter 1.

How Difficult it is to Define the Proper Influences of the Individual Planets.

In Section 1 of this Book, the proper *elemental* nature of the individual planets was stated; now it remain for us to discuss their proper *celestial* nature. But by the celestial nature we understand the baptismal influence of each planet defined by us in Book 12, Section 3, Chapter 20, which in Chapter 4 we distinguished from the substantial form of the planet, moreover, to flow from this; and therefore we have said that it is essential to a planet, namely it is the thing by which any planet gives out the proper effects of its own nature—the Sun giving solar effects, the Moon lunar effects, etc.

Next, this influence of any planet, although in itself it is a

[1] The reference is to the story in the Book of Jonah in which Jonah predicts to the citizens of Nineveh that the city will be destroyed by a tempest in 40 days, but then God chose to spare the contrite Ninevites.

unique and simple strength, nevertheless diffuses throughout the whole world; indeed it is universal in all things capable of generation, so that there is no natural effect, for which some planet cannot do something. From this it is certain, because from Book 12, Section 3, Chapter 6, that the influx of the planets penetrates the whole globe of the Earth, also from the highest and subterranean distances they affect the child being born on the Earth; given which, there is no natural effect that can conceal itself from the influx of a planet, as is said about the Sun in Psalm 18, 'And there is no one who hides himself from its heat',[1] and nature begets nothing, to the origin of which the planets do not concur; and because from such a concourse, it is not subject to a natural fate close to the experiences conformable to its own species. For the individual species of sublunar things are not subdued to fate by the influences in the same way, because a planet cannot do the same thing to a metal or a plant that it can to a man, even though it acts at the same time with the same strength on a single species or even on an individual; for the different arrangement of the steps stands in the way of those receiving the strength, which is received in the mode of the recipient. Whence, various effects are produced in the several species and in individuals, because this is also evident in the same heat of the Sun, which hardens clay and melts wax at the same instant.[2]

Having said these things in advance, since all the planets are different among themselves in nature and species, as in Book 9, Section 3, Chapter 1, and similarly the nature of things or of sublunar effects is different; it cannot be denied that the Sun, for example, has a greater natural affinity with some things or effects, and a lesser one with others; and no affinity at all with the rest. Whence the lion and the rooster among the animals, and gold among the metals, are thought to be solar things—namely, from the greater affinity of their nature with the Sun than with the rest of the planets—and yet all the planets join together for the generation

---

[1] Psalm 18:7 in Catholic Bibles, but Psalm 19:6 in Protestant Bibles.

[2] One of Morin's favorite observations. See Origen, *On the First Principles,* I, 1,13.

of a lion or of gold; but the stronger one wins and assimilates the subject to itself. And that assimilation is easier in subjects or effects that are allotted the greater natural affinity with the active cause. That which we are saying here about the Sun may also be understood to be said of any other planet.

Besides, to define with a proper name the influence or formal strength of any particular planet, which will explain clearly in its own way the essence of its strength seems to go beyond the capacity of man. For although the Sun's influence is said to be "Solar," and Jupiter's influence "Jovial," and neither one of them can be better expressed by us; nevertheless, it is not known from that [adjective] what the Solar influence is formally, or what its nature is, or what it consists of; indeed, the intellect is overpowered by the magnitude and preeminence of the cause that is indeed universal, or it causes mistiness in his understanding; and it judges that force, at least for men going about in this world, to be unutterable in its simplicity.

For to define this clearly by a name suitable to it, it would be necessary to contemplate the effects of its strength in individual kinds of things—certainly, in elements, minerals, vegetables, dumb animals,[1] and men; and it must be observed in the individual thing in which the effects coincide to what extent they are affected by the influence of the Sun. For if it should become known by a name appropriate to itself, it would reveal the nature of the solar influence. But since we can scarcely know what the influences of the planets perform in the human species; in fact, about [their performance in] the minerals, vegetables, and brute animals we have little or no experience—indeed, those influences have hitherto remained unknown or wrapped in the deepest obscurities on account of Aristotle and the other philosophers, who wrongly ascribed all sublunar effects to the light and the motion of the stars. We have certainly done much more, if, from the effects of the planets seen upon the human species, we have defined the influences of the in-

[1] Reading *Brutorum* 'dumb animals' instead of *Erutorum* 'rescuers', a simple typographical error.

dividual [planets] that disclose to us their natures and differences, according as the human species is affected by them; and vice versa, from these the individual human effects may be thus derived. But for the rest of the sublunar bodies or effects we shall at least cling to tradition for determining the planetary rulerships over them, just as those correspond to reason and the experiences of astrologers with regard to *analogy*, which will be explained below.

Chapter 2.

By what Theory, the Influences of the Planets, at least with Respect to Men, can be Investigated and Defined.

Let us begin with the Sun. It, therefore, seen in the sky, is considered to be the ornament and glory of the whole world, and its brightness of such great majesty that it is held to be the king of all the stars, not undeservedly, because all the rest of the Planets, with the exception of the Moon, are only its satellites that perpetually surround and pay respect to it in their own revolutions, being movable with respect to it; but it, although their ruler and prince, always brings them along with it.[1]

Moreover, viewed according to the way it affects men in their [bodily] composition, it appropriates for itself the heart among the other viscera by sympathetic analogy, of which more below. That is, it is the fount of vital heat, the primary seat of life, and the universal cause; and in sum, it is the noblest organ of the entire human body, and the foremost; and it is greatly analogous to the Sun itself; that is, it excels analogically in man, as the Sun does in the macrocosm.

But in the nativity of a man, if the Sun is found in a primary

[1] Another reference to Tycho Brahe's model of the solar system, in which the Sun revolves in an orbit about the Earth, but all the other planets revolve about the Sun; hence, they are carried along with it. As mentioned in a previous note, Morin had adopted that model because it avoided controversy with the Catholic Church, which did not favor a heliocentric model.

space, or is its ruler, at least [when it is] little debilitated by the malefic Planets, not only does it deliver up the heart itself more closely to itself through its particular influx, but it renders the [native's] temperament fiery after its own manner, a face notable for its splendor or majesty, his manner sincere and open; it bestows fame on his name, and always [gives] the native some eminence in his father's house or over his brothers. If it is in the 2nd house, it signifies splendid wealth or expenditures. But of persons, it always signifies royals, primates, notables, or those standing out over the rest, with regard paid to the family or condition of the Native. Of illnesses, strokes, heart-attacks, fevers; among the kinds of death, famous, public, or occurring in the common disaster of battle, shipwreck, the plague, etc., or something otherwise notable. And therefore, since in the proper individual effects of the Sun there are present fire, vitality, beneficence, fame, splendor, eminence, it is necessary that the Sun have these [qualities] itself, as will be clear from this example: if the Sun is found in the 11th house of a nativity, it presages the friends to be kings, princes, or magnates by the observation of Astrologers; and it does not have this [signification] from its site in the 11th considered by itself; for Saturn in that same house would not signify such things; nor does it have this [signification] from the sign in which it is placed, for in whatever sign the Sun is placed in the 11th house, it will signify the aforesaid friends. Nor yet does it have this [signification] from a corporeal conjunction, nor from an aspect with the other Planets, because, when it is not connected with these in any way, it will [still] signify those same [kinds of] friends very plainly. Therefore, it has this [signification] from itself – namely, because of persons it signifies kings and magnates rather than common people or those of low degree. Wherefore, ignition, vivification, benefaction, elevation, glorification, or if you prefer, igniting, vivifying, benefiting, elevating, making famous (if they please, grammarians may give names to a philosopher equivalent to these), will be words or attributes, by means of which the influence of the Sun is seen to be comprehended.

True as GOD, even very true, it may be said to be true, just, wise, etc., because we have known it to be of that particular sort by its effects, and by its infinite goodness, justice, wisdom, and the other things attributed to it without limit, we may try to define its nature, although, nevertheless, what it is in its simple essence, may remain unknown to us; so the celestial bodies, which in the likeness of GOD are universal causes, and images of Him (at least by the way of acting) compared with the rest, the noblest in universal corporeal nature, as will be made more clearly plain in what follows; although they were defined by us with some words [expressing] the properties or attributes apprehended in them from their effect and by experience; nevertheless, [exactly] what is the simple nature or the formal strength seen in them will remain unknown to us in this life, as we humbly direct our attention to the fog and weakness in this corruptible body. For seeing the Sun doing different things on different subjects—namely, in the first house on certain kinds of dispositions, in the eighth on a certain kind of death, in the twelfth on certain kinds of illnesses, etc.—and all of these coincide with it because they are not Saturnian effects but Solar ones; that is, they do not refer to the nature of Saturn, but to the nature of the Sun. Of course, reason dictates that all of these are [the result of] some simple nature of the Sun, but when one tries to investigate what that is, he is sunk into fog, if indeed the essences of things (as also that of GOD, which they represent by an essence) always remain as an inaccessible light for us, at least in this state of nature. For the Sun's influence is not properly incendiary and vivifying, exalting,[1] etc.; for these individual [characteristics] have individual and different formal concepts, none of which is a formal concept of influence, which is unique and very simple—equivalent to all the aforesaid things, or to those enfolded in itself—but as from the effects [caused by] GOD, His attributes become known to us, and from having recognized them, we may rightly consider then the works or effects of GOD; so from the effects of the planets we may [recognize] their attributes, and from their attributes, we may aptly deduce other similar effects, to the extent that is allowed

[1] Reading *exaltativitas* rather than *ex altativitas*.

in this life; where we may observe things not in themselves or intuitively, but only by their noticeable effects or the appearances of accidents. But in what follows it will be more evidently plain how that influence, very simple in its being, is so manifold in acting, and at the same time determinable in ways so varied, that from them the human intellect can not fail to be seized with the greatest admiration. And these things about the influences of all the other planets are going to be explained.

But the Moon, since it is also a primary Planet and free like the Sun—that is, its orbit is not bound to the orbit of another Planet—if it is seen in the *Caelum*, especially by night, among the Planets and stars that are then conspicuous, it appears to be like the ruler or the queen of the stars, even though it does not shine by its own light, but [by that] of the Sun, as do the rest of the Planets that are called minor Planets,[1] which if they were not illuminated by the Sun, neither they nor the Moon would be visible to us.

But in the makeup of a man, it principally rules the brain by analogy. And if it is found in a primary house in any nativity, it renders the temperament phlegmatic, his mentality somewhat dull, his morals inconstant, nevertheless a man illustrious in some way, but unsettled. Of riches, it signifies aquatic possessions or profits from waters. Of persons or dignities, magnates or illustrious persons, and especially feminine ones; then, couriers, go-betweens, hunters,[2] and common folk. Of illnesses, catarrhs, excessive menstrual flows, epilepsy, and such like. Which individual things, if they are carefully considered, we will perceive to be watery, benefic, notable, elevating, moveable—words or attributes by which the influence of the Moon is seen to be not separately but jointly comprehended; however, the simple essence of the influence does not become obvious to us from them, as was said above about the Sun.

---

[1] That is. Mercury, Venus, Mars, Jupiter, and Saturn— not today's *minor planets,* a now obsolete astronomical term for the asteroids. See the note on primary and secondary planets below.

[2] The Roman goddess Diana, identified with the Greek Moon goddess Artemis, was a huntress.

But the rest of the Planets are only said to be secondary Planets, because they do not primarily and independently revolve about the Earth,[1] like the Sun and the Moon, but only secondarily and dependently, and they emulate the nature of servants rather than that of lords; because in fact they are not free in their own motions like the Sun and the Moon, but they are bound to the motion of the Sun in its orbit. And yet two of these are more noteworthy, namely Saturn and Jupiter, both of which were also allotted satellites by the Author of Nature, since Saturn [has] two minor planets and Jupiter four, as is discerned by the optical tube.[2] Wherefore, it seems that it should be declared that Saturn and Jupiter are of great authority in mundane matters, and that they are principal [planets] after the Sun and the Moon.

Furthermore, if it is permissible to conjecture about the bodies of the Planets from the clarity and purity of their light; Saturn and his followers, exhibiting a dull and impure light, is perceived to be the darkest and most impure of the Planets.[3] From this it is obvious, because even if the Moon, [seen] backwards through the optical tube,[4] were not removed up to the distance of Saturn, so

---

[1] Remember that Morin had adopted Tycho Brahe's scheme of the solar system, in which the Earth is the center, the Moon and the Sun both revolve about the Earth, and the five planets revolve about the Sun. Hence, in this scheme both the Sun and the Moon are "primary planets," while the other five are "secondary planets."

[2] These are the first four *moons* of Jupiter, viz. Io, Europa, Ganymede, and Callisto, discovered by Galileo in 1610, and the *rings* of Saturn, which, being only indistinctly sighted in the primitive telescopes, were first supposed to be two small bodies close to Saturn on either side of it. The true nature of the rings and the first actual Satumian satellite. Titan, were discovered by Christiaan Huyghens (1629-1695) (who was a better lens-maker than his predecessors) and announced in 1656, but the *Astrologia Gallica* had already been written before that. The "optical tube" is of course the telescope.

[3] Saturn's appearance to the naked eye is dull and yellowish in comparison with Venus, Jupiter, and Mercury, which appear to be white. By *impurus* 'impure', Morin evidently refers to the fact that Saturn's color is not a pure white. Mars, of course is noticeably reddish when it is at its brightest, but Morin does not mention that.

[4] Morin apparently refers to looking at the Moon backwards through the telescope.

that it is seen still more remote; nevertheless, it is established by experience that the more the tube throws it higher,[1] the brighter and livelier its light appears, so that it excels the brightness of Venus in that way. Therefore, since Saturn, the highest of the Planets, shines for us with a very dull and impure light, this certainly argues that its body is very much more impure and darker than the body of the Moon,[2] in which black spaces [that are] neither few nor small are seen.[3] That same logic very probably proves that the Moon is purer than the rest of the bodies of Jupiter, Mars, Venus, and Mercury, whose light and mixture we have described in Book 9, Section 3, Chapter 8, asserting there that the earthy nature predominates to an intense degree in Saturn, the fiery in Mars, the airy in Venus; but the fiery nature predominates in Jupiter to a mild degree, and the earthy similarly in Mercury.

If, therefore, the effects of those Planets on men are noticed and gathered together in turn, as was already done for the Sun and the Moon above, it is perceived [that]:

Saturn in its influence is frightening, revolting, malefic, distressing, secretive, delaying, strengthening.[4]

Jupiter, igniting, beneficent, healing, dutiful, lawful, prudent, enriching, honoring, delighting.

Mars, igniting, arrogant, audacious, impatient, malefic, cruel, squandering, terrifying.

---

[1] Morin seems to be referring to the projection upon a card of the Moon's image through a reversed telescope, which would yield a very bright image, and, if the telescope were hand-held, a dancing image.

[2] This may have seemed logical in the early 17th century, but it is wrong. Most of the Moon's surface is a dull grey, brilliantly illuminated by the Sun, while Saturn's visible Surface is a sort of dirty yellow.

[3] These are the so-called *maria*, which appear dark to the naked eye.

[4] All of the epithets attributed to Saturn and the other planets are in the grammatical form of causative agents, e.g. *terrificum, ignificum, beneflcum, salvificum,* etc., thus representing the active force of the planets. Some of these are awkward to translate, so I have rendered them by the corresponding adjectives, and similarly for the other planets.

Venus, airy, beautifying, beneficent, healing, dutiful, amative, delighting, voluptuous, prolific.

Mercury, terrifying, acute, ingenious, knowledgeable, loquacious, crafty, adaptable, fickle. All of which terms produce an accomplishment of the causative agent.

But if by more or by fewer terms, it may seem to some that the influence of each planet can be explained better, or equally well, I would not deny that; for in [the case of] Mars, "arrogant" ("making proud") seems to embrace "acting bold," "being impatient," "evil-doing," "acting cruelly," and "tyrannizing"; indeed, because the latter are easily deduced from the former – even as the name Jesus embraces all the attributes or duties pertaining to "Savior." But I only suggest that to fashion a unique word that would explain the influence of a particular planet and satisfy its attributes as assigned above would, it seems to me, exceed the capability of man. It is true that until now the influences of the individual planets are known much more clearly – what in the individual kinds of things is principally or particularly subjected to the rule of each planet; but then, what the individual [planets] do especially with regard to the accidents of men will be more fully set forth in the table placed below, if we have first spoken about the analogical strength of the planets, on which that table itself also depends.

Finally, if it should be asked why Mars in the following table signifies soldiers, generals, or robbers, it is customary to reply that that is known by experience alone and not from the thing itself; if indeed posited in the ASC of the native, or if it is its ruler, it makes men of that sort conformably disposed; therefore, the answer will be for the cause à posteriori; moreover, the cause à priori is the proper nature of Mars, and its conformable celestial status, insofar as they are determined to the morals or the social position of the native. The same must be said about the Sun for kings, about Jupiter for bishops, about Saturn for monks, etc.

Chapter 3.

The Strength of the Planets by Analogy.

This [feature] of the planets is seen to be most worthy of admiration; namely because by its own nature, then by its location in the *Caelum*, and with respect to the earth, as well as by the mutual relationship by conjunctions, aspects and applications, and by other accidents or events, as if they premise future sublunar effects through some analogy or similitude already explained with sublunar things. Moreover, that such an analogy may be made between the celestial bodies and sublunar things will be shown here by a unique example, which will be like all [other cases].

It is known by experience that the Sun in the 11th house especially signifies friends at court, kings or princes, or magnates; in the 10th, splendid honors and royal dignities. And indeed it does not have [this influence] from the 11th house because friends of that sort are signified, no more than rustics, plebeians, or monks; therefore, will the Sun have [this influence] from the sign in which it is, or from the connection with other planets, or from its own self? Not the first, because posited in any sign in the 11th it will signify famous and illustrious friends; and not the second, because not connected with any others by rulership or aspect, it will [still signify] such friends. Therefore, it has it from itself that of persons it signifies kings and magnates, rather than plebeians and common people; moreover, Saturn is the reverse. And similarly it is shown in the individual houses that the Sun by itself signifies persons and things that are famous, illustrious, and royal; whence it is demonstrated that the Sun has conformity of analogy and agreement with those things; and the logic is the same with the other [planets].

Moreover, two kinds of analogy are universally found among the planets—namely, essential and accidental. And indeed essential analogy is [both] simple and composite. But it is simple especially by nature, dignity, or sex.

The *analogy by nature* consists of some similitude of *natures*, of the sort that is found between the Sun and something innately hot. For, just as in the macrocosm the Sun heats all these lower things, vivifies them, and governs them, so the native heat[1] in the microcosm, the heat and life and the functions of life are commanded in its own way and move forward to the whole body; and it is just like the Sun in its own microcosm. and the same analogy of nature is found between the Sun itself and the heart and the vital spirit; between the Moon and the brain and the phlegm; between Saturn and the spleen and melancholy; between Jupiter and the liver and the blood; between Mars and the bladder, the gall-bladder, and the bile; between Venus and the genitalia and the sperm; and between Mercury and the nerves and the animate spirit. Consequently, when they are determined to such things and located in the first house or when they are its ruler, they particularly signify such things; then in the twelfth they signify illnesses [affecting those things].

To these things, an *analogy by nature* is given between the Sun and gold, worthy of admiration. For just as the Sun is the first, purest, and noblest of the planets, so indeed is gold among the metals. And so also are the analogues, Moon and silver, Saturn and lead, Jupiter and tin, Mars and iron, Venus and copper, and Mercury and quicksilver. So that consequently not without reason the old alchemists wanted to distinguish these 7 metals by the names of the 7 planets analogous or sympathetic to them—namely, because they agree mutually in the purely natural effects; the magical understanding of which must not be disparaged.

Again, the *analogy by nature* comes between the Sun and dignities, honor, and fame; between the Moon and the common people; between Saturn and enclosures, prisons, and solitude; between Jupiter and riches; between Venus and pleasures; and between Mercury and mental ability, arts, and sciences. For the Sun is the glory of the macrocosm; Saturn the horror; Jupiter the riches; Mars the terror; Venus the delights; and Mercury the versatility; for as the Sun is conspicuous by its own splendor, it obscures the rest of the stars, so that honors, dignities, and fame make a man to stand

[1] Reading *calor nativus* 'native heat' rather than *color nativus* 'native color'.

out before the other commoners, whom he seems to overshadow. And, as the Moon is the lowest of the planets, very quickly changing her phases, so the commoner is the lowest kind of man, very rapidly changeable in his opinion and friendship. And so with the rest [of the planets].

The *analogy by dignity* consists of some similitude of *rulership*, of the sort that is found between the Sun and a king, a father, or a husband. For as the Sun shines in the middle of the planets, which are like satellites to it, perpetually surrounding, following, and observing it, so does a king shine in the midst of his own court and satellites; and the father and husband in the midst of his own family. And so the Moon, by analogy of dignity, refers to queens and great ladies, because these shine among other women, just as the Moon does among the stars when appearing by night. In a similar manner, since Jupiter and Saturn were allotted satellites, they refer by analogy to those among men who are lesser magnates, who because of dignity are surrounded by some assembly. And indeed Jupiter, the more splendid one with 4 followers, [indicates] more conspicuous persons, such as bishops, chancellors, governors, chieftains; but Saturn with only two more obscure satellites, and closer to the vast uninhabited area of the ether, [is indicative] of monks, those in charge of desolate regions or mines, and royal paymasters.

The *analogy by sex* consists of a certain similitude of *masculinity* or *femininity*. For, as having seen the Sun as the father of a family in the macrocosm, and the Moon as the mother, the rest of the planets must be held to be subordinate to the Sun, as if in slavery or as offspring, or as just the family of the Sun and the Moon—each one by reason of its own sex in accordance with Section 2, Chapter 1. There will, therefore, be an *analogy by sex* among Saturn, Jupiter, Mars, and Mercury as husbands, brothers, male servants, and the rest of the males; then, between Venus and wives, sisters, house maids, and the rest of the females of an inferior sort. For the Sun also signifies males and the Moon females by analogy, but strong and very superior, at least essentially; namely, the Sun, a king, father, or husband; the Moon, a queen, mother, or wife. And let these few [examples] of simple analogies suffice.

Moreover, *composite analogies* are born from these simple analogies. For the Sun, by reason of its dignity and sex, is analogous to kings, fathers, and husbands; the Moon to queens, mothers, and wives. By reason of its nature and sex, Mars is analogous to soldiers and robbers; Venus to lovers and whores; Mercury to astronomers and merchants. And in all of the above said [examples], there is this worthy of note and admiration—that an analogy agreeing with one planet does not agree with another; for Mars is not analogous to lovers, nor Venus to robbers; nor the Sun to monks; nor Saturn to Kings; but the above said individual analogies are appropriate to the [proper] individual planets, as experience teaches.

Besides, the essential *analogical strength* of a planet is not something really different from its influence, but they are the same thing; because what is said of the *analogical strength* by acting reveals subjects or effects with which that planet has a greater affinity. Indeed, in whatever space of the figure any planet acts analogically, it is from the things signified by that space that it chiefly affects whatever is more analogous to that planet; and that is nothing else than the planet acting in any space in accordance with its nature or proper influence on the things signified by that space; and this must be well noted.

Furthermore, Cardan in his *Commentary on the Quadripartite*, here and there, and then in his *Book of Revolutions*, Chapter 5, calls the planets *significators according to their substance*, of those things which it was said above that the planets themselves are analogous to; e.g. the Sun is a *significator according to substance* of a king, a father, or a husband; Jupiter of riches; etc.; moreover, the rulers of the Sun and Jupiter are significators of these same things by accident; and these *significators according to substance and accident* are those that are the principal foundation of judgment according to almost all the rest of the astrologers; and yet that it is false as it is commonly employed by Cardan and the rest of the astrologers, we shall prove most manifestly in its proper place. Here, let it suffice to note that we call all those things "Solar," for which the Sun has an essential analogy; "Lunar," for which the Moon has analogy; "Saturnine," for which Saturn has analogy, and so on with the rest [of the planets]; and it should be especially noted that the "Solar" effects are generally made in various ways according to the varied status of the Sun in the *Caelum*; the "Lunar" effects according to the varied status of the Moon; and thus with the rest [of the planets].

Moreover, the *accidental analogical strength* of the planets is that which comes as an extrinsic to them, and that happens in various ways.

First. From the quality of their own motion; for a planet that is swift in its own motion, or slow, direct, or retrograde is analogous to persons or things that in their own actions or motions are swift, slow, direct, or retrograde; and also by the force of analogy they make these that way; which you should understand about the things and persons to which these planets are determined in the celestial chart.

Second. From the method of approach of the planets; for if the ruler of the ASC, representing the native, applies to the ruler of the seventh space, which signifies the wife, the native will be concerned about taking a wife, and he will take a wife, unless somewhere else [in the chart] a celestial obstacle strongly interferes; but if both of the rulers have separated from each other, the native will avoid marriage, and he will not marry; or at least they will not agree between themselves, but divorces will occur, especially from [the action of] the malefics.

Third. By the *freedom of light*. For a combust planet—or one *under the Sun beams*—is analogous to hidden things; but, free from the Sun beams, it is analogous to visible things; and consequently it brings about such things.

Fourth. From the *heliacal rising or setting*. For a planet emerging from under the Sun beams is analogous to things that are new and free; but immersing itself under the Sun beams, it is analogous to the opposite of that.

But from these kinds of *analogies*, both accidental and essential, as set forth above, it will not be difficult to apprehend and understand the rest that will occur; and it is already sufficient to make [them] known.

Finally, *analogy* is also found in the *Caelum* itself or in the *Primum Mobile.* Since the part of the *Caelum* that is rising signifies the origin of life of the thing that is then being born; the culminating part its energy or action; the setting, its decline; and finally, the part that occupies the IMC, its destruction; if in fact this is the force and signification of the *Caelum*, it can more readily be referred to *analogy* than to any other cause, as is established in Book 18, Chapter 5.

TABLE OF THE UNIVERSAL RULERSHIPS OF THE PLANETS[1]

The Seven Planets are the Primary and Universal Causes of Physical Generation in the Family of Nature as a Whole. They are allotted an affinity with those things of a particular nature placed below, either from their own essence or because of analogy, and on this account they are said to rule them.

Parts of Heaven

Saturn: Capricorn, Aquarius.
Jupiter: Sagittarius, Pisces.
Mars: Aries, Scorpio.
The Sun: Leo.
Venus: Taurus, Libra.

[1] The material that follows is displayed in a large full-page tabular format on pp. 302-311 of the Latin original. Some of the print is large and some is very tiny and sometimes even printed sideways. Rather than attempting to reproduce the actual format of the tables on these much smaller pages, I have chosen to list the contents of the Table in sequential text format.

Mercury: Gemini, Virgo.
The Moon: Cancer.

Elements

Saturn: earth.
Jupiter: air, fire.
Mars: fire.
The Sun: ether, fire.
Venus: air.
Mercury: earth.
The Moon: water.

Elemental Qualities

Saturn: Intense cold, dryness, density, opacity, heaviness.
Jupiter: Moderation, with an excess of lightness, heat, and dryness.
Mars: Heat and dryness in intensity.
The Sun: Vital heat, rarity, lightness.
Venus: Moderation, with a little moistness.
Mercury: Cold and dryness in some degree.
The Moon: Cold, wetness, liquidity, density, and heaviness.

Colors[1]

Saturn: Black, dark, earth-colored, swarthy.
Jupiter: Blue.
Mars: Red.
The Sun: Yellow.
Venus: Green.
Mercury: Variegated.
The Moon: White, pale.

Odors

Saturn: Foul, narcotic.
Jupiter: Sweet.
Mars: Sharp.

[1] The printed text mistakenly has *Odores* 'Odors'.

The Sun: Fragrant, aromatic.
Venus: Delightfully sweet
Mercury: Mixed.
The Moon: Dull, imperceptible.

Flavors

Saturn: Sour, astringent.
Jupiter: Sweet.
Mars: Bitter.
The Sun: Salted just right.
Venus: Rich.
Mercury: Acid.
The Moon: Flat, watery.

Parts of the Year

Saturn: Fall.
Jupiter: Spring.
Mars: Summer.
The Sun: Summer.
Venus: Spring.
Mercury: Fall.
The Moon: Winter.

Weather Conditions and Effects in the Air

Saturn: Intense and frightful cold, and sometimes pestilence. Heavy, black clouds, dark rainstorms, snows, frosts, destructive winds, violent winds.
Jupiter: Mildness, healthy condition, moderate winds, fair weather, clouds turning from white to red.
Mars: Intemperate, hot, dry, very hot, pestiferous, wasting, fair weather, or red clouds, tawny, green, thunder, flashing, cloud-to-cloud lightning, thunderbolts, hail. Comets with tails, glowing impressions,[1] tornadoes, tempestuous, harmful, destructive winds.
The Sun: Heat, dryness, fair weather and sometimes very

[1] Probably the glowing trains of meteors.

hot, tawny clouds or turning tawny from red, moderate winds, dry and healthy.
Venus: Mildness, health, fair weather, dew, fog, mist, clouds completely white, light and healthy rain, moderate and somewhat humid winds.
Mercury: Dryness, sudden winds, strong, gusty, shifting; violent, damaging winds; variegated clouds, thunder, flashing, thunderbolts.
The Moon: Humidity and cold from itself.

In Waters and in the Sea

Saturn: Overflowing, floods, corruption, destruction or scarcity of fish, violent winds and raging storms, difficult voyages, shipwreck.
Jupiter: Moderate and useful increases in waters, abundance of fish, tranquility, or moderate winds, favorable and profitable passages of ships.
Mars: Drying up of waters, corruption, destruction of fish, violent winds, sudden shipwrecks, invasions of pirates.
The Sun: Droughts and decreases.
Venus: Useful increases and overflows, good health, great abundance of fish, easy, secure, and fortunate voyages.
Mercury: Violent winds and sudden storms that increase when it is matutine, and decrease when it is vespertine, plots of pirates.
The Moon: Increases, ebbing and flowing.

On the Earth

Saturn: Sterility of fruits and corruption of useful plants by malign air, cold, frost, rain storms, hail, floods, caterpillars, locusts; destruction of useful animals, appearance of harmful ones; earthquake, collapse of buildings and cities.
Jupiter: Abundance and health of plants, fruits, and useful animals, and the suppression of injurious ones, or those spawned from rotten material.[1]

[1] Maggots, etc.

Mars: Scarcity and unhealthiness of plants, fruits, and animals useful to man from intemperate heat and dryness or from the poisonous quality of the air; generation of venomous creatures, fires, earthquakes.
The Sun: Four parts of the year, but especially the summer per se; droughts, forest fires; the rest according to the characteristics of the ruler and the aspects.
Venus: The same as Jupiter, but with more fertility.
Mercury: Great earthquakes, but a diversity of other events, instability, and often, with Saturn or Mars, destruction of plants and animals.
The Moon: Putrefaction, but in accordance with its relation to the Sun and the other planets, whose configurations with the Moon ought to be carefully noticed, since the Moon is closest to the Earth.

Minerals

Saturn: Lead, black stones, dark-colored, field-stones.
Jupiter: Tin, sapphire, amethyst.
Mars: Iron, lodestone, jasper, bloodstone, reddish [stones].[1]
The Sun: Gold, carbuncle, hyacinth,[2] chrysolite.
Venus: Copper, emerald, turquoise, coral, pearl.
Mercury: Quicksilver, chalcedony, carnelian, *alecterius*.[3]
The Moon: Silver, crystal, beryl, diamond, pearl.

Plants

Saturn: The oak, medlar, quince,[4] rue, hellebore, narcotic [plants], and the rest of the thick substances, and those growing slowly.
Jupiter: The laurel, sandalwood, cinnamon, sugar, balsam,

---

[1] The Latin has *rubinus* 'reddish'.

[2] A hyacinth-colored precious or semiprecious stone, either a variety of amethyst or sapphire. Cf. Pliny, *Natural History,* XXXVII. 40 (Sect. 122).

[3] I cannot identify this mineral or stone, unless the reference is to the *alectoria* or "cock's stone" mentioned by Pliny, *Natural History,* XXXVII. 54 (Sect. 144).

[4] Reading *cydonius* 'quince' instead of *citonius* [unidentified].

frankincense.
Man: Pepper, ginger, mustard, radish, scammony, colocynth,[1] garlic, everything bitter, and hot poisonous [plants].
The Sun: The palm, rosemary, heliotrope, crocus, grain, and spices.
Venus: The date palm, olive, pine, lily, rose, pea.
Mercury: The hazel, yarrow.
The Moon: Gourds, cucumbers, pumpkins, lettuce.

Animals

Saturn: The camel, bear, goat, ass, cat, owl, bat, tortoise, mouse, beetle, and others that walk slowly, and those that roam about at night, the toad.
Jupiter: The elephant, deer, bull, stag, peacock, falcon.
Mars: The horse, wolf, boar, dog, ostrich, kite, hawk, venomous serpents, scorpion, spider.
The Sun: The lion, eagle, falcon, cock.
Venus: The nanny goat, sheep, pheasant, partridge, dove, turtledove, sparrow.
Mercury: The fox, ape, serpent, parrot, spider, bee, ant.
The Moon: The hare, swan, nightingale, frogs, fish, juicy snails, shellfish, crabs, slugs.

The Humors

Saturn: Melancholy, black bile.
Jupiter: Moisture, blood, semen.
Mars: Yellow, vitelline, aeruginous, [or] porraceous bile.[2]
The Sun: Vital spirit, bilious blood.
Venus: Phlegmatic blood, semen.
Mercury: Animal spirit.
The Moon: Phlegm, serum.

---

[1] The *Cucumis colocynthis* of Linnaeus, a wild cucumber used as a purgative. See Pliny, *Natural History,* XX. 8 (Sect. 14).

[2] Vitelline means yellowish; aeruginous, bluish-green; and porraceous, greenish.

Parts of the Body

Saturn: The bones, teeth, cartilage, right ear, spleen, bladder.
Jupiter: The liver, veins, lungs, diaphragm, sides, muscles.
Mars: The gall bladder, left ear, pudenda, kidneys.
The Sun: The heart, arteries, right eye, and the right side in men, but the left one in women.
Venus: The throat, breasts, belly, buttocks, womb, kidneys, genitalia.
Mercury: The legs and feet, arms, hands, fingers, tongue, nerves, ligaments.
The Moon: The brain, left eye, the left side in men, but the right one in women. Intestines, stomach, vulva, membranes.

The Faculties

Saturn: The retentive.
Jupiter: The digestive[1] and vegetal.[2]
Mars: The expulsive.
The Sun: The vital, attractive.
Venus: The generative.
Mercury: The animate, rational.
The Moon: The expulsive, vegetal, animate.

The Senses

Saturn: Hearing on the right.
Jupiter: Touch, smell.
Mars: Hearing on the left.
The Sun: Sight on the right in a man, especially by day; on the left in a woman.
Venus: Taste, smell, touch, the pleasures [arising] from these senses.
Mercury: Taste, hearing.
The Moon: Sight on the right in women; on the left in men.

---

[1] Literally, *coctrix* 'cooking'.

[2] The word *vegetal* is used in the sense of 'growing'

Parts of the Mind

Saturn: Memory.
Jupiter: Judgment, the concupiscible appetite.
Mars: The irascible appetite.
The Sun: The universal appetite for good.
Venus: The concupiscible appetite.
Mercury: Common sense, imagination, ingenuity, reason, or the rational appetite.
The Moon: Apprehension, the universal appetite.

The Natural Laws of Men and their Relations amongst Themselves by Analogy

Saturn: Great-grandfather, grandfather and father, then also a servant, a hidden enemy.
Jupiter: The master, children.
Man: The husband in women's charts, elder brothers, open enemies.
The Sun: The father and the husband in women's charts.
Venus: The wife and the mother by day, sisters, daughters, lovers, concubines.
Mercury: Younger brothers, servants.
The Moon: The mother and the wife especially by night, widows, pregnant women.[1]

Corporature

About which there can be no universal determination. For even though in general and everywhere on earth Martial types are drier and more slender; Jovial and Venusian types, moister, juicier, fairer-skinned, and more beautiful; Saturnians uglier and darker; etc.; still, the particular conformations of parts and colors do not always correspond equally to the natures of the planets, but there is a [particular] character of body native to each place on earth, as is obvious from the Ethiopians, the Tartars, and the Peruvians, who differ greatly among themselves in body, hair, and shape of face, but the Ethiopian in France begets an Ethiopian.

[1] Or, less likely, 'pregnant widows'.

Therefore, consider the region and the parents; and understand that the things given here [are mainly applicable] to the white men of Asia, Europe, etc.

Saturn Oriental: Cold, moist, moderate flesh, moderate in stature, a long face, large dark eyes, occasionally spotted, uneven teeth, an ugly and grim appearance, face and body rather dark in color, tawny,[1] honey-colored,[2] pallid, dark hair, thickset, rugged, crooked feet.

Occidental: Cold, dry, thin, short in stature, dark eyes, dark plain hair, scanty on the head and in the beard, the rest of the body hairless.

Jupiter Oriental: Moderately hot and moist, fleshy, round cheeks, moderate and elegant and majestic in stature, white in color, inclining to yellow or rose, eyes rather large [and] dark, handsome, with a mark in the right foot.

Occidental: Somewhat moister in temperament, moderate in stature, bald, with a mark in the left foot, which rarely fails.

Mars Oriental: Hot, dry, less fleshy, decently tall and well proportioned, in color from white to red, with bluish eyes, much hair between curly and straight, with hairiness of body.

Occidental: Drier, moderate in stature, with a big head, a round and freckled face, or with a mark on his forehead, small eyes, large nostrils, long teeth; red in color, red-haired, rigid, with a hairless body, and a long and military stride.

The Sun: Hot and not so dry, moderate in stature, a large head; a round, white, and shining face, eyes large and splendid and yellow in color, long hair but growing bald, a somewhat harsh voice.

Venus: Hot and moist, moderate in stature, plump, and the face especially full and delicate, white with a blush of red, beautiful, lovable, hair somewhat curly, tawny, or rather dark,

[1] Reading *fulvus* 'tawny' rather than *fulcus* [no such word].

[2] Latin *mellinus*.

tawny-colored eyes, handsome, happy, glancing charmingly, thin eyebrows and lips, narrow chest, full legs. And these features are more apparent when Venus is oriental.

Mercury Oriental: Somewhat hotter, moderate in stature and well proportioned, with good color, or honey-colored, small eyes, moderate, yellowish hair.

Occidental: Somewhat dry, thin, slim, with small teeth and fingers, scanty beard, a thin voice, small, quick steps, a very sharp mentality.

The Moon: Moist, tall stature, a beautiful face, white in color, gray eyes, fine hair, a becoming beard.

Note

Judge cautiously and carefully on the form of the body, for this part of judgment often fails, since it is not yet well understood. But through experience it can be perfected, namely by having looked at the planets in the first house and their lords and the lord of the Ascendant, along with the forms of the natives.

Character and Talents

Saturn well-placed.[1] Very talented, investigators of secret things, prudent, outstanding in counsel, secretive, rather solitary, suspicious and jealous, dissembling, hardworking, long-suffering, persevering, overcoming, violent, thrifty, eager for wealth, great accumulators, striving for dominion, fit for governorships, useful and dear to princes.

But badly disposed. Sad, melancholy, abject, repulsive, austere, shameless, sluggish, timid, nervous, envious, outstanding ineptitude in crime, wretched, complaining, or taciturn, those who hate association and light, very solitary, paupers, or trading in evil arts, very suspicious and jealous, liars, spiteful, fraudulent, plot-

[1] The Latin reads *bene affecto* 'well affected', which means "well placed by sign and house and well aspected." "Badly placed" is of course the reverse. More familiar terms (especially to Horary astrologers) would be *fortified* and *impedited.*

ters, traitors, and those who frequently suffer judicial punishment for their crimes.

Jupiter well-placed. Straightforward, upright, religious, just, faithful, courteous, merciful, clean, modest, cheerful, obliging, easy to talk to, moderately serious, frank, dutiful, prudent, sensible, strong in counsel, obliging, generous, illustrious, great in giving justice, in making laws, fit for magistracy, for first place, and for kingdom, fond of and partial to his own and his own things, truthful.

Badly disposed. Character in one way or another like the previous, but artificial and inclining to faults, as superstition in place of piety[1] and religion, silliness instead of courtesy, timidity instead of modesty, pretense instead of fidelity, prodigality instead of generosity, pride and arrogance instead of greatness—of course in accordance with the way of the planet by which it is afflicted by connection[2] or by rulership.

Mars well-placed. Brave, strong, spirited, noble, bold, arrogant, boastful, despising the praise of another, and full of contempt for other men, irascible, prone to strike and wound, eager for revenge, obeying no one, unable to endure servitude and injuries, eager for dominance, craving battles and conflicts, arrogant tyrants, reckless and scornful of danger, active, ready, in a hurry, self-confident, spurning wealth, generous, lucky, well-suited for commanding soldiers, ill-suited for ruling citizens, scornful of God or not concerned.

Badly placed. Unscrupulous, unjust, pitiless, arrogant, quarrelsome, seditious, loud-mouthed, reckless, mad, truculent, aggressive in challenging, cruel, assassins, murderers, tyrants, drunkards, destroying their own property and that of others, incendiaries, robbers, thieves, pirates, neglecting their own people.

The Sun well-placed. Upright, just, honest, faithful, clean, sensible, in one way or another irascible, great, very eager for hon-

[1] Reading *pro pietate* instead of *proprietate*.

[2] That is, by aspect.

ors and much honored, illustrious, grand, distinguished, famous, cultivators of friendships, but not overly fond of wife and children.

Badly placed. Silly, spiteful, less observant of honor, artificial, and degenerate from the things said above in accordance with the nature of the planet making it unfortunate by rulership or unfavorable connection.

Venus well-placed. Endowed with good character, charming, upright, and worshiping God religiously, merciful, peace-making, cheerful, sociable, fond of cleanliness and decoration, devoted to dancing, singing, music, and dining, elegant and charming in their actions, playful, and inclined towards all delights and pleasures, fortunate and cautious in love affairs and friendships, kind especially towards his own [people], unable to endure hard work, quarrels, anger, and misfortune, and easily reconciled.

Badly placed. Timid, idle, suitors, and bothersome in love affairs or friendships, imprudently and unfortunately jealous, womanizers, addicted to indecent desires, disreputable, and with many expenditures on account of women, mischances, bothersome to the wretched and bad; unless Venus herself rules most of the principal places of the geniture and is in an important angle.

Mercury well-placed. Endowed with outstanding character, excelling in shrewdness of intellect, easily capable [of learning] the sciences and arts of all kinds, but especially mathematics, readily conjecturing and reasoning; learning many things without a teacher, and finding unknown things first, finely differing and discussing, quick, wary, prudent, composed in behavior, readily adapting himself to any person, situation, or time, and therefore sociable and fit for getting things done.

Badly placed. Unstable, foolish, forgetful, addicted to mental wanderings, talkative, boastful, dull-witted, insolent, liars, stubborn, flatterers,[1] dissemblers, crafty, deceivers, treacherous, spite-

[1] And "yes-men."

ful, perjurers, plotters, slanderers, given to falsifications of writing, testimony, or money, disreputable, pimps, rudely embroiling themselves in matters of every sort, giving dangerous advice, and boldly undertaking crimes.

The Moon well-placed. Fine mental ability, famous, honored, well composed in behavior, honest, frank, honorable.

Badly placed. Dull in mental ability, timid, common, untruthful, vagabonds, artificial, and of no name, or servants, or fools.

Professions, or Characters Speaking to Them

Saturn well-placed. Great theologians, philosophers, treasurers, mine superintendents.

Moderately placed. Farmers, excavators, miners, potters, builders, leather-workers,[1] monks, hermits.

Badly placed. Practitioners of magic, fortunetellers, sorcerers, those who clean out cesspools and sewers, beggars, [and] executioners.

Jupiter well-placed. Advisers, senators, judges, presidents, executive secretaries,[2] high priests, generals of sacred orders, or provincials,[3] abbots, bishops, cardinals, popes, governors of provinces or cities.

Badly placed. Schoolmasters and athletic directors.

Mars well-placed. Knights, commanders-in-chief of armies, generals, and colonels,[4] hunters, lawyers, physicians, blacksmiths, founders,[5] [and] cooks.

---

[1] The Latin word *coriarii* 'tanners' or *'curriers'* designates those who work with raw hides rather than artisans who turn finished leather into consumer products.

[2] Not copyists and routine office workers, who are under Mercury (see below).

[3] Generals and provincials are the superiors and division superintendents of Catholic religious orders such as the Benedictines. The leader of the Salvation Army also holds the title General.

[4] The Latin has *Capitanei exercituum, Duces atque Praefecti.* The ranks mentioned in the translation are arbitrary. Certainly, military officials of higher rank than captain are meant. (Cf. the Spanish *capitan general.*)

[5] That is, those who make castings in a foundry.

Badly placed. Butchers, leather-workers, pirates, bandits, cattle-rustlers[1] [and] executioners.

The Sun well-placed. The Pope, emperors, kings, princes, governors, magnates, and all administrators with royal honors or dignities.

Venus well-placed. Spice-merchants, perfumers, druggists, painters, jewelers, musicians, tavern keepers, soothsayers, members of sacred orders.

Badly placed. Whores, seductresses, enchantresses, painted ladies,[2] beggar-women.

Mercury well-placed. Mathematicians, geometers, astronomers, astrologers, philosophers, orators, copyists, secretaries, poets, painters, merchants. All ingenious craftsmen, and inventors of new arts.

Badly placed. Pimps, thieves, counterfeiters, forgers, and sellers of fake goods.

The Moon well-placed. Queens, widows, couriers, sailors, fishermen, hunters, commoners.

Accidents of Fate

Saturn well-placed. High positions, governorships, authority, discovery of treasures, great wealth.

---

[1] The Latin text has *Lictores,* where I have translated 'cattle-rustlers'. Lictors were official attendants who walked before the high magistrates of Rome carrying an axe. This word is certainly wrong here. The Latin version of Ptolemy's *Tetrabiblos,* iv. 4, printed by Cardan has the following (Textus XVI, p. 324, col. 2) . . . *carnifices . . . raptores, latrones abactores. . .* 'executioners...robbers, bandits, cattle-rustlers . . .' I think what Morin wrote was *abactores* 'cattle-rustlers'. My second choice would be *luctatores* 'wrestlers', which appears a few lines up in the same text.

[2] The Latin word *fucatrices* is not in my lexicon. If it is not simply a misprint, it would seem to be derived from *fucatus* 'counterfeit' or 'artificial'. I suppose it refers to women who wear heavy makeup, but if the derived sense of *fucatus* is taken, it could be translated as 'deceivers'. And if *fucatrices* is a misprint, perhaps Morin wrote *fututrices,* a coarse word that could be translated as 'sluts'.

Badly placed. Fall from honor and high position, low status, poverty, servitude, bad luck with projects and actions, secret enemies, disgrace, imprisonment, exile, punishment, a sorrowful end.

Jupiter well-placed. Independence, riches, honors, high position, friends, servants, fortunate marriages, or high positions in the Church, fame, glory, an abundance of children, and from them happiness, profits. And, to sum it up, Jupiter well-placed bestows good luck in undertakings and in all things, and happy outcomes.

Badly placed. It denies these things, or lessens them, or gives merely the appearance of them, or makes them unfortunate.

Mars well-placed. Friendships with and cultivation of military men, fortunate in duels, positions of command in war, victories in battles when storming cities or attacking fleets of ships, spoils, [and] triumphs.

Badly placed. Enmities, lawsuits, fights, duels, battles and military assaults unluckily undertaken, losses of personal property and high position, robberies, squandering, destruction, plots, attacks, thefts, homicides, illicit intercourse, imprisonment, and frequently a violent death.

The Sun well-placed. Glory, fame, splendid status, honored appointments, public offices, high royal or ecclesiastical positions, in both cases, i.e., secular and ecclesiastical, with honor and outstanding respect, powerful friends, a name famous from death.[1]

Badly placed. It gives powerful enemies, and it renders unfortunate the things mentioned above, or else it denies them [altogether], and it portends misfortune in all things undertaken for himself.

Venus well-placed. Good will from everyone, profits, happy successes in love affairs, happy marriages, fortunate and numer-

[1] This could mean 'from the manner of death' or 'from [the time of] death', i.e., 'after death'.

ous offspring; high positions and exceptional good fortune in undertakings and actions.

Badly placed. It lessens, renders unfortunate, or even denies the things mentioned above.

Mercury well-placed. Successful business activities, profitable missions, fortunate contracts, outstanding and successful inventions, high positions, professions, and honor and profit from these, many and useful friends.

Badly placed. It corresponds to the opposite [of the preceding], then [it indicates] useless occupation in curious, arcane [activities], expenses and misfortunes, deceptions, falsifications, inconstant position in life[1] due to various unexpected events, and liable [to experience] an uncertain demise.

The Moon well-placed. A renowned name, wealth, happiness, honorable and lucrative missions, possessions of watery lands, many offspring, happy marriages, high positions and also royal positions, highly placed friends in both spheres.

Badly placed. It lessens, renders unfortunate, or even denies [altogether] the things mentioned above, and it gives a life of change, hardship, and liable [to experience] various unexpected events.

Ages

Saturn: Decrepitude extending to the end of life.
Jupiter: Old age to the 68th year
Mars: Virility to the 56th year.
The Sun: Youth to the 42nd year.
Venus: Adolescence to the 21st year.
Mercury: Boyhood to the 14th year.
The Moon: Infancy to the 4th year.

Illnesses[1]

Saturn: Of the parts of the body which Saturn itself rules. Then quartan ague[2] scabies,[3] leprosy,[4] wasting diseases, melancholy,[5] paralysis, the black jaundice,[6] dropsy, arthritis, cancer, cough, asthma, tuberculosis, and other serious catarrhs, deafness, toothache, lethargy,[7] apoplexy, hernia.

Jupiter: Of the parts over which it presides. Then chronic fever, variola, exanthema, angina, back pains,[8] inflammation of the liver, pleurisy, inflammation of the lungs,[9] spasms; then sick-

[1] The text seems to be falsely punctuated here. I have read *falsificationes. vitae status inconstans* as above, instead of *falsificationes vitae, status inconstans 'falsifications* of life, inconstant position.

[2] Morin was a medical doctor, so his list of the diseases peculiar to each planet should be reasonably reliable. However, medical terminology has changed considerably in the three centuries since he wrote. Consequently, it is not always possible to equate the names of the diseases and conditions he mentions with their present day names. And of course the reader must bear in mind that the real cause of most diseases or conditions was unknown to Morin and his contemporaries. The medicine of his time classified diseases according to their symptoms, thereby confounding different ailments that displayed similar symptoms but arose from different causes.

[2] Probably the *malariae* form of malaria. (Most of the medical notes that follow are from the introduction to W. H. S. Jones's translation of Books XX-XXIII of Pliny's *Natural History* [Loeb Classical Library, Pliny, N.H., vol. 6]).

[3] In Latin, *scabies,* but this term is now narrowed to mean an itchy skin eruption caused by the itch insect. The older usage was broader and referred to any ruddy hardening of the skin accompanied by itch.

[4] Not necessarily true leprosy, but any scaly condition of the skin resembling leprosy and accompanied by itch.

[5] Melancholy refers to a state of mental lassitude or depression, which can have either a physical or psychological cause. It is one of the manifestations of chronic malaria in certain patients.

[6] Probably the name used for a long-standing case of *yellow* jaundice, in which the skin has finally taken on a dark green or dark brown hue.

[7] Probably *coma* is meant, rather than sluggishness, although, from an astrological point of view, Saturn would rule both.

[8] Disregarding the comma in *passiones, spinae dorsi.*

[9] Latin *peripneumonia,* probably the disease we call pneumonia.

nesses [arising] from winds, stench and inflammation, phlegm.[1]

Mars: Of the parts over which it presides. Then acute, burning fevers, plague,[2] yellow jaundice, convulsions, hemorrhage, dysentery, carbuncles, anthrax, erysipelas, gangrene,[3] wounds, especially in the face, tertian fever.[4]

The Sun: Of the parts over which it presides. Then ephemeral fevers, spasm, fainting, catarrhs, illnesses of the eyes.

Venus: Of the parts over which it presides. Then venereal disease, gonorrhea, illnesses of the womb and the genitals, priapism, weaknesses of the belly arising from cold or moisture, and from that, diarrhea, inflammation.

Mercury: Of the parts over which it presides. Then intermittent and recurrent fevers, madness, frenzy, delirium, insanity, epilepsy, convulsion, stammering, catarrhs, cough, abundance of spittle.

The Moon: Of the parts over which it presides. Then quotidian fevers,[5] epilepsy, apoplexy, silliness, catarrhs, colic, vomiting, fluxes from the belly, excessive menstruation, dropsy, stroke, phlegm.

Death

Saturn well-placed. A natural death from the illnesses over which Saturn itself presides.

Badly placed. Sudden or violent death from the collapse [of

[1] In Morin's time, two hundred years before the adoption of the germ theory of disease, it was believed that various diseases were caused by winds or bad smells (from swamps, sewers and cesspools, or rotting garbage). Malaria (from the Italian *mala aria* 'bad air'), a disease now known to be caused by a protozoa! parasite is a case in point.

[2] Probably the bubonic plague or "black death." But the term would have also have been applied to outbreaks of typhus or malignant malaria.

[3] In the Latin, *ulcera phagedenica & serpentia.* These are eruptions on the skin that are round and putrefying or streaked.

[4] An attack of chills and fever that recurs every other day, as in vivax malaria.

[5] Daily attacks of chills and fever.

buildings), from a fall, a precipitous fall, drowning, shipwreck, suffocation, incarceration, hanging, lead shot; or with infamy, as by an executioner.

Jupiter well-placed. A natural death from the illnesses over which it presides.

Badly placed. A violent death from drowning, from war, a duel, or by order of a prince.

Mars well-placed. A natural death from the illnesses over which it presides.

Badly placed. A violent death from wounds [made] by iron, from fire, or catapults; from decapitation, mutilation of [bodily] members, being torn to pieces, strangulation, hanging, bites of animals, especially venomous ones, mangling or letting of blood by unskilled surgeons and physicians, [or] by being burnt up.

The Sun well-placed. A natural death from the milder illnesses over which it presides, such as fevers.

Badly placed. Sudden death from plague, [or] stroke; or a violent [death] from a public order of a prince, or in battle, or by being burnt up.

Venus well-placed. A natural death from the illnesses over which it presides.

Badly placed. A violent or premature death from poison, medicine, intoxication, an excess of intercourse or of women, or because of lust.

Mercury well-placed. Death from those illnesses over which it presides, and a natural one.

Badly placed. An unexpected and very violent death, by murder, poison, magic, or on account of counterfeiting, perjury, forgery, or misapplication of the law.

The Moon well-placed. A natural death from those illnesses over which it presides.

Badly placed. A violent death from the excessive [administration of] laxatives, from drowning, or murder, generally public or judicial.

Particular Places on the Earth

Saturn: Subterranean [places], pits, sewers, latrines, prisons, cemeteries, lonely [places], hermitages, deserted [places].

Jupiter: High [places], and lofty churches, palaces, [places] especially intended for judicial purposes.[1]

Mars: Foundries and machine shops, fortified places.

The Sun: Courts of kings and princes, auditoriums, churches, places of cities.[2]

Venus: Parks, greens, groves, gardens, banquet-houses, theatres, whorehouses.

Mercury: Markets, academies, colleges.

The Moon: Forests, seas, rivers, pools, and places dedicated to public gatherings.

Days of the Week

Saturn: The Sabbath.
Jupiter: Thursday.
Mars: Tuesday.
The Sun: The Lord's Day.
Venus: Friday.
Mercury: Wednesday.
The Moon: Monday.

And the things said here are sufficient for the general rulership of the planets over these lower things. But it must be carefully noted that:

1. In the tables above, I did not set forth all the rulerships pertaining to Saturn, but only the more common and notable ones, so

[1] Or, less likely, 'High and lofty palaces of the Church, especially intended for judicial purposes.'

[2] That is, a large open area in a city—*place* in French, *piazza* in Italian, *plaza* in Spanish, sometimes *square* in English.

that from them it may be clearly exposed what sort of influence Saturn has on rulerships. And the consideration is the same with regard to illnesses, accidents of fortune, death, etc. resulting from Saturn or coming forth from any other planets.

2. The rulerships of the planets over sublunar things that are set forth above are only the simple rulerships from the proper nature of each planet. And consequently, when many planets concur together in the rulership, e.g. of rulership itself, there must be a sagacious mixture of the strength and nature of the individual planets, having taken into account the one that predominates [over the others]. And so with the rest.

3. And judgment must not be made about [the native's] morals from all the planets together, nor from one separately according to the above said table, but only from the one or from those that will be determined in the natal figure to signifying behavior by body, rulership, or with connection by body or by aspect, as will be said in its own place. And the logic is the same in the case of corporature, profession, illness, etc.; and thus the faith of the table will be able to be applied. And when it is said that these kinds of accidents appear with regard to behavior from a planet well disposed, but those other kinds from a planet badly disposed, a good or bad disposition is understood to be both by reason of the sign and of the connection with other planets, or the celestial state of that planet, and by reason of its location in the figure. For even when a planet is said to do this or that with regard to behavior, it is already supposed to be determined to those things. Nevertheless, that planet will signify one thing about behavior if it is in the tenth, and another thing if it is in the fifth, or one thing if it is the ruler of the tenth and another if it is the ruler of the fifth. A planet by reason of its own location or rulership in a figure, is well or badly disposed to those things that it signifies.

Chapter 4.

The Influences of the Jovial Planets.[1]

There is no one of sane mind who would dare to assert that these planets are of no importance in the nature of things and of no use; therefore, either they serve us, or they serve those living in the Jovial world; and if this is asserted, it should similarly be said that Saturn, Jupiter, Mars, Venus, and Mercury serve those living in the solar world or on the Sun. But we experience that these [planets] are made to be causes for us and that they direct their own powers of acting toward us. Therefore, why not the Jovial ones? To these things, since they are made hypothetically on account of Jupiter, and Jupiter on account of us, as we experience it; it follows that these things are always made because of us, or if you prefer the system of Jupiter to have been established, as we experience that the system of the Sun was made for us, as Holy Scripture teaches. Therefore, they do serve us, not indeed by their own light, which is not noticeable to us; [and are] therefore, an influence very difficult to recognize, for the detection of which, we have nevertheless described a certain method elsewhere. The same thing must be judged about the two satellites of Saturn.[2]

Chapter 5.

The Proper Influences of the Fixed Stars.

Here it must frankly be said that the proper influences of all the fixed stars, as well as their elemental strengths, are not known

[1] Morin is speaking of the satellites of Jupiter, four of which were known in his time.

[2] Not *satellites* of Saturn, as Morin supposed them to be, but in fact the *rings* of Saturn, which to early observers such as Galileo appeared to be two appendages, one on each side of the planet, that some took to be satellites. It was not until 1656 that Saturn's big satellite Titan was discovered by Christiaan Huyghens (1629-1695), who in 1659 published the first drawing showing the Saturnian "appendages" to be in fact a ring about the planet. But Morin had died before these discoveries. Nevertheless, his statement that the same logic would apply to Saturnian satellites is valid.

to men; consequently, astrology—at least practical astrology—experiences no mean loss. For even if the seven planets are the primary governors of this inferior world, and their influx is not in governance, or if the secret laws of Saturn, Jupiter, Mars, Venus, and Mercury escape the light of philosophy (as Alexander de Angelis asserted in the Preface to Book 5 of his [treatise] *Against the Astrologers*), but rather the awkwardly and stupidly [made] obscurities of those who are philosophizing. Nevertheless, it is certain from the conjunctions of the planets with the fixed stars that their sublunar effects are varied. For which reason, Astrologers have not only made tables of [the stars] for recognizing future conditions of the air, from the true or heliacal rising and setting of the fixed stars, or tables of the applications of the Moon to the fixed stars. But Hippocrates himself in his *Book on Airs, Waters, and Places*,[1] text 30, prescribes that the observation of those risings and settings of the stars must be made in medicine, especially those of Sirius, Arcturus, and the Pleiades, whose powers he had experienced more than the others, teaching that the same thing should be done in the future in the case of the others, especially the more notable ones that to himself were then unknown. Therefore, to deny to the fixed stars powers and efficacies, both elemental as well as influential, on these lower things, does not seem to be of less inexperience than to take them away from Saturn, Jupiter, Mars, Venus, and Mercury, [which would] also be apart from experience, which alone produces those who are skilled in this art, just as inexperience produces unjust judges, who, attributing power over these lower things solely to the Sun and the Moon, consider the other stars to be made without effect, or only as decorations, or for the sake of illuminating.

And yet it is certain that those things that Ptolemy has in Book 1, Chapter 9, of the *Quadripartite* about the powers of the stars are no less uncertain than they are devoid of reason, and scarcely in agreement with the things that he put in Book 2, chapter 11, on the

[1] A treatise ascribed to Hippocrates (c.460-c.360) in the collection of his writings. Morin probably referred to the Latin translation by Fabius Calvus (Rome, 1525).

strength and nature of the signs. In those, therefore, he is counseled by experience. Moreover, how the force of only a few of the fixed stars, namely the influxes of the brighter ones, are however known to astrologers; and not to be trusted are the tables of the fixed stars handed down by the old astronomers for the nature of the fixed stars, which Cardan himself relied upon in his judgments of nativities, even for fixed stars of the fifth magnitude. From which no little advantage comes to astrology, especially with regard to the accidents of humans, which are certainly often produced by the brighter fixed stars, or evidently observed to be initiated, but not by the lesser ones, except rarely, or to the degree that they are accumulated in some constellation, such as the Pleiades, Delphinus,[1] etc. Nevertheless, since we already know more about the powers of the stars than Hippocrates did, or others who lived at the birth or in the youth of astrology, what forbids that it may not be of use now more fully to those following those things in recognition, if generous talents, either on their own or with the generosity of princes (which here, no less than in astronomy, should be carried out) have wished to undertake this sublime field.

Besides, we are now speaking in general about the influences of the fixed stars, those influences that act in a divided and conjoined manner on all these sublunar things, as was made plain above about illnesses and constitutions in air; but on man particularly, than which there is no subject in the elementary region that is more suitable for receiving influences. Consequently, some of the fixed stars are benefic to man by nature, but others are malefic, as was said about the planets in Section 2, Chapter 3. And besides, the individual [stars], just like the planets, differ in kind; nevertheless, they preserve along with these some affinity of nature, as has been shown diffusely by us in Book 9, Section 4, Chapters 1 & 3. And it is set forth in the table of the fixed stars set below, in which it happens that at least the brighter stars, which they call *royal*, con-

[1] The Pleiades are a little asterism of six stars within about one degree of each other, and Delphinus is a small constellation, whose principal stars are within about six degrees of each other in the northern part of the constellation.

joined to planets to which they are related by their own nature, especially in the principal spaces of the figure, very often produce great and stupendous effects in accordance with the property of the space. Both, if they rise or set with the planets, but especially with the lights, or if they are in the same circle of position with them, or if they are in angles of the figure, or in aspect with the Sun or the Moon.

But as for their kind, the Girdle of Orion, Canis Major, Canicula, Castor & Pollux, the Left Foot of Gemini, the Heart of Leo, Spica of Virgo, Arcturus, the bright star of Corona Gnosiae, the bright star of Lyra, Aquila, the Tail of Cygnus, Fomalhaut,[1] and others, are allotted benefic influxes, which they make manifest in conformable locations. But the Head of Medusa, the Eye of Taurus, the Pleiades, the Heart of Hydra, the Heart of Scorpio, Hercules, Delphinus,[2] and many others have been discovered to have malefic influxes in accordance with the property of the space in which they are found, or in accordance with the nature and the determination of the planet with which they are found, just as both of these can be confirmed by innumerable observations of astrologers and can be tested by anyone. See Junctinus's *Compendium*[3] on his observations of the fixed stars.

Besides, two things should not seem to be omitted here. First, that if the royal fixed stars in the principal houses of the nativity are strengthened by fortunate aspects from the planets, especially the lights, or of those that rule the angles themselves, or if planets are conjoined to the fixed stars themselves, it is certain that they produce stupendous and lasting effects; but if they are not

---

[1] The more customary names of these stars today are the Belt of Orion (consisting of Mintaka, Alnilam, and Alnitak), Canis Major (the constellation), Sirius, Castor, Pollux, Alhena, Regulus, Spica, Arcturus, Alphecca, Vega, Altair, Deneb, and Fomalhaut.

[2] The more customary names of these stars today are Algol, Aldebaran, the Pleiades, Alphard, Antares, Hercules (the constellation), and Delphinus (the constellation).

[3] Probably a reference to Francesco Giuntini's *Speculum astronomiae*... (Lyons: Philip Tinghi, 1573. repr. 1581).

strengthened by the conjunction or the aspects of the planets that exalt men, then they wretchedly depress them.[1]

Secondly, that when a planet is joined to any fixed star, it must be seen in which house or space of the figure that is done, or which house that planet rules, for it is to those houses that the notable accident signified pertains, especially when the planet rules the house that it occupies. As if the Sun was with the Heart of Leo, Jupiter with the Heart of Scorpio, Mercury with the Eye of Taurus, Venus with Spica of Virgo,[2] etc.

Moreover, on account of the previously unknown principles of astrology, both of the planets and of the fixed stars, with what perfection could it be known or could it be distinguished between them, even though the influxes of the planets are more accurately known to us; therefore, for determining the strengths of the fixed stars from now on, the following rules should be noted, at least for the brighter ones. For the lesser ones do not affect men noticeably; besides, effects also happen to be observed on individual days from the directions of significators to them, although however such effects only happen rarely from the brighter ones, but very frequently from the planets that are the primary rulers of this inferior world, and from their aspects. Here, moreover, it must be frankly stated that men do not discern anything in astrology but the more conspicuous things, but Demons also notice the little things.[1]

First, if there is no planet in a particular space of the nativity (which must always necessarily happen, since there are only 7 planets, but 12 spaces), look at the star that is brighter, and or what region is vertical to or which is closer to the ecliptic, and more

---

[1] These last phrases seem at first glance to be inconsistent with what is said earlier. One would expect the royal fixed stars to exalt the native to some degree—greatly if supported by the benefic planets, and somewhat less if they act alone—but one would not expect their influences to turn from good to bad if they lack that support.

[2] The Latin text has ☿ *cum oculo 8'*, ♀ *cum spica 8 &c.* The phrase *cum oculo 8'* is meaningless; I have assumed that we should read the symbol ♉ rather than 8'; and of course the symbol ♏ is a simple typographical error for the symbol ♍.

powerful, that occupies that space. For if there is anything happening to the native that is pertinent to that space, and it may be seen that it cannot be referred to its own influence or determination or to the planet that rules that space (about which determination we shall discuss [at length] in Book 21), it is probable that that particular accident is from the influx of that star. And if the same thing or something similar is observed many times, there must be no doubt about it; and so from the effect, the nature of the star can be discovered, especially if by its nature and influx it was not similar to that planet.

Second. If any planet is in a space and ruler of that space, look similarly at the brighter fixed star, and, as above, distinguish the influence of that planet, both by reason of its nature and its determination, so that you may be able to discern the force of the star if the two of them differ in nature.

Third. If any planet is in a space that is under the rulership of another planet (which is the middle mode between the two extremes mentioned above), the judgment will be more difficult, and more entangled. For what each planet can do by reason of its nature and determination will have to be distinguished individually, so that the influx of the principal fixed star can be distinguished. But this mode, and then others more complex, as when many planets are conjoined in the same space under the rulership of another, ought to be disregarded, since the first two should be abundantly sufficient. Moreover, the previous rules are especially valid for fixed stars that are found on the cusps of the spaces, but especially

---

[1] In this statement Morin refers to the Catholic doctrine, first enunciated by St. Augustine (354-430), in his *City of God* that Demons had some ability to see into the future and would sometimes whisper their observations into the ears of astrologers to enable them to make true predictions and thereby confound the faithful. (This was Augustine's sophistry to try to cope with the obvious fact that astrologers sometimes make true predictions, but also to preserve the Catholic dogma that only divine beings can see into the future, while men cannot.) So Morin seems to say that men overlook some effects of the fixed stars, perhaps unadvisedly, but Demons take note of them (thus offering an explanation of their ability to predict some future events that escape the notice of men).

on the angles, where the fixed stars act more powerfully.

And let what has already been said about the planets and the fixed stars suffice. But to the glory of GOD, the Creator of the fixed stars, it does not seem that the following ought to be overlooked: that since He himself is of infinite wisdom who established everything in weight, number, measure, and order, and since the individual stars differ among themselves, if not in species,[1] at least in individual properties; it then follows that each fixed star, in such-and-such a location and arrangement, both with respect to the other [stars] and to the earth, was located in the firmament by GOD himself, so that it could not be better done, and that particular location or arrangement cannot be changed, why then does the sublunar nature not also experience an extraordinary alteration, as it experiences from the location of the planets that are continuously varying their own daily alterations [of location]. Who, therefore, will not indeed admire the marvelous and perpetual agreement [in arrangement] of so many fixed stars determined for the government of these sublunar things?

Finally, it must be added that if the fixed stars were referred to the inhabitants, as on our Earth, just as some have supposed along with the Cardinal of Cusa,[2] it is certain that the whole solar system would affect those same inhabitants much more weakly and insensibly than we are affected by the system or satellites of Jupiter, since, as we have proven elsewhere, the Sun itself is invisible from the region of the fixed stars. It was, therefore, an outstanding artifice of GOD the Wisest, that in the creation of the World it consisted of the Moon and the Sun arranged around the earth,[1] and of the solar system that embraces the systems of Saturn and Jupiter.

---

[1] Here Morin probably refers to the fact that most of the stars look alike, differing only in their brilliance.

[2] Nicolaus Cusanus or Nicholas of Cusa (1401-1464), German cardinal, theologian, and scholar. Morin perhaps refers to his book *De docta ignorantia* 'On Ignorance that is Taught' (1440). He also wrote *Coniectura de novissimis diebus* 'A Conjecture on the Last Days', in which he predicted the end of the world to occur in 1734. These and other tracts were published in an omnibus edition of his works at Basel in 1565.

And the twelve signs of the *Primum Caelum*, the domiciles of the planets in the zodiac, their syzygies, and their approaches to the fixed stars (the strength of all of which is very conspicuous on Earth) testify that all the rest of the universe was made for the sake of that Earth, or rather for the sake of man living on it. And so the divine wisdom played about in the circle of lands, in which He also wanted to be born and to live among the sons of men and to die for them. Let there be glory to Him forever, amen.

End of Book Thirteen.

[1] Remember that Morin had accepted Tycho Brahe's plan of the solar system, in which both the Moon and the Sun were in orbit about the Earth, but the other planets were in orbit about the Sun.

APPENDIX 1

Table of the Bright Fixed Stars for 1 January 1600

Star Name	Catalogue	Magnitude	Longitude	Latitude
Mintaka	δ Ori	2.2	16 ♊ 47	23 S 36
Alnilam	ε Ori	1.7	17 ♊ 53	24 S 34
Alnitak	ζ Ori	2.0	19 ♊ 06	25 S 21
Alhena	γ Gem	1.9	3 ♋ 31	6 S 47
Sirius	α Cma	-1.5	8 ♋ 34	39 S 31
Castor	α Gem	1.1	14 ♋ 40	10 N 04
Pollux	β Gem	1.1	17 ♋ 42	6 N 39
Regulus	α Leo	1.3	24 ♌ 16	0 N 27
Spica	α Vir	1.0	18 ♎ 16	2 S 02
Arcturus	α Boo	-0.1	18 ♎ 39	31 N 01
Alphecca	α CrB	2.2	6 ♏ 39	44 N 22
Vega	α Lyr	0.0	9 ♑ 43	61 N 45
Altair	α Aql	0.8	26 ♑ 08	29 N 19
Fomalhaut	α PsA	1.2	28 ♒ 14	21 S 05
Deneb	α Cyg	1.3	29 ♒ 50	59 N 56
Algol	β Per	2.1	20 ♉ 36	22 N 23
Alcyone*	η Tau	2.9	24 ♉ 25	4 N 01
Alphard	α Hya	2.0	21 ♌ 43	22 S 25
Antares	α Sco	0.9	4 ♐ 11	4 S 31

The names of the stars shown in the table are those that are in common use today. Morin refers to some of them by other names, but the names in the table are mentioned in the footnotes.

The longitudes of these stars increase at about 50" per year; the latitudes remain nearly the same.

* Note. Alcyone is the brightest star of the Pleiades and is near the middle of the asterism.

APPENDIX 2

Table of the Bright Fixed Stars for 1 January 2000

Star Name	Catalogue	Magnitude	Longitude	Latitude
Mintaka	δ Ori	2.2	22 ♊ 22	23 S 33
Alnilam	ε Ori	1.7	23 ♊ 28	24 S 30
Alnitak	ζ Ori	2.0	24 ♊ 41	25 S 18
Alhena	γ Gem	1.9	9 ♋ 06	6 S 44
Sirius	α Cma	-1.5	14 ♋ 05	39 S 36
Castor	α Gem	1.1	20 ♋ 14	10 N 06
Pollux	β Gem	1.1	23 ♋ 13	6 N 41
Regulus	α Leo	1.3	29 ♌ 50	0 N 28
Spica	α Vir	1.0	23 ♎ 50	2 S 03
Arcturus	α Boo	-0.1	24 ♎ 14	30 N 44
Alphecca	α CrB	2.2	12 ♏ 18	44 N 19
Vega	α Lyr	0.0	15 ♑ 19	61 N 44
Altair	α Aql	0.8	1 ♑ 47	29 N 18
Fomalhaut	α PsA	1.2	3 ♒ 52	21 S 08
Deneb	α Cyg	1.3	5 ♒ 20	59 N 54
Algol	β Per	2.1	26 ♉ 10	22 N 26
Alcyone*	η Tau	2.9	29 ♉ 59	4 N 03
Alphard	α Hya	2.0	27 ♌ 17	22 S 23
Antares	α Sco	0.9	9 ♐ 46	4 S 34

The names of the stars shown in the table are those that are in common use today. Morin refers to some of them by other names, but the names in the table are mentioned in the footnotes.

The longitudes of these stars increase at about 50" per year; the latitudes remain nearly the same.

* Note. Alcyone is the brightest star of the Pleiades and is near the middle of the asterism.

Index of Persons

Note: the characterization given for each person is not necessarily complete, but it represents the type of work that he did to which reference is made in the Preface or in the Translation or the footnotes. Book publishers' names are not listed. They may be found in the Bibliography.

Bibliography

Alchabitius (Abû al-Saqr al-Qabîsî)
Alcabitii ad magisterium iudiciorum astrorum.
[Alchabitius's Book on the Art of Judgments of the Stars]
Paris: Simon de Colines, 1521.

Augustine, Saint
De civitate Dei.
[The City of God.]
[Latin text and English translation]
The Loeb Classical Library
London: Wm. Heinemann and
Cambridge, Mass.: Harvard Univ. Press, 1960. 7 vols. repr.

Cardan, Jerome
Claudii Ptolemaei Pelusiensis libri quatuor/
De astrorum iudiciis cum expositione Hieronymi Cardani.
[Cardan's Commentary on the Quadripartite.]
in vol. 5 of Cardan's
Opera Omnia.
Lyons: Huguetan & Ravaud, 1662. 10 vols.
London: Johnson Reprint, 1967. 10 vols. reprint

Cusa, Nicholas of, Cardinal
De docta ignorantia.
[On Ignorance that is Taught]
Coniectura de novissimis diebus.
[A Conjecture on the Last Days]
Basel, 1565. omnibus ed.

Haly (ˁAlî ibn abi al-Rijâl)
Liber completus de iudiciis astrorum.
[The Complete Book on the Judgments of the Stars]
Venice: J. B. Sessa, 1503. often reprinted

Hermes the Philosopher (actually Albumasar)
De revolutionibus nativitatum.
[The Revolutions of Nativities]
Basel: Petriana, 1559. folio

Magnus, Olaus
Historia de Gentibus Septentrionalibus.
[History of the Northern Peoples]
Rome, 1555.

Morin, Jean Baptiste
Astrologia Gallica.
The Hague: A. Vlacq, 1661. folio xxxvi,784 pp. portr. diagrs. tables

Book 18—The Strengths of the Planets.
trans. by Pepita Sanchis Llacer and Anthony Louis LaBruzza
Tempe, Az.: A.F.A., Inc., 2004. paper 101 pp. port. diagrs

Book 21—Determinations.
The Morinus System of Horoscopic Interpretation.
trans. by Richard S. Baldwin
Washington: A.F.A., Inc., 1974. paper [v],109 pp.

Book 22—Primary Directions.
trans. by James Herschel Holden
Tempe, Az.: A.F.A., Inc., 1992. paper xv,292 pp.
Tempe, Az.: A.F.A., Inc., 2005. repr. paper xv,292 pp.

Book 23—Revolutions.
trans. by James Herschel Holden
Tempe, Az.: A.F.A., Inc., 2003. 1st ed. paper x,142 pp. portr. diagrs. tables 28 cm.
Tempe, Az.: A.F.A., Inc., 2004. 2nd ed. rev. paper xi,147 pp. portr. diagrs. tables

Book 24—Progressions and Transits.
trans. by James Herschel Holden
Tempe, Az.: A.F.A., Inc., 2005. paper xii,112 pp. diagrs. tables

Offusius, JoFrancus
De divina astrorum facultate in
larvatam astrologiam.
[The Divine Power of the Stars Against
a Decadent Astrology]
Paris, 1570.

Origanus, David
Astrologia naturalis...
[Natural Astrology...]
Marseilles, 1645. 8vo. xxxvi,454 pp. diagrs.

Origen
Peri Archôn 'On first Principles'
trans. by Trannius Rufinus into Latin as
De Principiis 'On the Principles'
trans. into English as 'On the First Principles'
by G. W. Butterworth
New York Harper & Row, 1966.

Pliny the Elder
Natural History.
trans. by H. Rackham, W.H.S. Jones, and D.E. Eicholz
Loeb Classical Library
Cambridge, Mass.: Harvard Univ. Press, and
London: William Heinemann, 1962. 10 vols. repr.

Pontano, Giovanni Gioviano
De Rebus Coelestibus.
[Celestial Things]
Naples: Sigismund Mayr, 1512.

Proclus
Procli Diadochi paraphrasis in Ptolemaei
libros IV de siderum effectionibus.
[Proclus Diadochus's Paraphrase of Ptolemy's
Four Books on the Effects of the Stars]
Latin translation by Leo Allatius
Leiden: Elsevir, 1635.

Ptolemy, Claudius
Tetrabiblos.
ed. & trans. by F. E. Robbins
The Loeb Classical Library
London: Wm. Heinemann and
Cambridge, Mass.: Harvard Univ. Press, 1940. xxiv,466 pp.

Schöner, Johann
De Judiciis Nativitarum libri tres.
[Three Books on the Judgments of Nativities]
Nürnberg: J. Montani et Ulrici, 1545. viii,152 pp.

Jean-Baptiste Morin

Astrologia Gallica

Book Fourteen

The Primum Caelum and its Division into Twelve Parts

Translated from the Latin

By

James Herschel Holden, M.A.
Fellow of the American Federation of Astrologers

TABLE OF CONTENTS

Translator's Preface

In this Book Morin begins with an elaborate explanation of why the *Primum Caelum*[1] is divided into exactly twelve sections, called the Signs of the Zodiac, and he also discusses the several ways in which the Signs are classified. He repeats the assertion, made in earlier Books of the AG, that at the beginning of the world (roughly 6,000 years ago) the Sun was in the beginning of tropical Aries as was the solar apogee. And he cites these reasons as proving that Aries is the first Sign of the Zodiac. He also relates Aries to the season of spring, and he says that this is another reason for making it the first Sign. This brings up the fact that the seasons of the year are reversed south of the equator, and Morin briefly alludes to that, but he insists that Aries is Aries, both north and south.[2]

The four elements, the four qualities, and the triplicities of the Signs are mentioned. And in a digression into number symbolism, he adduces reasons why 3 is a prime number, which combined with the 4 of the elements, gives 12—the proper number for the division of the Zodiac into 12 Signs.

From time to time, objections to all of this by Pico della Mirandola (1463-1494) and Alexander de Angelis are mentioned and refuted. Those men wrote books in which they pointed out what they believed to be irrational beliefs held by astrologers. Their books were still familiar to readers in the first half of the 17th century, so Morin thought it necessary to deal with their com-

---

[1] Stated to be the outermost sphere of the universe.

[2] Morin takes up this matter at much greater length in Book 15. Modern southern astrologers agree with Morin's statement. I recall raising the question with the New Zealand astrologer Donn Forrest (1919-1987) in 1982. He retorted angrily that "we don't stand on our heads below the equator," and went on to assert that there was no reversal of the signs below the equator. But still, since the seasons are reversed, then either the signs must be reversed or else the arguments by Ptolemy and Morin that are based upon the seasons must be considered to be invalid.

plaints. Today their works are no longer read either by critics of astrology or by partisans of the art; and in fact even their names are scarcely known. Therefore, the present day astrologer may regret that Morin went to such lengths to present their criticisms and his refutations of them. Still, something can be learned from the discussion, even though it is now of mainly historical interest.

In the present Book 14 and in some of the later ones, the reader will notice that Morin talks a lot about the "Four Elements," which he says are Fire, Earth, Air, and Water, and occasionally about a sort of fifth element, "Ether." He also talks about the "Four Qualities," which he defines as Heat, Cold, Moistness, and Dryness. But both of these terms, as he uses them, are now out-of-date. They were current in the science of the first half of the 17th century, but both chemistry and physics were in their infancy then. The old philosophers had coined these terms to describe material substances and some of their obvious properties, but as science progressed, beginning in the 17th century and extending into the 18th century, new discoveries and theories eventually displaced these terms.

Morin's reason for talking so much about them is that in addition to teaching practical astrology, he had two other goals: (1) to demonstrate that astrology was soundly based upon physical science; and (2) to show that astrology was not at odds with Roman Catholic religious dogma. But we must recognize that science has changed a lot since Morin's time, and that the necessity for proving that astrology is not irreligious has largely vanished.

And while 21st century astrologers know that "elements" are now defined as material substances that are unique and not composite, they can still benefit from the older definition by analogy. The old Four Elements can also be viewed as Qualities of matter—"fiery heat," solid, gaseous, and liquid substances; and the term Ether was still in use as late as the 19th century, but has now been replaced by the more stylish term "space," which might be defined as a nothingness that has physical properties.

The reader will also note that Morin discusses magnets and

magnetism. This probably reflects John Kepler's speculations about them. It seemed to Kepler that there must be some attractive force in the universe, and he thought that it might either be magnetism or something similar to it. We now call it gravity, but it is still a mysterious force. Again, Morin's reason for discussing magnetism that he is trying to relate astrological influences to something physical.

As astrologers, we are mainly interested in learning Morin's methods of reading charts and using the auxiliary features of astrology to make predictions. Experience teaches us as it taught Morin that the methods he explains are valid and effective. And we are prepared to ignore the criticisms of people who know nothing of astrology and have had no experience with it. Consequently, the fact that Morin's concepts of physics and chemistry are now outdated does not detract from his exposition of his astrological methods. We do not understand the physical mechanism by which astrology works, but experience teaches us that it does work, and that is sufficient for us.

I would like to say something about the translation. I have tried to translate Morin's Latin as literally as possible, but sometimes I have thought it necessary to paraphrase his words, and I have often inserted some words that are common and needful in English sentences but less common or not found at all in his scholarly 17th century Latin. And since Morin had a large Latin vocabulary, he often uses uncommon Latin words for the sake of variety. I have preferred to render them by their more common English equivalents, so I have dulled his literary style to some extent.

He seldom uses italics except for his Preface, chapter titles, and quotations. I have retained the first two of these, but I have generally handled quotations by enclosing them in double quotation marks. And I have italicized a number of words to point up some of the items under discussion in the several chapters.

Morin uses a number of words in a technical sense. I have rendered them by their most common English equivalent, even when their most common present-day meaning is not what he had in mind. An example is the Latin word *virtus*, which I have translated as 'virtue'. The Latin word's root meaning is 'strength', but it carries the implication of a particular kind of strength arising from the condition of its possessor. The English word 'virtue' now means mainly 'moral uprightness'. But to translate *virtus* as 'strength' is not adequate, for to Morin it referred to the characteristics of a planet as well as to its active force—'strength' does not carry that implication. So I have rendered it simply as 'virtue', but I have added a footnote to explain the term more fully.

The word *determinatio* 'determination' is another similar case; it is a very important technical term in Morin's astrology. In classical Latin the word means 'boundary', 'conclusion', or 'end'. But Morin used it as a noun derived from the verb *determino*, whose secondary meaning was 'to fix or settle something'. Consequently, for him a 'determination' was the making of a particular Signification, especially by the action of a celestial house on a planet that was in it or was its ruler. The usual sense of the word in English is 'maintenance of a fixed purpose to do something', although in legal circles it means 'a judicial decision' or 'the logical resolution of a question', which is somewhat like Morin's meaning. I have explained its technical meaning in a footnote.

In the case of the Latin word *Caelum*, which means 'sky' or 'heavens', I have chosen to retain the Latin word in italics. Morin sometimes uses it to refer to the 'sky' in general, but more often he has in mind the orientation of the Zodiac and the placement in it of the planets at a particular time, when it could be translated as 'celestial configuration', but *Caelum* is simpler. In Morin's day the old term *Primum Caelum* 'first sky' was still in use. It referred to the outermost sphere of the universe, on which the Signs of the Zodiac, were thought to be located. Since the Earth was still considered by him to be the center of the universe, the sphere of the *Primum Caelum*, sometimes called the *Primum Mobile* or the 'First Mover', was thought to be in daily rotation about the Earth. Within the *Primum Caelum* was the sphere of the second *Caelum*, on which the constellations and the fixed stars were supposed to be located. It was dragged along by the motion of the *Primum Caelum*, so it also rotated once every day. These were old and now abandoned astronomical concepts, but they were still current to some extent in the first half of the 17th century.

The terms 'influence', 'element', and 'quality' are defined in the text.

There are a number of other technical terms whose meaning may differ somewhat from the more common meaning of the English word used to translate them, but, as with the two words above, I have explained them in a footnote at their first occurrence in the translation.

James Herschel Holden
3 July 2005

ASTROLOGIA GALLICA

BOOK FOURTEEN

PREFACE

In this Book the Primary and Supreme Arcana of Judicial Astrology is set forth and disclosed by us; namely, the division of the Primum Mobile *into 12 parts, differing among themselves in their elemental nature and disposed in a certain order. And yet what is the reason, indeed the faith of surpassing that may be seen; that the* Primum Mobile *is said by common consensus to be the simplest of all physical bodies and the most homogeneous; yet it has a foundation in nature similarly chosen by rational experience, as will be stated below. But for investigating the cause of that division, the work was for us not a meager or unhappy intellectual effort. But if the cause assigned by us will have been laughed at by any astrologer, let him assign a truer one; since astrology stands upon experience; seeing that in the truth of the matter the* Caelum *itself is divided into parts differing in their elemental natures.*

SECTION I.
The Prime Physical Cause and the Division into Twelfths.

Chapter 1.

Among the Effective Physical Causes, there is One that is First and Most Universal of All, and That is the Primum Caelum.

Since in nature there is a subordination of acting causes; therefore, either there will be a procession to infinity in the order of the causes, which is rejected by all the philosophers; or else there will be one prime cause of all things, which is proposed here. But now, that such a cause is the *Primum Caelum* is proved thus. The prime effective cause of all things, and the one that is most universal, must be said to lie in Nature, to which everything else is subordinated, but nature is subordinated to nothing else; or how would everything else be determined to a specific kind of action, but Nature to none. Or, what would be concurring with all natural effects, when none concurs with itself by a superior physical cause, according to Book 7, Chapter 10. And yet, such a one is the *Primum Caelum*, whose very simple and marvelous nature was stated in Book 3, Section 3, Chapter 3. For when man generates man, the elements of the seed determine per se the generation of a man; and those elements determine the Sun, the Moon, and the rest of the planets to acting in accordance with their own effects; that is, the individual planets make their influxes on the fetus in accordance with their own proper natures, as reasonable experience proves. Moreover, the Sun, the Moon, and the rest of the planets determine the *Primum Caelum* similarly to act upon the native, just as that part of the *Caelum*, under which the Sun is located at the beginning of his generation, acts like the Sun, in a solar manner,[1] with respect to that same fetus, at least until it is brought forth into the light.

---

[1] Here Morin is referring to the position of the Sun at the moment of conception. And he goes on to say that it acts in a solar manner on the fetus while it remains in the womb.

Moreover, in the actual moment of the nativity, which is the fetus's completed and full generation, the Sun again determines the *Primum Caelum* with respect to the native, so that that part under which the Sun was at the moment of the nativity is like another Sun, although one that is invisible and morally spiritual, that acts in a solar manner or makes its influx with respect to the native, subject to the rule of the *Caelum* so long as he lives his life, as is plain from the directions of that location of the Sun and the transits of the other planets through that same location, during the life of the native. And not only is the *Primum Caelum* determined to acting on the native with the nature of the Sun, the Moon, Jupiter, etc., but also according to the nature of the elements. For if in the native's ASC there is that part of the *Caelum* that is called Aries, it will cause the native to be of a fiery or bilious[1] temperament; if it is Cancer, of a watery temperament; and so on with the rest of the Signs, which will be more fully explained in its own place.

And so the *Primum Caelum* is actively determined to the nature of the planets, the elements, and the parents, seeing that with a man it generates a man, with the element of Water it moistens, and with the Sun it heats, and of these in acting as thus it completes its effects. And the same must be said about the *Caelum* itself and about the rest of the particular causes devoting attention to their own natural effects. Therefore, since so broad an active determination does not agree with any element, with the Ether, and the circle of the *Caelum*, or a planet, as does the *Primum Caelum*, and it does not actively determine any other physical body, it is plain that the *Primum Caelum* is the prime physical cause of all things and the most universal cause, which eminently contains the *virtues*[2] of all the other causes. But because the position of that first cause and its approval is of the greatest moment for astrology, we have proved those same things in another way. For since Aries and Cancer do

[1] The word *bilious* refers to one of the Four Humors, namely Yellow Bile, which in excess produces a charismatic, active temperament, sometimes called *choleric.* It does not refer here to its modem meaning "sickly."

[2] The technical term *virtue* is used to refer to the strength and characteristic of a planet.

not do the same things in the ASC, but different things—that is, Aries gives a bilious temperament and a martial character, but Cancer a phlegmatic temperament and a Lunar character—therefore, diverse virtues are inherent in the Signs themselves; and therefore, either *formally*, or *eminently*, or only *determinatively*; but not *formally*, for the *Primum Caelum* is homogeneous, because (otherwise) it would be heterogeneous; and it is not sufficient that it would be *eminent*, because since Aries and Cancer, as parts of the *Caelum* are essentially the same between themselves and all the rest; also the same eminent force is in (all of) them; notwithstanding that their strengths are diverse; therefore, they will have these with diverse *determinations*.[1] Since, therefore, the virtues of the elements and the planets are in the twelve divisions, Aries, Taurus, Gemini, etc., as experience proves; therefore, those Signs ought to be *determined* to those virtues or natures. It is therefore necessary for the Signs themselves that they should be parts of the *Primum Caelum*, or that there is an *eminent* force in the *Primum Caelum* itself, indiscriminatingly complicating those natures and *determinable* to the individual ones of them; which, moreover, is such that it is the prime and most universal physical cause of all things; for there is nothing else in nature with which a universal *determination* agrees more.

You will object. If the *Primum Caelum* is the prime physical cause, being strong with a virtue appropriate to itself, why does it not by means of this alter and change all the bodies that are inferior and subordinated to itself?

I reply. The proper virtue of the *Caelum* is not formally elemental or planetary, but another one surpassing them, contrary to no other virtue, but friendly to all of them. Therefore, from the *Primum Caelum* seen in all its own simplicity, nothing can be altered, corrupted, or changed, but rather all things that are in its abyss are fostered and conserved, just as fish in the sea—their own proper element—are fostered, nourished, and conserved, and only from

[1] The technical term *determination is* used to signify the effect that is characteristic of a Sign or a celestial house.

other causes are they altered and corrupted. And such a thing must the prime physical cause be, a thing that is contrary to none, but the friend of all, and determinable by everything, as by its own archetype; indeed, by a perfect analogy it agrees with God. But from the *Primum Caelum* seen beyond its simplicity, like its own determinations, as is said below, all these *inferior things*[1] are generated and corrupted, as will be proved in its own place.

Chapter 2.

The Primum Caelum Consists of Parts of Diverse Virtue.

Since all the planets always move by their own or second motion under the same course of the *Primum Caelum*, which they call the Zodiac; and consequently they affect sublunar things[2] in various ways, in accordance with each one's own different site under that Zodiac, it ought to be divided by Nature into parts of various powers with respect to the Globe of the Earth, from which the former are discovered and in which they are reduced to action. Otherwise, the same planet with an active virtue, moving with that same active virtue through the whole Zodiac, would accomplish different things in the same passive virtue, contrary to Axiom 9 of the Elements of Astrology, for which see Book 19.

Moreover, the same forces are twofold in kind—that is, *elemental* and *influential.* And the *elemental forces* correspond to the natures of the elements—namely, hot, cold, moist, and dry; for sublunar things experience such things, and the intensifications or relaxations of them from the places in the Zodiac and from the descent of the planets [to places] in the Zodiac; but the *influential forces* correspond to the proper natures of the planets; in fact, all the influences are generically reduced to the primary governors of the World—that is, the natures of the planets—not indeed excluding those that are proper to the fixed stars. And those forces in the

[1] By *inferior things,* i.e. 'lower things', Morin is referring to things *upon the earth* or 'sublunar things' as he sometimes calls them.

[2] Morin uses the expression *sublunar things to* refer to things on the earth.

Zodiac are not confounded, but are distinguished in such a way that experience, the faithful instructor of things, proves that each part of the Zodiac preserves its own constant nature—both *elemental* and *influential*. Therefore, this division of the Zodiac or of the *Caelum* must be inquired into by us, which inquiry indeed other than by fictitious reasons would therefore seem to be impossible; both, because the *Caelum* is a circular body, and circles by their nature have no beginning or end; and then because it is the simplest and most homogeneous in its material form and virtue. Truly, because for whatever is sought, Nature is never devoid of a light leading the way for our minds; if we have followed that lead, we shall finally enter into the sanctuary of that hitherto hidden truth. But it must be noted that when the discussion here is about the division of a spherical body that is the simplest and most homogeneous of all, the method of division will not be sought from the material, the form, or the figure, but from something beyond and above that, as something delicate and spiritual, acting from the purpose of the Creator of the World, which is the source and prime cause of all principles.

Chapter 3.

The Primary and Actual Division by Nature.

In the beginning, therefore, attention must be wisely directed to what thing Nature supplies to be divided; then in addition, to whether it appoints any primary divisions, since it would make nothing in vain, but it would put in front of the eyes of men the primary ways of things and the primary principles, from which, as running hither and thither from more familiar things to the less known, he might then proceed. Moreover, the *Primum Caelum* shows that it is divided in the first place by the *equator*, the primary circle of motion of the *Caelum* itself. But this circle is again divided first by nature into two equal parts by the *ecliptic*, the proper circle of motion of the second *Caelum*, or the sphere of the fixed stars; whence the ecliptic is called the circle of the second motion, common to all the stars, as the equator is the circle of the first motion, only proper to the *Primum Caelum*; and one half of the ecliptic inclines towards the north, the other half towards the south; but its points of division are called the *equinoctials*, and they are the most effective of the whole *Caelum*; because, situated in both circles, they are powerful from the strengths of both circles, and their power is plain from experience.

Besides, this division of the ecliptic would not yet suffice, unless that same nature had indicated another division established by the poles of the equator and the ecliptic, defined by way of another circle, which they call the solstitial colure, by which a certain union of the first and second circles is made. And both halves of the ecliptic are cut twice in two other points called *solstices*, so that the whole thing is seen to be divided into 4 equal parts by an act of nature, because these circles and their poles are real and not fictitious; therefore, this division is said by us to be a real one.

Therefore, since this division of the Zodiac or the *Caelum* is primary and complete, it would be stupid to think that it was made in vain by Nature. Therefore, it is necessary that it was made on account of the action of the *Caelum* and the stars on these inferior things. Moreover, the celestial bodies act with their elemental and influential qualities, for they transmit both of them; and the *Primum Caelum* eminently contains all of them, as stated in Chapter 1 above. Therefore, since the elemental qualities, heat, cold, dryness, and moistness, are the primary and most universal qualities of nature, indeed those to which every sublunary body is susceptible, but not to the influential qualities, Nature seems to invoke the four points of the above said division of the ecliptic to be appointed to the four sources of heat, cold, moistness, and dryness in the *Caelum*.

Chapter 4.

The Secondary and Virtual Division by Nature.

For this reason, that division is called secondary and virtual because it does not seem to be actually made by nature, but only to originate from the virtue of the primary division while that emanates into the ecliptic circle and multiplies itself. For each one of the four above said points or sources is perceived to have two others with them of the same nature—those namely by which it makes an equilateral triangle in the ecliptic, so that consequently the whole ecliptic is thus divided into twelve parts, each three of which posited in trine aspect (to each other) are all of the same elemental nature—of course, hot, cold, moist, and dry. Which, though it is confirmed by experience, yet reason can scarcely arrive at, on account of the subtlety of the thing, which is common to all first principles.

Two reasons are set forth by the old astrologers, the first of which is this: namely, that the Sun runs through the whole Zodiac in a period of one year, but meanwhile the Moon comes together with the Sun twelve times by twelve revolutions of the Moon itself, which are called months. So that, therefore, a year is divided into 12 months, and the annual motion of the Sun under the Zodiac is divided into 12 conjunctions with the Moon; so, that the Zodiac or the Sun's way must be divided into 12 parts by nature, which is rightly taught, so they have judged. But this division is not equal and exact, for the annual period is not exactly distributed into 12 conjunctions of the Moon with the Sun.[1]

The second reason is that in the year there are 4 primary parts differing in qualities among themselves, namely Spring, Summer, Autumn, and Winter, to which correspond the 4 quadrants of the Zodiac; but any one of these again admits manifest diversities of time—that is, in its own beginning, middle, and end. For the extremes of each quadrant participate in the qualities of their neigh-

[1] Since the length of the mean month is only 29.531 days, 12 mean months are completed in only 354.4 days, and 13th month begins.

bors on either side; but the middle preserves the exact temperature of the quadrant. Whence, even though Spring is hot and moist, nevertheless its beginning, on account of Winter, is more moist than hot, but its end, on account of the Summer immediately following, is more hot than moist. And so on with the rest of the quadrants. So that as a result there are twelve differences of weather in the whole year. Therefore, since both the year and the differences of its parts are [resulting] from the different parts of the Zodiac that the Sun runs through, it is not without logic that they have judged that the Zodiac itself is naturally divided into twelve parts. And this reasoning seems to me to be more accurate than the one above, at least in the temperate zones; but in the torrid zone, especially under the equator, when Summer, Winter, and the other parts of the year are duplicated, it does not satisfy them, even in accordance with the twelve part division. Moreover, neither of these provides a reason, why the parts of the ecliptic that are placed in trine aspect are allotted the same nature among themselves.

And so we must try to raise up the sharpness of the mind a little higher with regard to the causes of this division and the finest and simplest principles, which is the nature of the principles; for the first principles are (based) upon reason, and there is no reason for them except only God—the supreme principle of all principles and the simplest truth, embracing the truths of all the sciences in itself. And consequently, for us it suffices here to be from the natures of things and from experiences, or to expound things agreeing with the phenomena, from which neither in discourse nor in Nature are absurdities introduced, and especially not in the science of astrology itself. But if any insolent person rejects our concepts, let him produce some truer one, and ones more conformable to experiences on the parts of the *Caelum*. For here there are only sought reasons for those things which are perceived in the *Caelum*; namely, that one part of the *Caelum* is of a fiery nature and the domicile of Mars; another part is of the nature of Water and is the domicile of the Moon, etc.; and I do not think that anyone would be happier for his success than I, who do not even attribute these things to my intellect, but I consider that they must be referred to the Father of Lights.

Because, therefore, whatever point is taken in the ecliptic, even aside from any consideration of a planet, it determines the other eleven points in the same circle, and in those twelve points, it can thus be conceived that there are triplicities of the same nature. For since whatever point of the greatest circle on a sphere has its own essence from a pole, from which that circle is described, just as both that whole circle, and therefore with the pole itself, the point above has an essential connection, the circle of connection is drawn from the point itself to the pole; and two circles are made cutting themselves into two halves, the poles of which, because again they are mutually from themselves, just as they are derived from the poles in essence, as points of the circles; if again they are connected by another circle drawn from the prime point taken as a pole; there will now be 3 circles dividing themselves; and not from the first point taken above, but beyond the third it can advance this mutual connection of the poles. And because from what was said above, the circle has its own essence from the pole from which it is drawn; therefore, the circle's essence and virtue will eminently belong to that pole. And consequently, since from the three circles above having been divided in turn into quarters, each one of the 4 sectional points of each circle, is the pole, and as far as the point of that same circle, it has its own essence from two other poles, and that in turn; and therefore, in any sectional point of the circle itself, the virtue of the pole is threefold in number, which nevertheless is of one kind and nature, because in those poles and circles there is no inherent diversity of nature; if from any such point as a pole the threefold virtue into the circle of which it is the pole is conceived to be poured out, there arise in that same circle four times three virtues of the same nature taken three times, and consequently twelve in the whole circle itself. And therefore, since each one of these four sectional points is thus equal to another in virtue and prerogative; there will not be any reason why from these individual points there should not be an equal effusion of that threefold virtue onto the whole circle; therefore, from the four threefold virtues of these points, the whole circle may be divided into twelve equal parts. And because each of these parts unfolds its own threefold virtue on the whole circle, and that equally among themselves, therefore the parts of the circle that are placed in trine aspect will be of the same nature among themselves, for otherwise the effusion of the virtue of that triplicity would be made unequally in the whole circle by those four sectional points; contrary to the hypothesis.

Furthermore, both divisions of the *Caelum* are similarly explained here, namely the primary or the actual, and the secondary or virtual; for the former is made by the two circles dividing the superimposed circle at four points, distant by quadrants. But the latter by the effusion of virtue of each of those four points onto the others, by trine aspect from the effusing remote ones. Whence, from these there arises the identity of natures or properties in the circle, and from the former ones the opposite.

Besides, lest any incapacity of the higher mind disfigure the speculative reasoning, let him see how many masters of the speculative numerical science, who, along with Pythagoras and Plato have asserted that they eminently comprehend the unity of all numbers, their virtues and properties; let him see Proclus *On Euclid* about the dignity of a point, but especially let him read Kepler, *Copernican Astronomy*, Book I, pp. 48 & 49, on the dignity of the center, when he says:

> The center is the origin of the sphere, which taken away, there is no sphere or circle; and that center is indivisible and not investigatible. Moreover, the spherical surface is the character and image of the center and like a lightning flash from it and the way to it. And who sees the surface, sees in it itself and the center not otherwise.

and other things there set forth, as it shows to be inherent in the sphere of the TRINITY that must be adored as a marvelously expressed image that is plain from those things that we have said above.

Indeed, the eternal TRINITY is from infinite Love, and it is the source and substance of infinite Love; in which the one who loves is first, the one who is loved is second; and there comes forth from both of them Love, which is third, (but) they are one in number in Nature; and therefore it is the simplest and most perfected in Love, whose infinite perfection pours out with itself onto all things; and yet more perfectly in itself more by analogy is poured out the sort of things that are those that stand together in the union of the Three; whence it is said "the whole Three perfected"; first, that is, and the most universal of the prime Three by that perfection that exists in Love, which all the Three with nature's own capacity participates in various ways. And this is the first essential and hidden cause, why, when the Zodiac or the Ecliptic from the fourfold creation of the primary qualities, led into the divine Ternary of Love, is perfectly and absolutely divided into twelve parts, some of which are opposed, others square, others in trine aspect, etc. The wiser ones of the more recent astrologers, instructed by their experiences, have discovered in the twelve parts of that same ecliptic aspecting each other by trine, a general identity of Nature; in those the perfection of the Trine, that is Love is indeed manifestly flourishing; so that, in the kind of effective aspects discovered in the circle, they have claimed the trine to be an aspect of the identity of Nature, or perfected amity, and among other things of good and natural felicity greatly diffused upon sublunar things, as daily experience here and there proves in natal figures.

And let these things that have been said be sufficient about the cause of the secondary division of the *Caelum* into parts, and into neither more nor less than twelve parts; which are therefore called *Twelfths*, commonly too the *Signs of the Zodiac* and the *domiciles* of the planets, under which the individual planets make their own revolutions. Moreover, their names and their order, begun from the intersection of the ecliptic and the equator, towards the northern part of the World are Aries, Taurus, Gemini, Cancer, Leo, Virgo, Libra, Scorpio, Sagittarius, Capricorn, Aquarius, and Pisces; of which the characters are also put here in the same order: ♈, ♉, ♊, ♋, ♌, ♍, ♎, ♏, ♐, ♑, ♒, ♓. But note that these names fabulously imposed (on them) by the Heathen do not express the true natures of the Signs,[1] which ought to be expressed by means of the natures of the planets, as is stated in the following Book, in the second chapter.

Chapter 5.

The Proper Elemental Natures of the Individual Signs are Investigated and Proved.

Having stated the things above as known, it must be more fully determined from which of these four cardinal points *heat* is derived, from which *moistness*, and from which *cold* or *dryness* (acting) upon these inferior things. But this task, this labor, must yet be conquered by the light of Nature.

Since, therefore, the cutting of the ecliptic by the equator is the first and most evident of all; indeed it is also the cause of another that is made through the poles of both circles, that will be the *equinoctial points*, which, among others, not only of the ecliptic, but also of the whole *Caelum* are the primary and most powerful ones; that is because at the same time there exist in both the ecliptic and the equator, the celestial circles that are altogether primary in their virtue, the latter in moving, and the former in influencing. And since there are also middle places in the World, but the solstices face the extremes of the World or the poles, (then) rightly and wisely there ought to be assigned to the equinoctial points qualities that are between the others in the dignity of the primary and the nature of the middle places; and consequently, all those of nature that are most friendly and rejoice in the middle—such as *heat* and *moistness* are—from which there is generation and life for sublunar things, and the name for the Zodiac itself,[2] as corruption and death are from *cold* and *dryness*, which are also deadly to living things, hence from this they are relegated to the extremes of

---

[1] Morin means that the nature of a Sign should *not* be taken from its name, but in this he differs from most other astrologers both ancient and modern.

[2] The word *Zodiac, ho zôdiakos* in Greek, means literally 'the thing containing living creatures'.

the World; and therefore it seems to have been of the highest wisdom that a dispersed virtue is weaker than a united one; for if in the middle of the World the sources of *cold* and *dryness* had existed, it is by no means doubtful that the corruptive causes would have prevailed over the generative ones, especially because both equinoctial points are mutually opposed to each other as *antiscions*, which gives strength to both of them. And from that, not only would generations have been rarer, but a fitting duration would also have been denied to the things generated because of the strength of the corruptive virtues. For, just as *moistness* is pre-eminent over the birth of things, but especially of animals, and *heat* is pre-eminent over their vigor, so *dryness* is pre-eminent over their decline, and *cold* over their demise. But on the contrary, God had indeed from the beginning of creation intended for frequent generations and a fitting duration for generated things, so that the individual species might be multiplied, like that divine saying *Increase and multiply yourselves and fill up the earth.*[1] Very wisely, therefore, did God Himself arrange these causes—namely, by locating the primary generative causes in the middle of the World and the primary corruptive ones towards its extremes. Therefore, the sources of heat and moistness will be inherent in the equinoctial points, whence under the equator *heat* and *moistness* flourish at their greatest, and it heats up very much and rains very much. But the solstices are the sources of *cold* and *dryness*, whence towards the extremes of the World there is a greater intensification of *cold* and *dryness*.

Finally, led thus by that same Nature, we shall find in which equinoctial point *heat* is inherent and in which one *cold* is inherent (which seems to be the target of our investigation).

It is therefore certain that the one of the equinoctial points, to which *heat* is suitable with respect to the Earth, will have it either from itself or from another. Because, since the *Primum Caelum* is certainly homogeneous, as has already been shown, those points in it only differ (so that) one is not another, but one is in one part of

[1] Genesis, 1. 22 "Increase and multiply yourselves and fill up the waters of the sea; and let the birds be multiplied on the earth."

the *Caelum* and the other is in the opposite part; wherefore, since all things are equal in these, *heat* cannot agree with one of them more than with the other; but even though both of them are disposed to *heat* or *moistness* according to what was said above, both of those qualities will be inherent in whichever one is innately neither the one nor the other. But no other point in the whole *Caelum* will have it, because the *Caelum* displays itself in the same way to both (points). And finally, not from any other part of the *Caelum* itself, because of its homogeneity, by reason of which it is not suitable to confer *heat* on that point which is neither one point nor the other. Therefore, that by which *heat* is conferred upon the other point will be *extrinsic* to that point and to the whole *Caelum*.

And consequently, since those qualities are assigned to parts of the *Caelum* that are not seen in them, either intrinsically, because of the homogeneity of the *Caelum*, but (rather) with respect to the Earth, it must be seen whether from the Terrestrial Globe either one of the equinoxes can be determined to *heat* or *moistness*, or to a *fiery* or an *airy* nature, with respect to it. And so, it will either be determined for the whole globe of the Earth or from that part of it that is turned towards that point at the beginning of the World, rather than the one opposed or another, for the application of the one that is turned toward it is more perfected and consequently more effective. Not from the whole globe, because since it is in the center of the *Primum Caelum*, it is equally placed with regard to any point of it; therefore, it will determine itself neither to *heat* in preference to any other quality. But not even from the part that is turned toward it, because both equinoctial points had a turned part of that same globe at the beginning of the World; and therefore, when those points and the parts of the globe turned to them, in that they existed altogether equal at the beginning of the World, there is no reason why one of the points was determined from the turned part to *heat* rather than to *moistness*. Which is confirmed by this: because on the first day of Creation, the Terrestrial Globe was homogeneous everywhere on its surface; the whole Water-Earth, and the surrounding sphere, were not yet fertile with the seeds of things and with the divine blessing, as can be concluded from the first chapter of Genesis. Therefore, at the beginning of the World, neither of these points was determined to *heat* by the Terrestrial Globe or to *moistness*, or to a *fiery* or *airy* nature. Nor indeed was it rather determined to *cold* and *dryness* or to a *watery* and *earthy* nature by the nature of that same Globe. And by the same reasoning it will be proved that it was not determined by the elements *Air* or *Fire*.

Moreover, it stands among all the masters of the astronomy that was finally restored by us that not only was the solar apogee at the beginning of Aries at the beginning of the World, but from Exodus, Chapter 12,[1] the body of the Sun is also the substantial source of celestial heat, because the month of Nisan or March is truly the first month of the year, as was shown by us in Book 2, Chapter 4, so that consequently the Sun will be between the beginning of Aries and the middle of the Terrestrial Globe; and the Earth, from all the parts of the *Caelum*, (but) only from the beginning of Aries, was first noticeably heated by the *heat* of the *Caelum*. Moreover, by reason of these things the beginning of Aries is made much more important than the beginning of Libra, and that between the two I have determined the greatest difference with respect to the Earth, no one of sound mind will deny. Therefore, the beginning of Aries will be the beginning of the Earth itself, as long as this will be subject to alteration, the source and cause of the planetary or celestial *heat*; not formally and per se, but only extrinsically and determinatively. Even so, as in a natal figure the point of the *Caelum* under which the Sun is placed with respect to the native, and to that native through the determination by the Sun, (is) the source and cause of the solar force, both elemental

[1] Probably the reference is to Exodus 12:2 *Mensis iste, vobis principium mensium; primus erit in mensibus anni* 'This month, for you the first of the months; it will be the first among the months of the year'. The month is named in Exodus 13:4 *Hodie egredimini mense novarum frugum* 'Today you are going out in the month of new fruits'. The phrase 'new fruits' is a translation of the Hebrew month name *Abib,* which after the Exile was renamed *Nisan.* The original name refers of course to the swelling of buds on plants and trees at the beginning of spring.

and influential, so long as that native lives; or the ascending point of the *Caelum* is to that same native the source and cause of life by the common consent of astrologers, who from that point judge on the duration and quality of his life—a thing that is certainly entirely wonderful that will be explained in detail in Book 21. Consequently therefore, from what was said previously, the beginning of Libra will be the similar source of *moistness*.

Furthermore, since the source of heat in Nature is the greatest *heat*, and similarly with the moistness; moreover, a moderate *dryness* (goes) with the greatest *heat*, and a moderate *heat* with the greatest *dryness* from the elemental nature that is in the planets and Signs; and the intense *heat* will be at the beginning of Aries, having put aside the *dryness*, and consequently *fiery* in nature, which is also inherent in the determined Sun. Moreover, in the opposite point (there is) intense *moistness* and having put aside *heat*, and (it is) therefore of an *airy* nature.

Truly, it would hardly have been sufficient at the beginning of the World for the Sun to have been established under any other one of the aforesaid points for the sake of determining that, since the Sun will not determine that point that was put there first, unless as the point and the beginning, to which therefore it is only the beginning of virtue and that virtue itself is not proper; but from the twelve aforesaid parts of the *Caelum* that are called Signs it is proper for anything to be determined, since they had to differ in virtue, and they were individually determinable in their virtue, in so far as the parts of the first cause, to which it is only capable of being actively determined by all the others, as was said above. Moreover, the Sun at the beginning of the World, posited under the same equinoctial point, was in the middle between two Signs, one northern and the other southern. To which, since it holds itself per se equally by body and apogee, it was able to determine neither per se to *heat*; therefore, it was still the task for another (cause), by which the Sun might finally determine another one of the Signs. This moreover was the motion given to that same Sun by God, by which, since it could have equally aimed at a southern part through the Sign that is said to be Pisces, and to the northern part through Aries; it could also have equally determined both of them to *heat*; but, because by the sole will of God it turned to the north, and an indifference of motion was taken away from it, therefore the Sign that it first began to traverse, and which is called Aries, it made the source of heat, or *fiery* in its nature, wherefore the one opposed to it was also *airy*.

But with these things being thus, the Sign beginning from the northern solstitial point next to the invasion of the Sun, that is called Cancer, will be the source of the greatest *cold*,[1] with *moistness* abated, or *watery*; but Capricorn is opposed to it in the southern part—the source of the greatest *dryness*, with *cold* abated, and consequently *earthy*; and so, Aries, Cancer, Libra, and Capricorn will be the primary sources and the celestial origins of vigor, decline, and the destruction of things that are generateable and corruptible. Moreover, this is the reason: because when both halves of the Zodiac, the northern and the southern, are divided into two sources, they ought to contain all those qualities in turn that are necessary for generation, lest the first division in Nature be accused of imperfection or error. Moreover, the primary source of the northern half, Aries, is *hot* and *dry*; therefore, there will be another, namely Cancer, that is *cold* and *moist*; and similarly, the primary source of the southern half, Libra, is *moist* and *hot*; therefore, the remaining one, Capricorn, will be *cold* and *dry*. For thus, in the sources of both halves, heat, cold, moistness, and dryness will be found, as far as it greatly suits the generations and corruptions in both parts of the World. And because the first qualities are primarily divided into active and passive, therefore the Sun, the most active of all the celestial bodies, by its first position and motion in the northern part of the World, has determined it to the active qualities, such as Aries to *heat* because it is hot.

But finally, from the virtue of the trine set forth above, of the whole World, but especially of the celestial, divine impressed,

[1] This certainly does not agree with the facts in the northern hemisphere. Morin's reason for making this statement is not clear.

four triplicities of Signs of the same elemental nature arise, that is *fiery* from Aries, *airy* from Libra, *watery* from Cancer, and *earthy* from Capricorn—not fictitious, as many think, but from what was said before, the true foundation allotted in Nature that has until now been unknown; however, by very frequent experience it has become known that planets posited in the trine of Aries act elementally as if (they were) in Aries itself, although not influentially, as will be more fully explained in its own place; and so with the rest of the cardinal Signs. Nevertheless, it must be noted that the ecliptic or the path of the Sun and the planets having been placed as has already been seen, the natures of the Signs of the Zodiac were able to be varied in four ways at the beginning of the World. First, with the Sun placed in the beginning of Aries and its motion to the north contrary to the motion of the *Primum Caelum,* as it was done. Second, with that same Sun left in that very point that was said to be the beginning of Aries, but its motion inclined to the south in accordance with the prime motion. Third, with the Sun located in the beginning of Libra, and with its own motion to the south, contrary to the motion of the *Primum Caelum*. Fourth, with that same (planet) placed in that same place, with its own motion to the north in accordance with the prime motion. But now the second and fourth modes were contrary to the decree of the Divine Mind from their opposition to the first and second motions; of which this is not only the cause that the planets remain longer above the horizon, and thus operate more effectively on sublunar things. But in addition, it expresses the motion of a sensitive approach that in the *Cabala of the Houses* or Spaces[1] is more fully explained by us. Moreover, of the first and the third, God wanted the first, for the sake of ennobling the northern part of the World, as will be set forth more evidently below.

Therefore, from these causes it is established that the elemental forces of the Signs are not formally inherent in the *Caelum*, but

[1] A reference to Morin's early book, *Astrologicarum domorum cabala detecta a Joanne Baptista Morino...* 'The Cabala of the Astrological Houses disclosed by Jean Baptiste Morin...' (Paris: J. Moreau, 1623).

in another twofold scheme, certainly *eminently* since those very Signs are parts of the first physical cause; then *determinatively* from the location of the Sun at the beginning of the World, which was pleasing to God. And because that first determination of the *Caelum* was a general one with respect to the Earth or to the region elemental at a birth; therefore, to it are subject all things from the elements immediately after they were generated—and especially man, for whom nevertheless all his own and particular force is also inherent in his birth for the determining of the prime physical cause, by which the *Caelum* itself through its own location with respect to that man being born, and through the planets, are *determined* to those things that are the own things of that man, as is shown in its own place and may be confirmed by experience. And consequently that opinion of Kepler's is false, when in Chapter 6 of his *Book on the Fiery Triplicity*, (he says that) the denomination of the triplicities or the Signs of the Zodiac from the elements, namely those that are otherwise said to be *fiery*, *watery*, etc., are not from the nature of things, but from human judgment, and which he does not prove, nor can it be proved. And if from the above said division of the *Caelum*, approved by experiences, anyone can think up any better reasons, he will without doubt merit a bravo! But I don't see that there can be given better reasons that are self-consistent and more conformable to the division of the houses and the aspects than those which I do not doubt must be adhered to.[1]

Chapter 6.

The Twelve Divisions or the Signs of the Zodiac Cannot be Established in any other Caelum *than the* Primum Caelum; *and What a Twelfth Part is.*

That any *Caelum* other than the highest one cannot be divided into the Signs or domiciles of the planets is plainly proved from this: because whatever Sign or domicile of a planet (about which

[1] However, it should be noted that all of Morin's arguments based upon the seasons are only valid for the northern hemisphere.

we shall speak below) is established in such a way by the constant and immutable location of that Sign with respect to the intersection of the ecliptic and the equator, which is only conceived by astronomers to be in the *Primum Caelum*. But no part of any *Caelum* other than the supreme one can retain itself invariable. For the sphere of the fixed stars is moved under the *Primum Caelum* in the sequence of the Signs, that is from the beginning of Aries to Taurus, Gemini, etc. And if between the sphere of the fixed stars and the *Primum Caelum* other *Caeli* are given because of the motion of trepidation,[1] as many astronomers wrongly suppose, the trepidation of these would also take away the superior constancy of the site. Therefore, those Signs can only be established in the *Primum Caelum*. For them, each Sign has these two things—namely, that the same Sign always exists in its own place; then, that it is in mobile, diurnal motion around the Earth, with the stillness of the Earth shown by us.[2] But these things cannot be obtained from spheres lower than the *Primum Caelum*, as has already been said; and also not from that space of the whole World; first, because no part of it is mobile around the Earth; and then because the equinoxes always occur at no place on Earth under the same point of mundane space; consequently, they are not fixed in any (part) of that space. But they ought to be fixed in a fixed location in the Signs; therefore, it is necessary that a Sign have those two (requirements) from another (source), which cannot be (anything else

[1] This refers to the so-called "Trepidation of the Equinoxes," a theory mentioned by the late classical astronomer Theon of Alexandria. He said that according to the "old astrologers," the equinoxes moved back and form through an arc of plus or minus 8 degrees. The original purpose of this theory was to state the difference between the fixed Zodiac of the Alexandrian astrologers and the tropical Zodiac introduced by Hipparchus and adopted by Ptolemy. But the astronomers, beginning with Theon himself, did not understand its purpose, and so it continued to confuse astronomers down to the 16th century.

[2] Morin steadfastly adhered to the old belief that the sky rotated about the Earth, while the Earth stood still in the middle of the Universe. This had the advantage of not conflicting with Roman Catholic religious dogma. In 1616 the Inquisitors had declared the motion of the Earth to be heretical. Copernicus's book had been placed upon the Index, and the Church absolutely forbade any assertion that the Earth moved.

than) the *Primum Caelum* itself with a mobile, diurnal motion, and in which the equinoctial points are fixed. Therefore, the *Primum Caelum* is that one that is divided into domiciles or twelve Signs for the seven planets.

Moreover, that division is made through the poles of the ecliptic and not through those of the equator; because since the *Caelum* itself is divided on account of the planets, as is established below, it must have been divided for them not according to the motion of that *Caelum* or equator, but with the proper oblique motion of the planets, which is about the poles of the ecliptic. For thus, any planet and especially the Sun is most aptly carried through the middle of its own Sign, in which the virtue of that Sign flourishes more intensely, and from which it would perpetually diverge too much if, with a division made by circles passing through the poles of the equator, the middle of each Sign would stand on the equator.

Therefore, a Sign is *a twelfth part of the* Primum Caelum*, divided from a fixed equinox by circles passing through the poles of the ecliptic, with a virtue appropriate to itself provided by a determination.* Since it is said to be "a twelfth part of the *Primum Mobile*," it is removed from lower spheres and from the mundane space. Since it is said to be "divided from a fixed equinox," the location of each Sign is denoted, and its invariability (of position) with respect to the equinox. Since it is said to be "by circles passing through the poles of the ecliptic," it teaches that the ecliptic is in the middle of each Sign and (that it is) the shortest way from the location of that Sign to the equinoctial point. Therefore, certainly in the ecliptic itself the virtue of each Sign ought to flourish by reason of its location, but less beyond it, which squares with experience. Then, besides that, it also teaches the division of the *Primum Caelum* into twelfths, not agreeing per se with the *Caelum* itself, but only through determination. Finally, since it is said "with a provided virtue appropriate to itself," it is declared that each Sign is distinguished from every other Sign and also from the *Caelum* as a whole by a particular virtue by reason of its determination.

Besides, someone might argue thus against the superior division of the *Primum Caelum* and the determination of its parts by the Sun: "If the Sun, because it is hot, has determined Aries to heat by its presence and motion, it has therefore also determined it to its own influential nature." But both of these (arguments) are false, since Aries is determined to the elemental nature of Mars, which is fiery, as is Aries itself, and then to the influential nature of Mars itself, of which Aries is said by astrologers to be its domicile; therefore, it has not determined Aries to heat.

But it could (also) be said in reply: It is certain from what has been said previously that heat, cold, moistness, and dryness are prime *qualities* in the corruptible World, which comprises the elementary & ethereal or planetary region; and therefore the division of the *Caelum* into these prime and common qualities of all corruptible Nature ought to be before any other; moreover, the Sun, by its own position in the beginning of Aries, made this first division and determination primarily, certainly determining Aries to its own elemental nature, which is also fiery like the nature of Mars; moreover, the rest of the Signs (to their determinations), as was said above. But secondarily, it also determined it to its own influential nature, which especially becomes known by the twofold essential dignity of each planet in the *Caelum* – that is, by its *rulership* and *exaltation*; and these, since for the Sun they are in different and separate Signs, in which the former cannot naturally be placed together, it is sufficient that with respect to the Earth it has determined Aries to its natural element, namely fire, then to the influential (nature) of the exaltation; for Aries is the exaltation of the Sun, as the astrologers say, because its influential virtue is very much exalted especially in Aries, as (is stated) more fully about these things in their own place.

As for these things, since in the realm of astrology nothing is more evident than that in particular nativities of men the individual planets determine to their own influential nature those places of the *Caelum* in which they are located with respect to the individual natives; moreover, they act along with those very places or Signs of the *Caelum*, according to the nature of each one of them, that exists invariably in it from the origin of the World. Indeed, from Venus in Aries a mixed action of the nature of Venus and Aries comes forth; and from that same Venus in Gemini there is another mixed action of the nature of Gemini; and it is certain that the *Primum Caelum* of itself is homogeneous and only determinable to different things by causes inferior to itself, which are the planets, that in individual moments are prominent with respect to the inferior things being born, as was said above. And that determination cannot be harmonized by many planets at the same time, on account of the greatest confusion that would arise from it. For which planet shall I like best among the rest? Rightly and deservedly that one will be qualified first, and also for the whole Earth from its origin, it will be a universal and perpetual determination, certainly it will be the Sun, which is not only of a fiery nature and an elemental heat, with an abundance no less than its light and mass of body, but it far and away surpasses everything, so that it also burns, but besides that it obtains the principle place among them, as their chorus-master and moderator; indeed, five of them, Saturn, Jupiter, Mars, Venus, and Mercury are its satellites, but the Moon is like its spouse, namely because the Sun and the Moon have their own orbits arranged around the Earth, but the planets around the Sun itself?[1] Moreover, that thing is entirely confirmed by (the fact that) the apogee and the body of the Sun at the beginning of the World was located at the beginning of Aries,[2] which the Sacred Scriptures or the *(Rudolphine) Tables* do not show for any other planet.

More shrewdly will that one seem to urge at the outset, who says from the first chapter of Genesis that the Sun was only created on the fourth day, but that the Earth had also produced living

---

[1] This is the scheme of the solar system devised by Tycho Brahe and adopted by Morin.

[2] Morin had already discussed this in *Astrologia Gallica,* Book 2, Chapter 3. See the translation of that chapter in an addendum to my translation of Book 22, pp. 207-208. In it he adopted Kepler's estimate of the creation of the world as having taken place 3,968 years before the birth of Christ. Modem figures would put the Solar apogee at 0 degrees in the tropical Zodiac at about 4075 B.C., which is fairly close to Kepler's 400-year old estimate.

plants and other things; and consequently, neither the Sun nor the Signs of the *Primum Caelum* were in charge at the beginning of the World.

To which objection, we may reply first: that chapter of Genesis on the creation of the World[1] is explained in very different ways by various theologians and philosophers; and they have engaged greatly in controversy among themselves as to whether the light created on the first day was a substance of the Sun or not; indeed, whether the entire World and its arrangement was made at that same moment of time. Second. It follows from the text of that chapter that the water was not made on the second day, but was only divided from the middle of the firmament; and similarly, the Earth was not made on the third day but only revealed from the waters; and by consequence, the Earth, the water, and the entire elemental region were made on the first day simultaneously with the *Caelum* and light; because, moreover, that light is the globe of the Sun itself, not yet condensed as it is now, or (as) the material of the planets, still covered up in such a way as the Earth was covered up until the third day, so that only imperfectly did it illuminate; from which it is proved, because it is established from the literal sense of the words—to which it is safer to adhere—that when it is said that evening and morning were made on days one, two, three, etc., those days are understood to be with reference to the Earth or the elemental region. But this cannot be the case, unless there was some globe that was at least obscurely luminous, (which) by the diurnal motion of the *Caelum* circling around the Earth had made the evening and morning and had divided the diurnal light from the

---

[1] Here, it may be helpful to give a summary of the Creation according to Genesis, Chapters 1&2: "On the first day, God created light, and evening and morning were made; on the second day, He divided the firmament (the *Caelum)* from the waters, and evening and morning were made; on the third day, He created the dry land separated from the waters and seeded it with plants, and evening and morning were made; on the fourth day. He created the luminaries in the *Caelum,* and evening and morning were made; on the fifth day He created animal life, and evening and morning were made; on the sixth day He created male and female humans to rule the Earth and all that was in it, and evening and morning were made; on the seventh day. He completed his work and blessed it."

nocturnal darkness. Since therefore the light that was made on the first day provided that, and on the fourth day that same duty was in general entrusted to the Sun, which ever since has performed by dividing the day from the night or the light from the darkness, to be sure it seems that it must be proposed that the light created on the first day was nothing else than the body of the Sun itself, either not yet condensed or more truly covered up with that material, from which on the fourth day the rest of the planets were made; and that on the fourth day it was completed or disclosed, as the Earth was on the third day. For, as in an elementary region, so in the ethereal or planetary region, it is entirely probable that in the first days there was a confusion that is called Chaos by the poets. But now, either all things were made at the same moment, or the light that was created on the first day was the globe of the Sun upon them, (so) the doctrine stated above by us holds. For always in the birth of the Earth, the Sun is found in the beginning of Aries with its own motion towards the northern part of the ecliptic; and so the *Primum Caelum*, in itself homogeneous, has determined (itself) into different parts with elemental qualities, as was stated above.

Chapter 7.

What Kind of Error Concerning the Elemental Natures of the Signs was Introduced by Ptolemy and Cardan.

Ptolemy, the ancient prince of astrology, in Book 1, Chapter 10 of the *Quadripartite,*[1] says of the "general things," i.e. the elemental powers of the Signs, with their times, that they correspond

[1] This reference is to *Tetrabiblos i.* 10 "Of the Effects of the Seasons and of the Four Angles', which begins "Of the four seasons of the year, spring, summer, autumn, and winter, spring exceeds in moisture on account of its diffusion after the cold has passed and warmth is setting in; the summer, in heat, because of the sucking up of the moisture during the hot season just past' and winter exceeds in cold, because the sun is farthest away from the zenith. For this reason, although there is no natural beginning of the Zodiac, since it is a circle, they assume that the Sign which begins with the vernal equinox, that of Aries, is the starting-point of them all..." (Robbins's translation).

to the quarters of the year; and consequently the vernal Signs are Aries, Taurus, and Gemini, as spring, hot and moist, and therefore of an airy nature. The summer, moreover, (embraces) Cancer, Leo, and Virgo, hot and dry, and therefore fiery." And (he speaks) about the rest (of the seasons) in the same manner. Which he certainly confirms in the 10th Chapter, saying that the ancients established the first Sign as Aries, in which the vernal equinox is, so that they might start the moist nature of spring just as a live animation. Cardan explains that same thing at length in his *Commentary*, asserting that Taurus is the most temperate Sign that is in the *Caelum*, or the hottest and most moist according to its substance, for he talks about it thus because the homogeneity of the *Primum Caelum* was unknown to him, and its extrinsic determination, about which (see) above; and he thinks that the parts of the *Primum Caelum* are substantially and intrinsically different. Moreover, Cardan's rationale about Taurus is because it is the most temperate Sign of the vernal quarter, which is more temperate that all the other (quarters); and he philosophizes about the rest (of the Signs) in the same manner, concluding that the natures of the twelve Signs are had down to the marrow. But Ptolemy professes the same thing a second time in *Quadripartite*, Book 1, Chapter 17, when he says: "for since of the twelve Signs the two northern ones come closest to our summit, and Cancer and Leo make the greatest heats and the summer, etc." and a little after that he says "the opposite Signs Capricorn and Aquarius are cold and wintry." But that this opinion about the nature of the Signs is false is proved by this: that according to Ptolemy's and Cardan's reasons, the Sign Taurus in the southern part of the world will be the coldest and driest because it is in the middle of autumn; and Scorpio will be the hottest and most moist because it is in the middle of spring; and consequently, if this is agreed, the nature of the Signs is mutable; and this does not agree with them intrinsically and according to their substance, as Cardan says (it does), but rather accidentally and extrinsically from the part of the years and the place on the Earth; whence, it is plain that the accidental nature of the Signs was only unknown to Ptolemy and Cardan, which nature is not even inherent in them by impression or determination, as those things were explained above, but only by their designation, so far as a Sign that in one place on Earth is named hot, because when the Sun is in it is summer in that place, but by a contrary cause in an opposite place on Earth it is also said to be at the same time cold. But they are completely ignorant of the essential thing that coincides with them—either in so far as the parts of the *Primum Caelum*, or in so far as the Signs,. And with regard to this, we shall prove in its own place that the Signs are immutable in any place on Earth.

Moreover, all the Arabs, observing more accurately the essential natures of the Signs from their effects, have agreed on this: that some of the Signs are a fiery triplicity, others airy, others watery, and others earthy, but because they have assigned no cause for this division, it seems that they did not know any; and only through the Cabala was that very doctrine, nevertheless concordant with experiences, received from the bequeathed knowledge of Adam.

And so, from the doctrine set forth above, it is concluded that the Signs, as parts of the *Primum Caelum*, are formally of the same nature among themselves because they are of the same (stuff) as the entire *Caelum*, which is homogeneous; moreover, the Signs, as Signs, are formally of diverse natures among themselves. Namely this happens to the parts of the *Primum Caelum* through their extrinsic determination, so that the Signs are of diverse natures; and therefore that diversity of natures is thus *accidental* for the parts of the *Caelum*; moreover, it is *essential* with regard to the Signs; and therefore it will have to be judged thus about the nature of the Signs, as the Signs, are, by what is here and what follows.

Chapter 8.

What Objections were Made by Pico Mirandola and Alexander de Angelis to the Division of the Zodiac into Twelve Signs.

Besides our own objections to the superior division of the Zodiac as set forth in Chapter 6, it doesn't seem that those proposed in addition by Pico Mirandola should be omitted here, in order to overturn this fundamental basis of astrology; for if we should determine that those reasons are false and absurd, from that it will be doubtful to no one that that division would stand more firmly, however de Angelis forces upon us here and there the twice cooked cabbage that is the cooked over objections of Pico.

And so, first Pico: In Book 6, chapter 4, and in de Angelis, Book 4, Chapter 2, they say:

> "Astrologers, before the time of King Alphonso [1226-1284] did not know that above the *Eighth Caelum* there were innumerable stars shining, among which the twelve Signs of the starry Zodiac[1] made up a certain number, and they used these in (making) judgments of the stars at the time of that Alphonso. But more recent astrologers have thought up another *Caelum* above the fixed stars, only so that they might give a reason for the apparent movement of the fixed stars away from the equinoctial points; and they have divided that fictitious *Caelum* into twelve Signs, called by the same names as the stellar (Signs) and with their same powers; and consequently, some astrologers use the starry Signs, but others the imaginary ones for the purpose of (making) judgments, which cannot be done without tangible ignorance and absurdity; both because the imaginary Aries can be of no real virtue, and because the starry Aries differs in its location very much from the fictitious one, and on account of the motion of the fixed stars it does not preserve the same location with respect to the equinoctial points, which nevertheless the astrologers require in their own division of the Zodiac. Whence, it is (certain) that both Zodiacs are useless for astrologers."

[1] That is, the constellations.

But I reply that de Angelis almost always fights against astrologers with bad faith. For the motion of the fixed stars began to be noticed by Timocharis [3rd cent. B.C] even 330 years before Christ, but afterwards it was plainly known to Hipparchus and then to Ptolemy from the fixed stars observed in Signs that were immovable with respect to the equinoctial points. For these astronomers did not use any other Zodiac in assigning true places to the fixed stars than the immobile one, as is plain from Ptolemy's *Almagest*. But, having apprehended the motion of the fixed stars in that same Zodiac, it was necessary for them to conclude that either the fixed stars have a duplex motion per se, contrary to the laws of physics, or to create another *Caelum* above the fixed stars, in which that Zodiac would be immobile, which down to this day both astronomers and astrologers have used. Therefore, although both the constellations and the Signs were once confused, or although the Chaldeans observed only the starry Signs,[1] which de Angelis throws up to us, namely because then, at least as far as was noticeable, the constellations coincided with the true and immobile Signs; nevertheless, after their motion had been detected, they were distinguished one from the other, and they were entirely distinguished, lest to the fictitious images the real powers of the Signs be attributed, or to the Signs themselves those (powers) of the images of a fictitious nature, which is still wrongly done by many astrologers, who say of the Signs of the true and immovable Zodiac that some are human, others animal, some mute, others of good voice, etc., only because they have the same names as the spurious starry Signs that have such natures. But no one of sound mind can fail to see that this is the greatest ignorance; and it must be greatly lamented that the true names of the Signs are unknown to us, and that they were distinguished by the names of the fictitious constellations, since the true names of the Signs would disclose their true nature; although it can rightly be said that Leo must be called a Solar Sign, Cancer a Lunar one, Aries manifestly a Martial one, Scor-

[1] It is now known that the Babylonians (Chaldeans, as Morin calls them) used a fixed zodiac, but that it consisted of twelve 30-degree Signs with the same names as the zodiacal constellations (which are of very unequal length).

pio a hidden or internal one, and so on with the rest (of the planets).

Second. They assert that a division of the *Caelum* into twelve Signs, and each degree into sixty minutes, etc., is only an arbitrary and imaginary one for the more ready calculation of the celestial motions, but not a natural one. And de Angelis attempts to prove this both from the authority of Kepler and Avenezra[1] and by reason; because (he says) the *Primum Caelum* ought to be a simple and homogeneous body, and consequently it cannot be divided into parts of a diverse nature, just as that same simple motion does not agree with parts diverse in nature.

But I reply that Kepler wavered in his approval of astrology, because he did not profess or make any trial of this science that was hitherto devoid of true reasons. But Avenezra did not say that the division of the *Caelum* into twelve Signs is arbitrary, as de Angelis says he did, but only that the division of the Signs into thirty degrees and each degree into sixty minutes is arbitrary, which we also freely concede, but this does not cause us any difficulty, since we only deny that the division of the *Caelum* into twelve Signs is an arbitrary one. But I say this about de Angelis's reason: In the previous chapters we assert that the *Primum Caelum* is the simplest and most homogeneous body of all Nature, and yet it is divided into 12 parts or Signs that among themselves are of a diverse nature—not to be sure formally, but only determinatively, as was explained above; and de Angelis does not have anything that he can put in opposition to that division, since experience proves that in individual hours—indeed, in individual moments—it is similarly divided in nativities, namely into Solar parts, Lunar parts, Saturnian parts, Jovial parts, etc., by the planets that are moving in it.

Third. They say that astrologers have been deceived in their division of the *Caelum* because they have observed that the planets do something in one Sign and something else in another. For example, the Sun in Aries produces a temperature vivifying all

[1] Abraham Ibn Ezra (1089?-1167), famous Jewish scholar and astrologer.

things, but in Leo it emits a violent heat that consumes and burns up everything. And again, in mid-summer sudden cold occurs, and in mid-winter heat, which astrologers insist cannot be referred to anything other than the diverse nature of the Signs through which the Sun is passing. And yet, since these things are produced by the approach of that same Sun to our zenith and its departure there from, or from a particular combination of sublunar causes.

But I reply. The *Caelum* is not divided into parts of diverse nature principally on account of these elemental alterations, but rather on account of the influential effects, which, as de Angelis was unaware of them, he did not even hit upon the word here, for to bring in the heat of the Sun by its approach and to withdraw it by its departure is known to everyone; but for astrologers, that alteration of the elemental heat is not from any division of the *Caelum*.

Fourth. Finally, de Angelis tries with this ultimate battering-ram to attack and demolish that division of the *Caelum*.

> "Let us give (he says) to the astrologers that there are various properties of the Signs; let us concede that the planets produce various effects in accordance with the Sign in which they are located; still they have got nothing that can act as a cause. For if the planets borrow all their efficacy from the Signs, as the horoscope-makers dream, it is plain that the astrologers cannot say first by thought or predict what they will do or not do, unless it is known to them what Signs the planets are running through at individual moments of time; however, they don't know that, for let it be supposed that Jupiter is in 29° 59' 59" ♊, then it is judged to be in its own detriment and to have 5 black points. After a minute of time it has entered the first minute of Cancer—now exalted and fortunate, it is thought to rejoice with 4 white points. But now it is unknown to the horoscope-makers that (exact) minute in which Jupiter emigrates

> from Gemini to Cancer; therefore, it ought to be unknown to them what Jupiter will do from Gemini, and what from Cancer."

But I reply first that de Angelis himself has dreamed that all the efficacy of a planet is borrowed from the Signs, and he imposes that (notion) upon horoscope-makers; for if so, the planets would of themselves be of no virtue or efficacy, contrary to the understanding of all horoscope-makers who hand down the strengths of each planet, with a planet having been seen for itself, and according as it removes from any Sign, as can be seen in Ptolemy, *Quadripartite*, Book 1, Chapter 5, and other places, where it must incidentally be noted that if the *Caelum* were not divided into Signs of a diverse nature, and if the planets did not receive some force from the *Caelum*, the individual ones would receive only the same force and (that) perpetually; and so, no diversity of effects could arise from the *Caelum* itself; and the reason is that the Caelum itself is innately homogeneous and the simplest in its substance and virtue. But (we speak) about these things elsewhere.

I reply secondly. The previous demonstration of Alexander de Angelis is absurd, for during the whole year in which Jupiter remains in Gemini, could it not be observed what it performs in Gemini? Because if he could, which is foolish, want to look for that moment of time, in which Jupiter goes out of Gemini and is no more in Gemini? Similarly, during the whole year in which Jupiter will remain in Cancer, could it not be observed what it does in Cancer? Why, therefore, is there any need to take note of that moment in time, in which Jupiter is entering Cancer and is not yet in Cancer? So indeed like some man staying in cold water—the moment of time when he is coming out of the water will have to be looked for, so that it may be known whether the water is cold, as if it can only be apprehended in that moment. Now de Angelis cries out: "Madness, it is madness, to attribute various kinds of power to parts fastened together in the tenth sphere by the decision of the astrologers" and other such like (statements) in his own manner (of speaking). And it is sufficient for us to make it plain to everyone in opposition to these weapons of straw and Alexander's madness that astrology remains unshaken; and not by the unsubstantial words with which de Angelis overflows, but necessarily by including solid reasons (in which he is perpetually lacking, and cannot fail to be lacking) the overthrow of astrology must be undertaken, if of course it can be overthrown.

Perhaps, moreover, someone might force Lucius Bellantius[1] on us, an astrologer of no small reputation, who, in Question 7, Article 4, (says) the Sun in Cancer or in other Signs acts to vivify these things with its own heat and influx, and that the Signs are like material things, the Sun moreover and the planets (adopting) the form of the Signs. And consequently, the Signs themselves are of nothing per se, or at least they appear to be of different virtues among themselves. But here Bellantius made a big mistake. For since there is always the same virtue of the Sun and the individual planets, therefore any one of these Signs always vivifies anything in the same manner; and consequently the same planet in any particular Sign would only do the same thing, at least when it is alone in the Sign; but this is contrary to experience, which states that a particular planet does one thing with one Sign and something else with another one; therefore, the diversity of action, since it cannot be from the identity of the planet's virtue, it must be from the contrariety of the Signs, in which consequently a diverse virtue is inherent.

Chapter 9.

How Outstanding are Those Things that Follow from the Causes of the Division of the Caelum Assigned Above.

Since from true things nothing but truth and agreement are accustomed to result, but from false things nothing but falsity and contradictions; it must already be seen what results from the causes of the division of the *Caelum* assigned above. First, there-

[1] Lucius Bellantius, *De astrologica veritate* "The Truth of Astrology' (Florence: Gerard of Harlem, 1498. folio; repr. Basel, 1554).

fore, it follows that the prime cause or the *Caelum* does not act upon these inferior things unless in accordance with all the subordinate causes that are determined to some particular effect that is especially proper to that prime cause.

Second. There is the greatest agreement on the universal determination of the *Caelum* itself by the Sun with respect to the Earth that was set forth above, along with its particular determination with regard to men in their nativities. For just as the Sun in its own location in the beginning of Aries at the birth of the Earth determined the points of the *Caelum* to differing elemental natures with respect to the Earth, so that same Sun or any other planet, by its own position under any point of the *Caelum*, when a man is being born, has determined 12 points of that same *Caelum*, that is 12 aspects of that planet, to various influential forces with respect to man himself, as will be more fully explained in its own place.[1]

Third. The homogeneity of the *Primum Caelum* is confirmed more effectively from this: an outstanding virtue to marvel at, and one that is indifferent to agreeing with any other cause inferior to itself; and that, while remaining the same in its simplicity, it is made very diversified through the determination of its own parts—not indeed formally and intrinsically, but accidentally and extrinsically by the determination.

Fourth. Because even if the apogee of the Sun had been at the beginning of Libra at the beginning of the World, nevertheless, from the Sun's having been posited in the beginning of Aries, the Sign Aries would have always been fiery; and therefore from the motion of the apogee itself and its passage into the southern part of the World with the succession of the centuries, no change in the nature of the Signs is to be feared. But in turn, if at the time of the creation the Sun's apogee in the beginning of Aries (as many important men will have it, and Longomontanus, Origanus, and Kepler among the astronomers) had been in the beginning of Libra, there is no doubt that the Sign Libra would have been fiery, con-

[1] The aspects of the Planets are discussed in detail in Book 16.

trary to all the opinions of astrologers, which is (a fact) most worthy of note. And these things most strongly confirm the creation of the world at the time of the vernal equinox; and consequently, they support the Roman Church entirely against the Greek and Jewish (religions).

Five. Therefore, these twelfths or Signs are of these sorts; that is, fiery, airy, etc., with respect to the whole Earth because the Sun was at the beginning of the World of the whole Earth in the beginning of Aries; and hence the whole Earth received the celestial heat first, and the Sun's influence that penetrates the whole Earth, as was said elsewhere; Moreover, from the determination by Aries, the determination of the other Signs followed, also with respect to the whole Earth, as was explained above.

Sixth. In the Triplicities of the Signs of the same nature, the Signs and the cardinal points, Aries, Cancer, Libra, and Capricorn are of principal virtue, as in the fiery (Triplicity), Aries, but especially its beginning; in the watery (Triplicity), Cancer, especially its beginning; and so on with the others. But from the cardinal (Signs), the equinoctials push forward to the solstitials, and from the equinoctials, Aries to Libra; so that consequently, Aries is the first Sign in Nature, then the first in nobility, then in virtue; and not only by its number, as is believed by many; but of the solstitial (Signs), Cancer prevails over Capricorn, because in the latter there is a passive dry quality, and in the former an active cold reigns. Moreover, of the other Signs of the same Triplicity, that one will be second in virtue that is the one after the cardinal Sign, participating more in the nature of that Triplicity because it follows the cardinal itself in that same Triplicity, or it occupies the sinister trine of that cardinal (Sign).

Seventh. The northern part of the World is hotter and dryer, for in it there are two fire Signs and two earth Signs; but in the southern part there are two air Signs and two water Signs; and therefore, the northern part will be masculine and the southern part feminine—subordinated to the former because the latter is moister.

Eighth. From the fact that in one half of the Zodiac the active northern qualities, heat and cold, rule the cardinal points, but in the opposite southern qualities, only the passive qualities, moistness and dryness; from which the primary physical reason is made manifest: (we can see) why the northern part of the Zodiac was truly said to be *commanding* by the ancients, but the southern part *obeying*. And from the beginning of the World, each half was allotted its own effect as the stronger one on the globe of the Earth; in the northern part of which they always flourished, and so far the first and most important commands still flourish; but not in the southern part, all of which will therefore be subjugated by the northern part, and the northern part will never be subjugated by the southern part. But about the dignity of the northern part over the southern part, it will be stated more fully below, and then in Book 10, Chapter 5.

Section II.
The General Divisions of the Signs for the Whole Earth.

Chapter 1.

The Fire, Air, Water, and Earth Signs.

Since in a Sign there are two characters; namely, the formal nature of the Sign, and its location in the world or the ecliptic; therefore, by reason of each of these, the Signs of the Zodiac are divided in various ways.

First therefore, by reason of their nature they are divided into Fire, Air, Water, and Earth Signs. And the Fire Signs are Aries, Leo, and Sagittarius, of which Aries is cardinal, hotter, and the source of heat, which is followed in the order of virtue by Leo, then by Sagittarius, the least hot of the Fire Signs. Similarly, the Air Signs are Libra, Aquarius, and Gemini,[1] of which Libra, the

[1] The Latin text has the Sign □ by mistake for the Sign ♊ both here and twice more below in this paragraph.

cardinal Sign, is the moistest of all, then Aquarius, and finally Gemini. And so on in the rest of the triplicities, beginning from the cardinal Sign in accordance with the succession of the Signs. But it must be noted that although these things are said generally and with respect to the whole Earth, they are nevertheless true for us in the northern regions, Leo is a hotter Sign, because it is closer to the rest of the Fires and a summer Sign. It is moreover of a quarter of the year, and the greatest accidental virtue of nearness to the Zenith, in extending effectively the proper and essential natures of the Signs; seeing that from the vernal quarter alone Ptolemy along with Cardan wanted Aries, Taurus, and Gemini[1] to be formally or according to their substance hot and moist. Thence, therefore, in the southern part of the world, Sagittarius will be hotter than Leo. And by which reason it is said above that the northern part of the world is hotter and drier than the southern part. And by that reason it is said above that the northern part of the world is hotter and drier than the southern part; here we say those same things—(namely), that the heat in the northern part of the world—at least beyond the zone that they once called torrid—is hotter and drier than in the southern part of the same latitude; namely, because in the summer quarter of the north, the Sun runs through a Fire Sign; however, not in the south. There will be for us similarly from the Air Signs a more moist Sign, with airy moistness, because it is closer to us than the others, and especially the Vernal Sign; but Pisces will be principally of Water because for us (it is a Sign) of winter; but for those in the south, Cancer will be particularly Water. And one must philosophize in the same way about the rest of the Signs.

Chapter 2.

The Choleric, Sanguinary, Phlegmatic, and Melancholy Signs.

From the superior division of the Signs into the elemental natures, all the rest are deduced by reason of the nature. And this division corresponds entirely to the prior one. For the *choleric* Signs

[1] Again, the Latin text has the Sign □ instead of the Sign ♊.

are the same as the Fire Signs Aries, Leo, and Sagittarius; the *sanguinary* Signs are the same as the Air Signs Libra, Aquarius, and Gemini; the *phlegmatic* Signs are the same as the Water Signs Cancer, Scorpio, and Pisces; and the *melancholic* Signs are the same as the Earth Signs. For that which is Fire in the elements is *choler* in the humors, and they are the same qualities in both. And so with the rest of them.[1]

Chapter 3.

The Masculine and Feminine Signs.

The Fire and Air Signs are *masculine*, but the Water and Earth Signs are *feminine*. This would not hold otherwise if you only look at astrology as from its own principal or cardinal points; for the more effective principals are attributed to the masculine sex. But the Fire and Air Signs are allotted to be the principal and most effective (Signs) of the *Caelum* because they are equinoctial points, which are simultaneously in the equator and the ecliptic, the most effective of all (the Signs) in the celestial circles—the former in moving, the latter in influencing; namely, the Fire is the beginning of Aries, and the Air is the beginning of Libra; from this cause, therefore, the Fire and Air Signs are masculine; as Fire and Air; and therefore, because of the opposite cause, the Water and Earth Signs will be feminine; that is because they arise from the beginnings or from the points of the ecliptic most remote from the equator, and consequently from the weaker ones, namely from the solstices; the Water certainly from the beginning of Cancer, and the Earth from the beginning of Capricorn. However, if you look at the sublunar physical (scene), the Fire and Air Signs will also be masculine on account of the elements to which they refer; for indeed, Fire and Air are masculine, but Earth and Water are feminine; and

[1] Hippocrates (c.468-c.377) postulated that the human body contained four fluids or *humors:* phlegm, blood, choler, and melancholy. So long as these remained in their proper balance, health was maintained; but if one of them was excessive, then health, human appearance, and behavior was affected. This theory has long since been abandoned by physicians, but it was still alive in Morin's day.

therefore the latter are subject to the former, and from them they receive the force for producing their own fruits; not the other way around; for clouds, rain, hail, and lightning bolts are the fruits of air, but (also fruits) of the Terrestrial Globe, which are carried out in the air; for their material is raised up from the Terrestrial Globe.

Hence it is rightly deduced that as primacy in order is due to the masculine sex as the more active one, so the first of the Signs, namely Aries, is masculine, Taurus is feminine, Gemini is masculine; and so, with the sex alternating, each succeeds by the force of the 4 Triplicities mentioned above, so that it was not without reason that the Pythagoreans thought that those Signs are masculine for which a masculine and more effective number harmonized, namely an odd number—an offspring of *unity*; but feminine Signs for which the number, taking its origin from *two*, which among the numbers is female, just as unity is masculine. Anyhow, moreover, the reasons offered by Ptolemy and Cardan about this sex of the Signs are worthless, and not undeservedly they are derided by Pico Mirandola (1463-1494) in Book 6, chapter 15.[1] Indeed, of these also the one that is apparently more valid is that which is taken from the active motion near the equator, because thus the Sign Gemini would be with respect to Taurus feminine, and Taurus masculine; for under Taurus the motion is more active than under Gemini, which is contrary to the division handed down by them.[2]

You will object to the doctrine put above that the active quality *cold* predominates in Cancer and the *passive moistness* in Libra, but the active qualities are masculine and the passive ones are feminine; therefore, Libra, Scorpio, and Pisces will be masculine Signs, and Libra, Cancer, and Gemini feminine ones.

---

[1] The reference is probably to the posthumously published book by Count Giovanni Pico della Mirandola, *Disputationes adversus astrologiam* 'Disputations Against Astrology' (Bologna: Benedictus Hecteris, 1496.

[2] This is not altogether clear to me. I suppose Morin refers to the fact that the ecliptic in Gemini is further from the equator than the ecliptic in Taurus; but if so, then the ecliptic in Aries would be closer still.

I reply to this, not at all scorning the difficulty that although the cardinal Signs of the Zodiac were divided above by sex by reason of their own nobler and more effective site in the world, and not moreover by reason of their active and passive qualities, yet the former division is not contrary to the division by qualities, if this matter is understood with a sound mind and correct reason.

For, since besides those things that have a physical mark of their own sex (such as man or woman), the rest are said to be masculine or feminine only by a comparison of the nobler or more effective virtue among themselves; it is certain that among the elemental qualities both active and passive compared one by one, there will also be one that is masculine and another that is feminine. Therefore, having compared the active qualities heat & cold in turn, it is plain that heat is masculine in nobility and activity, but cold is feminine. For males of whatever species are universally hotter than females. Similarly, having compared the passive qualities moistness and dryness among themselves, dryness will be masculine and moistness feminine; then, because females are universally moister and softer than males; then, because dryness strengthens the force of acting and resists those things that weaken and obstruct by moistness.

Having understood these things, it is fitting that the hot twelfths[1] are said to be masculine, but the others either combine the maximum amount of cold and moistness from the passive qualities of the feminine; or, having set aside the cold for dryness from the passive qualities, they are said to be feminine. For the cold Signs to be able to be said masculine, it is necessary that cold should not only be combined with dryness but it should also be superior to it; which granted, Saturn, intensely cold and dry, is easily said to be a masculine planet. Capricorn, however, moderately cold and very dry like the Earth, is said to be feminine.

But against this explanation, someone might again argue that Venus was said by us to be hot and moist like the Sign Libra, and

[1] That is, the 12 signs.

yet feminine; therefore, the Sign Libra will also be feminine, or at least Venus will be masculine.

I reply that the Sign Libra refers to the nature of Air, which by the philosophers is held to be twice as moist as it is hot; moreover, Mercury is put by us to be four times more moist than hot—and also according to Ptolemy; from this, therefore, it is manifestly plain that Venus is farther away from a masculine nature than Libra is; and with respect to Libra's being said to be feminine, add the fact that Libra does not have its own essence as masculine from the elemental qualities of the Sun, but especially from its nobler location in the world, as was said above. Moreover, those things that are asserted here about the cardinal Signs, should also be understood to be asserted about their entire Triplicities.

For this reason, moreover, this division must be noted, because, other things being equal, the masculine Signs are more active than the female Signs, and in the latter the planets incline to feminine or weaker effects, in the former to masculine or more intense effects.

Chapter 4.

The Diurnal and Nocturnal Signs.

The *diurnal* Signs are masculine as was explained above, but the *nocturnal* Signs are feminine. Since the diurnal sect harmonizes with the masculine sex, the nocturnal sect harmonizes with the feminine one due to the nature of the active or passive virtue. But it must be known that there is a *duplex sect* within the Signs, that is an *intrins*ic and an *extrinsic* one. The former is from its own nature, and it is *simplex*; for each Sign is per se only masculine or feminine, and only *diurnal* or *nocturnal*; but the *extrinsic* sect is due to the location of the Sign above (or below) the horizon, which, since it can occur by day or by night, there will also be a *duplex extrinsic* sect of each Sign, namely *diurnal* or *nocturnal*.

Chapter 5.

The Northern and Southern Signs.

Having explained the division of the Signs according to nature, now there follows their divisions due to their location in the World or in the ecliptic.

And so they are first divided into *northern* and *southern* Signs. The former are those that are located in the northern part of the *Caelum* or the World—namely, Aries, Taurus, Gemini, Cancer, Leo, and Virgo. But the southern ones are those that occupy the southern part of the World, of course Libra, Scorpio, Sagittarius, Capricorn, Aquarius, and Pisces. And it should be noted that the celestial influxes penetrate the whole Earth, as we have said in Book 12, Chapter 32. And yet even as the subterranean influxes are weaker than the superterranean ones and those closer to the remoter parts of the vertex, so the northern Signs affect the southern part of the Earth less than the northern; and the southern are the other way around—less northern than southern; and therefore the oblique placement of the Zodiac is due to the equator, so that for both parts of the Earth the celestial influences are equally distributed.

Chapter 6.

The Mobile, Fixed, and Common Signs.

The *mobile* Signs, which are also called *cardinal*, are those that begin from the 4 cardinal points of the ecliptic, namely Aries, Cancer, Libra, and Capricorn; moreover, they are called *mobile* because more than the rest of the Signs they cause *changes* in things; and in these, the universal nature causes its own changes primarily through the position of the Sun and the rest of the planets. Then, because things that begin under their influx are of short duration, or the changes are obnoxious. And indeed the position of the Sun makes the changes of the seasons noticeable; namely, of winter into spring, of spring into summer, of summer into autumn, and of that into winter; which seasons of the year seem to begin from those 4 places, like doors opened by nature, and moving around their own hinges. But those points are divided into *equinoctial* and *solstitial* or *tropical*. The former are Aries and Libra, so called because they begin from the equator, and when the Sun in the beginning of them makes the day and night equal like a pair of scales everywhere on Earth; and thereafter the excesses of day and night begin and end in turn. They are also accustomed, not without reason, to be called Signs of religion or ecclesiastic Signs; both, because it is well known in histories that outstanding changes of religion have occurred with the superior planets or the Sun running through those Signs; and then, because just as between the Signs Aries and Libra[1] they lay claim to the primacy for themselves, as we have said above; so (they relate to) religion among human affairs. But the tropical Signs are Cancer and Capricorn, so called because they constitute the terminals towards the poles,[2] from which the Sun itself is converted to the equator; standing through some days in the solstitial points as if it were immovable to the judgment of the senses. Moreover, they are also called *political*; both because in histories it is well known that great changes in kingdoms and empires have happened from the superior planets or the Sun, penetrating those Signs; and then because just as the planets extending their own courses towards the north and south finally stand in the tropical points, and from there they go back to the equator; so, kingdoms and empires expand themselves up to certain limits, where, if at any time they stop, they are finally contracted to their own beginnings; if in fact they are given the origins of all the temporary things to which the increment pertains—vigor or standing still, decline and destruction. Furthermore, those things that are subject to the mobile Signs are either *not lasting* or they are very much exposed to *change* and *instability*. But those things which they rule either because of celestial charts or because

[1] The Latin text has "between Capricorn and Libra," which does not appear to make sense. So I have changed it to "between Aries and Libra."

[2] My photocopy is blurred in the area at the top of p. 326, column 2, but I think I have read the words correctly.

of the planets' traversing through them, or because of their verticality,[1] are subject to those (circumstances); and so, those that detect under the tropics are particularly subject to the Signs Cancer and Capricorn.

The *fixed* Signs are Taurus, Leo, Scorpio, and Aquarius—so called because in them nature celebrates a standing still from changes or vigor; and when the Sun is in them a change in the air, once begun, lasts; then, because things that are begun under their influx are of *long duration* or are entirely *stable*. But among them the more fixed are the masculine Signs Leo[2] and Aquarius, in which the steady states of heat and cold occur for us. Moreover, there is a property of the *fixed* Signs by which they confer *stability* and *durability* on the things that they rule.

Finally, the *common* Signs are Gemini, Virgo, Sagittarius, and Pisces—so called because (they are) a *middle mode* between the *mobile* and the *fixed* Signs, with regard to the effects that they have; and when the Sun is in them, it already inclines toward the nature of the following quarter; and consequently it serves as a mean between two quarters.

Chapter 7.

The Commanding and Obeying Signs.

This division of the Signs, and those divisions that follow, in addition to the fact of their location in the Zodiac, also comprises those of the Signs that have a certain relationship among themselves.

And so, the *commanding Signs* are Aries, Taurus, Gemini, Cancer, Leo, and Virgo—so called because they are in the northern part of the Zodiac or the world, which part is masculine and more active than the southern part, on account of the two sources of the active qualities of heat and cold, which are located in the

[1] I suppose he means "when they are at the highest point of the ecliptic."

[2] The Latin text has the symbol ☊ instead of ♌.

northern part and therefore belong to that right of dominating or commanding.

But the *obedient Signs* are Libra, Scorpio, Sagittarius, Capricorn, Aquarius, and Pisces—so called because they only contain the sources of the passive qualities, moistness and dryness; whence they agree with being subject to the southern part of the Earth and to obeying that which is subordinated to the obedient Signs; but the reasons of Ptolemy, Proclus, Pontanus, and Cardan for this division are worthless and not universal; indeed, for the southern Signs they are contrary, and null under the equator, when they say that the northern Signs are commanding because the Sun in them makes the days longer than the nights, and the southern Signs are obedient for the opposite reason.

Moreover, the old astrologers wanted the northern Signs to command the southern ones that are equidistant from the equator, not however having just any but having equal and parallel right ascensions. And also because Aries brought in Libra and Pisces. Truly, the rulership is duplex, that is legitimate or friendly and (at the same time) tyrannical or hostile. *Friendship* is between the Signs that are equidistant from the same equinoctial point, if indeed between them they are joined together by any bond of association and sympathy, of which sort are Aries and Pisces, mutually (friendly) to each other since they are from either side of the equator in the middle. *Hostility* is between the Signs that are equidistant from the opposite equinoctial points and therefore opposed to each other, of which sort are Aries and Libra; and these achieve an antipathy (to each other) from the opposition. And here Taurus commands Aquarius in a friendly manner, but is hostile to Scorpio; Gemini is friendly to Capricorn, but hostile to Sagittarius, and so with the rest of the Signs. In such a way however that the first degree of Aries commands the last degree of Pisces, and the 2nd degree of Aries the next to the last of Pisces; and similarly with the rest.

Moreover, it is (characteristic) of the commanding Signs (that) they stimulate and exalt to rulership subjacent regions, and also men whose life and actions they rule; but it is (characteristic) of the obedient ones that they are subjected and suppressed. And so, Cardan in his *Commentary*, Book 1, chapter 14, rightly notes from Aristotle that of men, by nature some are born free, but others are born slaves. And that someone having all or his principal Significators in commanding Signs will scarcely ever obey anyone unless he is forced to do so, and he will always seek command. However, if he has Significators in the obedient Signs, he will find himself in an opposite mode, and scarcely anyone will obey him unless from force or fear. And this is worthy of note between masters and servants.

Chapter 8.

The Antiscion Signs.

Those Signs are mutually *antiscions* to each other, that in the same part of the northern or southern *Caelum* are equidistant from the same solstitial point. As Aries and Virgo, Taurus and Leo,[1] Gemini and Cancer in the northern part. then, Libra and Pisces, Scorpio and Aquarius, and finally Sagittarius and Capricorn in the southern part. These Signs are not only mutual antiscions, but much more effectively their degrees are taken equidistant from the same solstitial point, as are the first degree of Cancer and the last degree of Gemini, the 2nd of Cancer and the 29th Gemini, and so on thereafter; which nevertheless you should so understand that the beginning of the first degree of Gemini is the antiscion of the end of the last degree of Cancer; and the end of the first degree is the antiscion of the beginning of the last degree; or if it is more than the first minute of Cancer, it is the antiscion of the last minute of Gemini; for only thus is the equidistance of the antiscions from the same solstitial point maintained.

Besides, those Signs themselves are said to be *antiscions* because from opposite sides they are casting a shadow[2]; namely, be-

[1] Here again the Latin text has the symbol ☊ instead of ♌.

[2] This is an exact definition of *antiscion,* which is a compound of the Greek words *anti* 'opposite' and *skia* 'shadow'.

cause when the Sun is in them, it makes the days among themselves and the nights among themselves equal in the whole terrestrial globe, even so as the day and the night among themselves (with the Sun) in the equinoctial points; nevertheless, with this difference—that where on Earth the days are increasing from the Sun in one Sign, in that same place the days are equally decreasing from the Sun in its antiscion, which is the reason why they are said to cast opposing shadows.

Moreover, by Ptolemy[1] and others they are also called *Signs seeing each other*, and those that *command and obey*, (and) *Signs hearing each other*, because they say sight only differs from hearing in mobility and certitude; only the antiscions differ in efficacy from the commanding and obeying; and it is not surprising, since the latter are in different halves and parallels of the world, while the former are in the same half and parallel; consequently, they are more united, and their virtue is more strongly united. But that logic and appellation of *seeing and hearing Signs* is so barbarous and inept that it rightly offers an opportunity to the haters of astrology for laughing and jeering.

Furthermore, these two things should be noted about the antiscions and the commanding and obeying Signs. First, that having found the antiscion of any point of the ecliptic, there is always a commanding or obeying point for it in the opposition to the antiscion, so that therefore the commanding or obeying (point) is what is called a *contra-antiscion* by others, to which they also attribute no little virtue, which however it seems ought to be ascribed to the abovementioned logic of the commanding and obeying Signs. and so, the antiscion of the 2nd degree of Taurus is the 28th degree of Leo, but its contra-antiscion or obedient (point) is the 28th degree of Aquarius. Moreover, the Signs that are equidistant from the same equinoctial point are, in the motion of the world and the *Caelum*, just like two oxen pulling under the same yoke, and mutually helping each other. Second, that the closer the

[1] Ptolemy does not mention antisicons, but he does devote a chapter *(Tetrabiblos* i. 14) to "Commanding and Obeying Signs."

antiscions and the commanding Signs are to the tropical points, the more powerful they are to a great extent. Because the degrees of the ecliptic near the tropics differ very little in declination or in rising and setting. But around the equinoctials, because it is the opposite, therefore the virtue of the degrees is not thus extended, and the antiscions ought then to correspond partilely to the commanding and obeying Signs; otherwise, their effect will either be null or small.

Chapter 9.

The Signs that Aspect Each Other and Those that do Not.

The Signs that aspect each other (which must also be understood about their individual degrees) are called those that are distant in turn from some part of the circle that taken many times exactly makes up a whole circle; and that particular distance is called an *aspect*, which by Ptolemy and the rest of the old astrologers was stated to be only fourfold; namely, opposition, trine, square, and sextile,[1] having only taken their reasons from harmonic proportions. Therefore, the sextile aspect is between Signs whose beginnings are distant from each other by an arc of 60 degrees. Such as Aries and Gemini, Taurus and Cancer, etc.; for that arc taken six times equals the whole circle. The square is between Signs whose beginnings differ from each other by 90 degrees; which, having been taken four times, equals the circle. The trine has a mutual distance of 120 degrees, or the third part of the circle; but the opposition between the distant (points) by a semicircle. But I, taught by reason and long experience, am adding to them the *semi-sextile*[2] aspect; namely one between Signs whose beginnings differ mutually by an arc of 30 degrees, since having taken this twelve times

[1] Modern astrologers consider the conjunction to be an aspect, but the ancients did not; for them it was a *position*. The Latin words that we translate as *aspect* imply a *view* of something at a distance, such as from one Sign to another.

[2] Morin calls this aspect a *dodectile* (i.e. a 'twelfth'), but here and below I will translate it as *semi-sextile,* since that is its modern name.

makes the whole circle; and therefore this agrees with the previous logic of aspects; and besides, I have very frequently observed that planets distant by the semi-sextile communicate their main forces to each other. This is especially true when they are oriental to the Sun or occidental to the Moon; but we shall discuss these positions more fully when we will be treating of the aspects of the planets.[1] Moreover, what we are saying here about the Signs and their beginnings must also be understood about the degrees of any Sign. Namely, the 2nd degree of Aries, for example, aspects by semi-sextile the 2nd degree of Taurus, by sextile the 2nd degree of Gemini, by square the 2nd degree of Cancer, by trine the 2nd degree of Leo,[2] and by opposition the 2nd degree of Libra; and thus with the rest of the Signs.

But it should be noted that by physicians, by Kepler, and some other astrologers, many other aspects are conceived—if not among the 12 Signs, at least among their parts—such as the octile, the decile, the quindecile, etc., but these are fictions without any foundation in nature. For every point of the Caelum determined by inferior causes determines not more than 11 others along with it, as was said above; and among those 12 points, only the aspects listed above as aspects are here defined.

Finally, there are Signs not aspecting each other, which in turn are distant from some part of the circle, which taken a number of times does not complete the whole circle—which sort are the 5th and the 7th from any Sign s s s[3] numbered is Virgo and Scorpio with respect to Aries, Libra and Sagittarius with respect to Taurus, etc. for the distance between the beginnings of Aries and Virgo taken twice is less than a circle, but three times is more; but I shall teach more fully about aspects elsewhere, where we shall also admit the *quincunx*.

---

[1] In Book 16.

[2] The Latin text has the symbol ♉ instead of ♌.

[3] The Latin text has *Signo s s s numeratus* 'Sign s s s numbered'. I do not know what the three s's signify unless they were put in place of a fraction such as 5/12.

Chapter 10.

The Conjunct and Inconjunct Signs.

Those Signs are said to be *conjunct* that are connected by any of the above said three modes—namely, by an aspect defined above, an antiscion, or by rulership; but those are *inconjunct* that are not mutually related by any one of those modes.[1]

Moreover, for any cardinal or mobile Sign, it is *unconnected* because it is opposed by the cardinal succeeding it, as for example Aries and Scorpio opposed to Taurus which succeeds Aries. Also, Cancer and Aquarius, Libra and Taurus, Capricorn and Leo. To any fixed Sign are those Signs inconjunct that are opposed to it, among which that one holds the middle place, as for example Taurus is unconnected with Libra and Sagittarius, which are opposed by Aries and Gemini, between which Taurus is located; And so Leo is unconnected to Capricorn and Pisces; and finally Scorpio to Aries and Gemini. Finally, any common Sign is inconjunct that one that is opposed to the common Sign preceding it. So, Gemini is unconnected with Scorpio, Virgo with Aquarius, and Pisces with Leo; for Leo is opposed to Aquarius, which precedes Pisces.

But it must be noted that those Signs are said to be unconnected that are distant by a part of the circle that taken several times is not exactly restored to its own beginning in one circuit; and they constitute the *quincunx* aspect between themselves. Those Signs are therefore said to aspect each other inadequately, and therefore they are inadequately conjunct, but the other Signs are adequately conjunct.

---

[1] The older astrologers called those Signs that were not related by a sextile, square, trine, or opposition *inconjunct,* that is to say *unrelated to* each other by one of the classical aspects.

Chapter 11.

Some Other Divisions of the Signs that Should Plainly be Rejected.

Besides the above true and physical divisions of the Signs, others were introduced in addition from the nature of the bodies, the images of which, affixed to the starry Zodiac, are believed by ignorant persons, and the names of which are attached to the true Signs of the Zodiac after the proper motion of the images or the fixed stars was noticed; and so, some of the Signs are said to be *human* and *rational*, such as Gemini, Virgo, Aquarius, because the constellations with that sort of name are believed to be images of humans; some are animals, such as Aries, Taurus, Leo, Cancer, etc.; some are mixed, such as Sagittarius; some are *beautiful*, such as Gemini and Virgo; some are *deformed*, such as Taurus, Cancer, and Capricorn; some are *mute* or *lacking a voice*, such as Cancer, Scorpio, and Pisces; some *having a good voice*, such as Gemini, Virgo, Aquarius, and Libra, but nevertheless it is often said of Libra that it *lacks a voice*; some *having a moderate voice*, such as Aries, Taurus, Leo, and Capricorn, since these animals surpass Gemini, Virgo, and Aquarius, etc.

Truly, in these divisions a manifold ignorance and stupidity is perceived. For in the first place it is established from Stoeffler's *Commentaries on the Sphere of Proclus*[1] that the images of the Zodiac and of the whole *Caelum* were only introduced by the fables of the old pagans, which I believe were suggested to the minds of men by the iniquity of the Devil, so that the *Caelum*, having been

[1] Johann Stoeffler (1452-1531). He was Professor of Mathematics at Tübingen, the author of almanacs and ephemerides, and a well-known astrologer. Morin refers to his book ...*Procli Diadochi, authoris grauissimi Sphaeram mundi...* 'The Sphere of the World by Proclus Diadochus, a most Important Author' (Tubingen: H. Morhardinis, 1534. folio). O. Neugebauer, *A History of Ancient Mathematical Astronomy* (New York Heidelberg Berlin: Springer Veriag, 1975. 3 vols.), vol. 2, p. 1036, says that this treatise, falsely ascribed to Proclus, is actually an excerpt from Geminus, *Eisagoge eis ta Phainomena* 'Introduction to the Phenomena'. See the edition and French translation of that work by Germaine Aujac, *Introduction aux Phenomenes* (Paris: Société d'Éditon 'Les Belles Lettres', 1975).

polluted with monsters and fables, Divine Providence might be hidden more scattered, (and also) noble knowledge—from which now at last the major laughing-stocks are exposed—and what should be attributed to God would be attributed to creatures.

Secondly. There is no constellation that refers to that body of whose image it is said to be, which entirely convicts the comment of the images; how, therefore, does it refer to a virtue, even though it refers to an image? The idea that the Signs themselves have borrowed their own force from sublunar bodies, especially at the beginning of the world, when animals and man had not yet been produced, which was only done in Days 5 and 6, is nonsense!

Thirdly. Since the images successively migrate from one Sign to another,[1] even if the credited virtue is inherent in these fictitious images (which of course cannot be the case), would it not be stupid to characterize the Signs with the virtue of a (now) absent image rather than the present one?

Therefore, on account of these reasons, the aforesaid divisions must absolutely be rejected,[2] and the Signs must only be called, either from the causes of the divisions explained by us above, or by the natures and properties of the planets ruling those Signs, as is shown below.

Chapter 12.

The Constellations of the Firmament.

Since the *constellations* were seen under the Zodiac, and they were once held to be the true and immobile *Signs* of the Zodiac; it will not be improper here to add this chapter on the constellations.

---

[1] Morin refers to the fact that due to precession many of the stars of a Zodiacal *constellation* have moved into the next *Sign,* which bears the same name as the next constellation.

[2] But Morin's argument against tradition was largely unsuccessful, since the majority of astrologers from his own time down to the present day continue to apply the Significations of the constellation images to the Signs of the Zodiac.

And so I say that the entire firmament is divided into those schemata of the fixed stars that are called constellations, which are like certain regions of the *Caelum*, differing among themselves in powers and natures. For it appears to the senses that the stars making up the constellation of Orion pertain thus to that image or schema, so that they truly separate it from any neighboring schema. And so with the constellation of Scorpio and many others that are seen in the serene *Caelum* and with the Moon in the meridian; although not all the constellations are so perfectly seen to be separated from the others, especially in the absence of the Moon, and the major part of them have their names solely from men's fantasies.

But now it cannot be denied that just as the whole Earth does not show all things, but the regions of Earth differ among themselves in their properties, because some are sandy, others clayey, others covered with stones and flints, etc., so diverse regions of the starry *Caelum* differ among themselves in their properties and influences. Moreover, the proper influences of the constellations are unknown to us—a great loss to astrology—and only the proper strengths of a few of the principal fixed stars are known to us. For just as it is absurd to suppose as many do that every kind of mineral, vegetable, and animal has in the *Caelum* a fixed star or particular constellation peculiar to itself, by which it is ruled in its origin, life, and death, since that is not even true of a man, who is subject to the influences of all the planets and fixed stars, so it is absurd to suppose that the constellations are similar in nature and virtue to the things by which they are designated. For example, that the constellation of *Aries* is similar in nature to the animal *ram*, the constellation of *Taurus* to a *bull* or a *bovine* animal, etc., which was nevertheless credited by the ancients and wrongly handed down by their successors. And much more disgracefully even now are those astrologers in error, who say that the effects of an eclipse of the Sun that occurs in the Sign Taurus pertains to bulls or bovines—thereby taking the *Sign* Taurus for the *constellation* of Taurus, which is now in the Sign Gemini!

So, however, the nature and virtue of the constellations could be discovered in the long succession of the centuries. And firstly of those that are under the Zodiac[1] of the *Primum Mobile* by noticing the New Moons, Eclipses, Great Conjunctions, Comets, and other similar things that occur in them; and by observing what effects they have, not only by reason of the Sign and the ruling planets, but also by the constellation and the fixed stars that are in it, and on what kinds of things they act most powerfully; indeed, in the nativities of men by observing the places of the ASC, the MC, and the planets in the constellations. But for those constellations that are beyond the Zodiac, their powers cannot be discerned by means of the planets; for otherwise the forces of the constellations that are beyond the Zodiac to the north or the south would be confounded with those that are within the Zodiac, and the latter could not be discerned separately from the former. And so, only those of them posited in celestial charts, or Comets rising or moving under them, can disclose their force on these inferior things. But to explore these things by means of accidents in the past or future of the world throughout the entire Globe of the Earth would be too much of a task, even for many astrologers making observations at the same time in different parts of the Earth, on account of the very slow motion of the fixed stars, which hinders our being able to discern the proper virtue of a constellation (as distinct) from the proper virtue of the Sign that it occupies. And I do not suppose that men will ever be able to acquire that knowledge.[2]

END OF THE FOURTEENTH BOOK.

---

[1] He refers here to the so-called *Zodiacal constellations*—Aries, Taurus, Gemini, etc.—as distinct from the extra Zodiacal ones.

[2] However, in the 450 years that have passed since astrologers began to publish their collections of natal horoscopes in the 16th century, the stars have moved forward more than 6 degrees, and that is probably a sufficient change for their individual natures to be detectable by careful analysis.

INDEX OF PERSONS

Note: the characterization given for each person is not necessarily complete, but it represents the type of work that he did to which reference is made in the Preface or in the Translation or the footnotes. Book publishers' names are not listed. They may be found in the Bibliography.

BIBLIOGRAPHY

Angelis, Alexander de (Angeli, Allesandro)
In Astrologos coniectores. Libri Quinque.
[Conjectures against the Astrologers. Five Books.]
Lyons: H. Cardon, 1615. 4to xxviii,351,xxxi pp.
Rome: B. Zanetti, 1615. 2nd ed. 4to

Bellantius, Lucius (Bellanti, Lucio)
Responsiones in disputationes Johannis Pici
adversus astrologicam veritatem.
[Reply to the Disputation of Giovanni Pico
Against the Truth of Astrology]
published together with:
De astrologica veritate.
[The Truth of Astrology]
Florence: Gerard of Harlem, 1498. folio
Basel, 1554. reprinted

Mirandola, Giovanni Pico della, Count
Disputationes adversus astrologiam.
[Disputations Against Astrology]
Bologna: Benedictus Hectoris, 1496.

Morin, Jean Baptiste
Astrologicarum domorum cabala detecta a Joanne Baptista Morino.
[The Cabala of the Astrological Houses disclosed by Jean Baptiste Morin]
Paris: J. Moreau, 1623. 8vo 38 pp.

Astrologia Gallica.
[French Astrology]
The Hague: A. Vlacq, 1661. folio pref (xxxvi), 784 pp.

Astrologia Gallica: Book Twenty-Two Directions.
trans. from the Latin by James Herschel Holden
Tempe, Az.: A.F.A., Inc., 1994. paper xv,292 pp.

Neugebauer, O.
A History of Ancient Mathematical Astronomy.
New York Heidelberg Berlin: Springer Verlag, 1975. 3 vols.

Stoeffler, Johann
Procli Diadochi, authoris grauissimi Sphaeram mundi…
[The Sphere of the World by Proclus Diadochus, a most Important Author]
Tübingen: H. Morhardinis, 1534. folio.

Jean-Baptiste Morin

Astrologia Gallica

Book Fifteen

The Essential Dignities of the Planets

Translated from the Latin

By

James Herschel Holden, M.A.
Fellow of the American Federation of Astrologers

TABLE OF CONTENTS

Translator's Preface

In this Book, Morin explains the various classifications and subdivisions of the Signs and gives his opinion as to why some of them should be changed or rejected altogether. He gives what seems to him to be logical reasons for these features of the Zodiac. And as usual he quotes Holy Scripture from time to time. We should be aware that he was also primarily motivated by two things in astrology: (1) a dislike of anything that did not have a definite relationship to astronomy; and (2) a distrust of anything that seemed to him to have been originated by Arabian astrologers.

Unfortunately, Morin's knowledge of the history of the World and the history of astrology, while consistent with what his 17th century contemporaries believed, was inferior to our knowledge today. Therefore, some of his "proofs" are no longer valid. And some of the subdivisions of the Zodiac that he discusses have fallen out of use and are hardly even known to modern astrologers. Still, his observations and comments are interesting, displaying as always his determination to put every facet of astrology on a logical basis. And unlike the majority of astrological writers, he does not simply enunciate a rule, but he also gives an explanation of why he believes it to be valid.

In Chapter 1 Morin resumes his argument that the signs are the same both above and below the equator. And we are surprised to learn that he held a mistaken idea of how to calculate house cusps for places in the southern hemisphere. In the examples that he gives, he has simply taken the house cusps from the House Tables as if the Southern latitude was Northern latitude, which is of course incorrect. The proper procedure is to add 180 degrees to the RAMC and then copy the degree numbers of the cusps but reverse the Signs shown with them in the table. However, since he apparently only had two horoscopes of persons born in the southern hemisphere, this error did not affect his practice of astrology in Paris. It seems that he was so intent upon asserting that the Zodiacal Signs were not reversed below the equator, as some astrologers had suggested, that he was reluctant to change the procedure for using the House Tables, since that would imply that there was something different about astrology in the southern hemisphere.

In order to make my translation of Morin's text easier to comprehend, I have italicized a number of technical terms. And I have broken up some of his long sentences into shorter ones. I have also added some words in parentheses, since he sometimes speaks rather shortly, especially towards the ends of sentences. And I have added some footnotes either to clarify the text or to provide my own comments.

James Herschel Holden
25 November 2006

ASTROLOGIA GALLICA

Book Fifteen
The Essential Dignities of the Planets.

Preface.

If in Book Fourteen it was especially difficult to investigate the important causes of the division of the Primum Mobile *into 12 parts, differing among themselves in their elemental natures, and to assign such natures to them as cannot be made more probable; it would certainly seem to be very much more sublime and difficult to have undertaken these things that are taken up to define and put them on a firm basis with reasons: Namely, whether the Signs are of the same nature and virtue throughout the whole Earth. Then, whether at the beginning of the World the Zodiac was divided by the Sun into parts conformable in elemental and influential nature to the individual Planets, and some other things that follow from that. For these are the prime and more abstruse fundamentals of astrology. Moreover, we hope that we shall enter upon this book, and with Divine light favoring, bring it to a favorable completion.*

Chapter 1.

Whether the Signs of the Zodiac are of the same Nature and Virtue throughout the Whole Earth.

After having explained in the previous book the division of the *Caelum* into elemental natures, it must now be seen in this book by what reason that same *Caelum* in its 12 Signs is divided among the influential natures of the Planets with respect to the globe of the Earth, so that from this it may be plain with which of them the individual Planets agree, and with which they disagree; and so, the dignities and debilities of the Planets that are called *essential* are disclosed and established; not only against those who debauch astrology, but also against those who, while affecting the name of astrologer, nevertheless overturn these divisions, not noticing that they only produce arbitrary ones, and thus overturn the whole doctrine of astrological judgments.

Moreover, Ptolemy first took an opportunity to display this error in *Quadripartite*, Book 1, chapter 17, where he says this about the domiciles of the Planets:

> "The domiciles are distributed by a natural reason. for since of the 12 Signs two northern ones come close to our pole, and in particular Cancer and Leo make heat, these two Signs must be judged to have the greatest and most effective light; Leo indeed is the Sun's, because it is a masculine Sign, but Cancer is the Moon's because it is feminine."

Moreover, to each one of the rest of the Signs he gives two domiciles as is seen in that same chapter.

As for the rest of that division of the Zodiac into the Planetary domiciles, which has subsisted solely on tradition down to our times, Ptolemy did not know the causes; for if he had brought forward reasons there that were natural and true; [then] certainly from those same causes, Capricorn and Aquarius will in the southern part of the World be Signs that are especially hot and summery, and the domiciles of the luminaries will indeed be Aquarius for the Sun because it is a masculine Sign, but Capricorn for the Moon because it is feminine; moreover, Cancer and Leo will be the domiciles of Saturn, into which what is surely an altogether absurd opinion I marvel that Cardan has fallen in his *Commentary* with these words: "From this it finally follows that in the southern half (of the World) Capricorn will be the domicile of the Moon and

Aquarius of the Sun, Pisces and Sagittarius of Mercury, Aries and Scorpio of Venus, Taurus and Libra of Mars, Gemini and Virgo of Jupiter, and Cancer and Leo of Saturn.[1]

But Campanella (1568-1639), the great corrupter of the sciences (which I would like to have stated as a caution to those who take delight in his books that are full of novelties) amplified Cardan's error in his *Astrology*,[2] Book 1, Chapter 3, Article 3, where he offers this:

> "the early astrologers only considered our latitudes; and therefore, the Spaniards who established colonies beyond the tropic of Capricorn have need of a new astrology." Moreover, in Chapter 6, Article 3, he says: "It is not a symbol for the Planets, with certain Signs of the *Caelum*, but to those who dwell beyond the equator, equidistant with us from the equator, to have the domiciles of the Planets in an opposite location—and the domicile of the Sun is in Aquarius, the domicile of the Moon in Capricorn, of Saturn in Cancer and Leo, and the domiciles of the rest of them as above."

But under the equator (which Cardan had not foreseen) the two and the same domiciles he attributes to the Sun and the Moon, namely Aries and Libra, to Saturn Cancer and Capricorn; and to the rest of the Planets he attributes two whole Signs, he says it is impossible.

But of such weight is the truth of this thing in this science, that there is a notable foundation for all judgments; and consequently they must be diligently considered. Moreover, we shall begin with Cardan's opinion, which indeed consists of fewer ambiguities; and

[1] Not well stated. If the signs are reversed south of the equator, Cancer and Leo will still be the domiciles of the Moon and the Sun. For when the Sun is in Capricorn and Aquarius in the northern hemisphere, it will at the same time be in Cancer and Leo in the southern hemisphere.

[2] Tommaso Campanella, *Astrologicarum libri VII* (Frankfurt, 1630).

that, so that it may be made more evidently to be avoided; then we think of the error of Ptolemy, then of the error all the astrologers until now, who, thinking that of the whole globe of the Earth only the northern part that contained Europe, Asia, and Africa is habitable, which is not a fifth part of the globe, have not (thereby) made astrology a universal science, but only a particular observation for Asia, Europe, and Africa; for which alone Ptolemy wrongly divides the whole Zodiac in *Quadripartite*, Book 2, chapter 2. But for an astrologer meditating on a universal science for the whole Earth, neither inclining towards the north nor the south, but it must be standing under the equator, where on account of that it is necessary that he establish himself at least mentally, and from a position held with respect to no part of the north or the south, with the natures of the Signs and the Planets having been looked at, not unless a thing is universal for the whole globe, he will therefore pronounce them common to both parts.

Therefore, having postulated the action of the stars on these inferior things, he will consider that light of Nature; there is no place of Earth that is not subject to the influxes of the celestial bodies, and before the others, the places of the right sphere, which among the other places of the Earth are more perfectly applied and subjected to the influences of the Zodiac and the Planets. Therefore, since the right sphere is the norm both for itself and for both oblique spheres, then it will declare that they are immutable—not some to the north and others to the south, and there are the same elemental natures of the Signs everywhere on Earth, and consequently the same rulerships by the Planets. Moreover, this will be the reason for it: for if some were to the north and others to the south as Cardan [1501-1576] will have it, therefore it is necessary that none of them are in the right sphere, since those that are to the north cannot be there, nor those which are to the south; and there is no reason why some of them are rather with the northern (parts) than with the southern ones. No nature, therefore, will be able to be assigned there nor the qualities of the effects from the celestial causes, as from eclipses of the Sun or the conjunctions of the lights. For from Ptolemy, *Quadripartite*, Book 2, Chapters 6 & 7, and all the rest of the astrologers, the nature of such effects must be taken from the natures of the Signs of the eclipses or the conjunctions, then from the Signs of the Planets ruling them; but the quality, whether of goodness or evil, from the benefic or malefic state of the Planets ruling those Signs, none of which naturally is found in the right sphere. For there, having been affected by the natures of the Signs, and consequently the rulership of the Planets, the primary cause of the status of the Planets would be taken away; but in fact this cannot be said about any one of them, whether it is in its own domicile or exaltation, or in its contrary position of exile or fall; in fact, whether it is in the places of the benefic or the malefic Planets; that is in no place that any Planet rules; therefore, in that place no nature or quality of effect can be assigned. Therefore, no effects will occur, since none can happen anywhere whose nature and quality cannot be determined. But from eclipses and conjunctions of the lights or syzygies no one denies that effects are produced in the right sphere. And of the uniform status of the things in the sphere itself, let us not suspect confusions of the natures, Signs, and rulerships there, from which they would produce monsters and continuous prodigies, against experience. And the same reasoning can be established with regard to the particular constitutions of those who are born in that sphere. From which nothing could be foreseen about the native's temperament, habits, intelligence, riches, honors, death, and the rest of his accidents, with the essential dignities and debilities of the Planets taken away, and also the rulers of the individual houses of the figure. Therefore, the natures of the Signs and the rulerships of the Planets must not be put some to the north and others to the south, contrary to Cardan's opinion.

Let us come now to Campanella, who seems to have wanted to remedy Cardan's disadvantage, and nevertheless fell into Scylla while trying to avoid Charybdis.[1] If, therefore, as he will have it, there is no conformity or symbol with certain Signs of the *Caelum*, why in the region of the north up to the arctic pole will Cancer be the domicile of the Moon, not of the Sun, and Leo will be the domi-

[1] That is, while trying to avoid one disaster, he fell into another one.

cile of the Sun, and not of the Moon? Or why is there not the same domicile for the Sun and the Moon? Here it was necessary for Campanella to become silent or to say something only absurd. Besides, if from the Tropic of Cancer to the arctic pole, Cancer and Leo are the domiciles of the lights, and from the Tropic of Capricorn to the Antarctic pole, Capricorn and Aquarius are their domiciles, as he says, relying on Ptolemy's reason; moreover, below the equator Aries and Libra are given to the Sun and the Moon for domiciles, it is plain that he wants the domiciles of the lights to be established solely by their greater approach to the zenith; and he says that in Chapter 7, Article 3, saying these express words:

> "Therefore, since the Sun, when it appears the most powerful, and when the Moon appears to be the closest, will make great effects of the sort that are appropriate to the lights, because they are the domiciles of the lights, everywhere that sort of nearness and strength of theirs is (directed) to their own inferiors."

Granted that, at least it follows from those statements that for those who live between the equator and the tropics, it is necessary to construct other domiciles for the Sun and the Moon, namely in Taurus, Gemini, and Virgo for the northern peoples, for whom those Signs are vertical, and in Virgo, Sagittarius, and Pisces[1] for those in the south. And so all the Signs that are the domiciles of the lights will be ambulatory and local, only serving to designate the proximities of the Sun and the Moon with respect to the vertical, although these could be defined without the Signs simply by their declinations, but otherwise they are plainly of no virtue, because Campanella himself seems to have been driven by that opinion to declare (that) in distinct words, when he said above that there is no symbol for the Planets with certain Signs of the *Caelum*. For if any

[1] These sets of three signs seem to be incorrect if verticality is the criterion. You would expect Gemini and Cancer in the first set and Sagittarius and Capricorn in the second set. Why Taurus and Scorpio are included is not clear. Taurus is of course the exaltation of the Moon, but if that is mentioned, why not Aries?

celestial virtue is inherent in the Signs, it cannot be denied that because of that they harmonize with some Planets and not with others. But it is plain that inherent in the Signs are great virtues from somewhere else, as from that same Campanella, that is in Book 2, Chapter 2, Article 3, where he says: "Aries makes fierce, very lively, savage, bold, perverse, treacherous persons." Therefore, since Mars also makes such persons according to that same Campanella, in Book 4, Chapter 7, Article 4, it is established from that that it is the symbol of Mars with Aries; and the reasoning is the same for the rest of the Signs and Planets according to those chapters. Therefore, since this doctrine of Campanella destroys itself by its evident contradiction and only affects a particular or localized astrology, but not astrology in general, or astrology for the whole Earth, which he promises in Book 1, Chapter 3, Article 3, there is no need to spend any more time to refute these statements, especially since, with the rulerships of the Planets taken away—which would only be imaginary if the virtues of the Signs were taken away—the universal astrology of Campanella, which is concerned with those two angles, collapses.

Nevertheless, this can be sought from Campanella, or from the supporter of his absurd imaginings—if that Sign with respect to each race is the domicile of the Sun, through which the Sun itself is nearer to the vertex of that same race, will that Sign be the domicile of the Sun for that same race during the whole year, or only during that month in which it moves through that Sign? For why would it be for the whole year? With regard to this, since in the two antiscion Signs of the Sun and the Moon they are made equally near to the vertex, since of the antiscions it will be the domicile of the Sun and the Moon for any race throughout the whole globe of the Earth, and why not another? Then, why under the equator are two domiciles attributed to the Sun, otherwise unique? The solution of which questions certainly no astrologer of a sound mind would accept.

And so, having omitted the rest of the absurdities which this opinion produces, solely for its more evident falsity, we are putting here the horoscope of Zaga-Christ, Prince of the Abyssinians,[1] born at Corcora, under a 6 degree elevation of the North Pole and a difference of longitude from Paris of 36 degrees.[2] He was driven out by his uncle, so he said, and was carried through various regions and finally into France, where recognized by the King, by Cardinal Richelieu, and by the whole royal court and also by me, at last worn out by poverty and destitution he died at Ruel on 21 April 1638 from an unfortunate direction of Saturn to his ASC to the square of the Moon, ruler of the 4th.

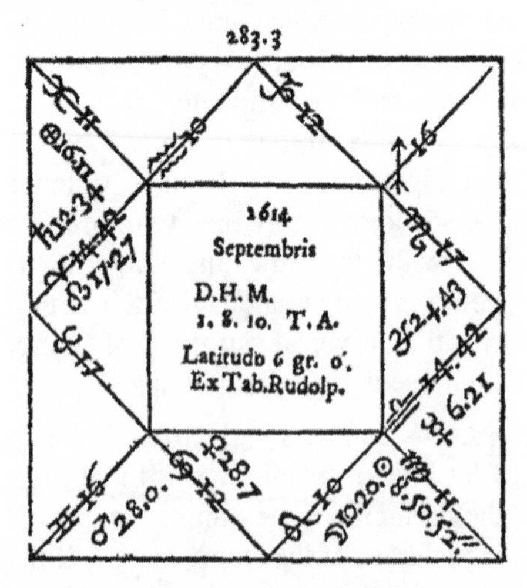

Prince Zaga-Christ,
Corcora 6N 38E, 1 September 1614 8:10 P.M.

[1] An account of the life of Zaga Christ is given in Father Eugène Roger's book *La Terre Saincte ou Description topographique.-.des Saincts Lieux...et une relation veritable de Zaga Christ, prince d'Ethyopie, qui mourut a Ruel prez Paris* (Paris: Antoine Bertier, 1646. 4to 440 pp.). But I think we should wonder whether the birth data that Morin gives for him is correct. He may have obtained it from the prince himself, or he may have found it in Roger's book., but considering the difference between the Abyssinian calendar and the Western calendar and the possible difference in the way in which Abyssinians counted their age, there were opportunities for error. Still, right or wrong, Morin's discussion of the horoscope gives a good example of his methods of interpretation.

[2] Perhaps the town Adi Corcora, Tigré, at 13N05 39E28. Geographical coordinates were not accurately known in Morin's time.

All the Planets are peregrine, with the exception of Mercury, and connected by no benefic aspect, if you make an exception of the corrupted sextile of Mercury and also the corrupted trine of the Moon and Saturn. Furthermore, Saturn ruler of the MC is in exile and particularly in the ASC on account of its southern latitude of 2°43',[1] and the Sun and the Moon are unfriendly to the 10th space (house),[2] and the Sun is opposite the Lot [of Fortune] in the 12th. All of which argued that the man would be unfortunate in his dignities, his actions undertaken, and his general fortune. And because Mercury, ruler of the 3rd which is the house of relatives, was square the MC and opposite Saturn, ruler of the MC, and also the ASC, and also square Mars,[3] ruler of the ASC, it Signified relatives not kindly disposed to the person and dignity of the native, and it also Signified enemies, especially because Mercury in the 6th would also indicate enemies; moreover, Jupiter, ruler of the Sun, in the 7th subjected his fortune to the power of enemies, more especially because Jupiter itself applies to the square of Venus, ruler of the 2nd. He was a talented and refined person on account of Mercury in sextile to the Moon under the rulership of Venus, and the Moon in trine to Saturn and to the ASC from the 5th house, being strong in reasoning and eloquence, but stubborn on account of that same Mercury opposed to Saturn and to the ASC; he was also extravagant on account of the Moon ruler of Venus in the 5th. And with the Sign of Leo in trine to Saturn and the ASC, indeed and Mercury ruler of the 5th and the Sun in the 6th, on account of a lover of senatorial rank it caused him to be imprisoned at Paris, from which however by order of the king he was freed. He was

[1] Calculation from the coordinates of Saturn given by Morin shows that Saturn would rise with 14°04′ Aries, which as he says would be in partile conjunction with the ASC in 14°42′ Aries.

[2] I am not sure why he says this. The Moon is in Leo and the Sun is in Virgo. Since the 10th house contains parts of both Capricorn and Aquarius, the Moon in Leo opposes the Aquarius portion; but the Sun in Virgo is trine the Capricorn portion and only quincunx the Aquarius portion.

[3] But this is a "heads and tails" aspect with a wide orb or more than 8 degrees, since Mars is in 28 Gemini, and Mercury is in 6°21′ Libra.

also very sad and melancholy on account of Saturn's being in exile in the ASC, and he was very prone to anger on account of Mars ruler of the ASC, and a fiery Sign in the ASC. And because Mars was found in the 3rd in trine to Jupiter ruler of the 9th and the 7th; and they are all angular in mobile Signs; therefore, long and varied journeys and inconsistencies of fortune and life were Signified. Finally, Mars, ruler of the ASC and the 8th, in the 3rd, was plainly portending at the least a wretched death outside his native land because by nature it is malefic, but not a violent one, because neither is the ASC injured by Mars, nor Mars by Saturn, nor are the lights injured by the malefics, nor were these in violent Signs. Moreover, Father Eugène Roger, a devout missionary to barbarous countries, (in his *La Terre Saincte*), Book 2, Chapter 2, of his own travels in the Holy Land, sets forth Zaga-Christ's life and the misfortunes of his circumstances. From which it is plain that Zaga-Christ was not an imposter, as many thought, but truly a very unfortunate prince of the Abyssinians, as his chart sufficiently testifies.

This figure therefore is very conformable to the fates of this Prince according to the domiciles of the Planets given out hitherto by Ptolemy and the rest (of the astrologers); and consequently by this experience near the equator; and then the reasons given above prove that the Signs of the Zodiac are per se of the same nature and virtue for the whole Earth; moreover, the domiciles of the Planets are also the same in the northern sphere, the southern sphere, and the right sphere; contrary to that which Cardan and Campanella have handed down from simple opinion devoid of experiences and reasons. Indeed, one could be more certain of this thing by having notices from celestial charts of persons born in the southern part of the World, of which until now I was unable to see any; but because no experience is ever contrary to reason, and moreover reason entirely favors our opinion, and also I certainly think that it would be true in the southern World and conformable to experience, as is plain here from the nativity of Zaga-Christ.

But at last, having passed more than 20 years from the time in which I gave out a letter transmitted by me to the northern and southern astrologers, that most generous and especially learned in astrology Mr. N. de Groenembergue, Commander of the Fleet of the King of Portugal, sent to me the birth times of two men born on the far side of the equator, along with their character, intellect, and some accidents; for which times I erected the celestial charts, which I have drawn to be added here, in a confirmation most worthy of note of the doctrine given by us above.

The first is that of Francisco Gomez Cortez, born on the 4th of the month of October in the year 1627, called the day of St. Francis, at the rising of the Sun at Olinda Pernambuco, 8 degrees on the other side of the equator. He was inclined to painting, arithmetic, music, dances, and the gladiatorial art; and yet he followed the military calling from his youth. He has many yellowish marks on his face, hands, and body, which are called Jewish Signs; he also has reddish hair; and he had a quarrel with someone whom, while not wanting to, he (nevertheless) killed.

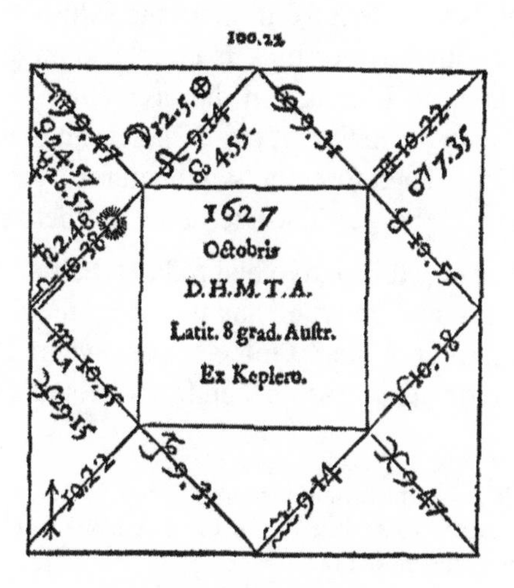

Francisco Gomez Cortez
Pernambuco, Brazil 8S09 34W59, 4 October 1627 Sunrise[1]

[1] This chart is drawn incorrectly! Morin has mistakenly calculated all of the intermediate house cusps for 8 degrees *north* latitude instead of for 8 degrees *south* latitude. Calculation from modern figures shows that Sunrise occurred at 5:57

His propensity was to arithmetic, writing, painting, music, and dancing, since Venus, ruler of the ASC is in the domicile of Mercury and joined to it. These things, however, would not have been if Venus had not been ruler of the ASC;[1] therefore, Libra is the domicile of Venus and Virgo is the domicile of Mercury. But if they had been inverted in the southern part (of the World), Mars would have been the ruler of the ASC in a domicile of Jupiter, from which the inclination given above could not have been produced, as is sufficiently plain from the nature of the Planets, which agree with their Signs, as is proved with reasons in its own place, in addition to the experience that is very well known to all astrologers.

In addition, he followed the gladiatorial and military (profession), since Mars, ruler of the 1st house, which is the house of character on account of Scorpio in the 1st,[2] and then ruler of the 7th, which is quarrels, and Mars is in the 8th conjunct the Eye of Taurus,[3] a bright and violent fixed star of the nature of Mars, in trine to the ASC. But with the rulerships inverted, that ought to have been from Venus joined to Mercury in the domicile of Jupiter, which does not agree with the nature of these Planets and their Signs—indeed it is contrary. Therefore, the same natures of the Signs are in the southern part of the World as are in the northern part.

Finally, because this native had reddish hair and had freckles on his face, hands, and body, he had that from the Sun in the ASC in trine to Mars, ruler of the 1st joined to the eye of Taurus, a fixed Martian star, in trine to the ASC, then from the square of the Moon

---

LAT or 5:46 LMT, at which time the RAMC was 99°15′, and the ASC was 10°45′ Libra. (If refraction is taken into account, Sunrise would have occurred 2 or 3 minutes earlier than those times.)

[1] But in the following paragraph, Mars is said to be the ruler of the ASC!

[2] With Libra on the cusp of the 1st, and 20 degrees of Libra in the 1st, and only 10 degrees of Scorpio in the 1st, it hardly seems appropriate to call Mars the ruler of the 1st house. On the contrary, if the signs had been reversed, Aries would have been on the cusp of the 1st, and Mars would have been its ruler.

[3] Aldebaran or a Tauri was at 4°35′ Gemini.

to Saturn[1] and the Sun in the ASC. Everything, therefore, agrees.

The second (chart) is that of Felipe Bandeyra de Mello, concerning whom Mr. de Groenembergue wrote these words for me:

Felipe Bandeyra de Mello was born in the year 1612 on the 15th of the month of April, Palm Sunday, at 5 A.M. or 1 hour before Sunrise at Pernambuco.

He was always inclined to arms, and he followed a military career from childhood; he had many quarrels with various persons; and in the year 1635 he killed a man with whom he had had a quarrel; and this happened on a riotous evening. He traveled through various parts of Europe; he experienced many storms at sea and also shipwrecks; in the year 1638, having been shipwrecked, he escaped by swimming. He was captured three times by the Dutch, and he has had little good fortune.

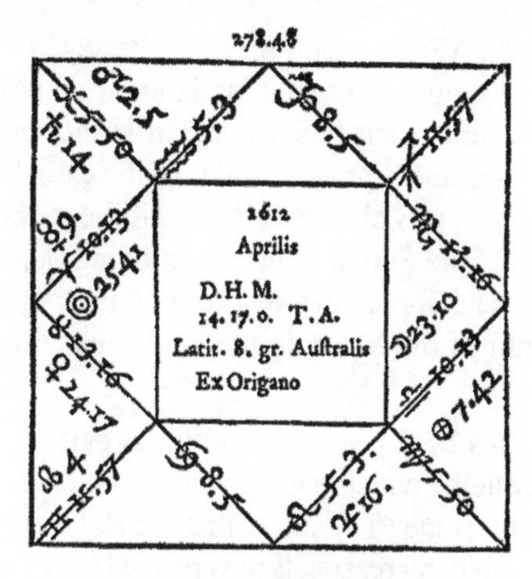

Felipe Bandeyra de Mello
Pernambuco, Brazil 8S09 34W59, 15 April 1612 5:00 A.M.[2]

[1] But the Moon is not square Saturn and the Sun; it is sextile Saturn and the Sun. Probably Morin still had in mind the fact that part of Scorpio was in the 1st house, and he reckoned that the Moon in Leo was square Scorpio.

[2] This chart is also drawn incorrectly! Again Morin has mistakenly calculated all of the intermediate house cusps for 8 degrees *north* latitude instead of for 8 degrees *south* latitude.

This native was dedicated to a military career from childhood, with many quarrels and a homicide, because Mars was the ruler of the ASC and of the Sun which was exalted in the 1st house, which is the house of character, then the 7th and 8th houses,[1] which are the houses of quarrels and wars and dangers of death; with Mars's exaltation in the MC, which is the house of actions and profession, and applying to Saturn, the ruler of the MC; and consequently, both of the malefics rule his actions and profession.

He suffered in the sea many dangers to his life and shipwrecks, since Mars, ruler of the ASC, is also ruler of the 8th, on account of Scorpio, a water Sign; and both Mars and Saturn, rulers of the MC, are conjoined in Pisces, a water Sign, and Mars is applying to Saturn. And yet he escaped on account of Jupiter, ruler of the 9th, and then Mars and Saturn in trine to the ASC and the Sun.[2]

Many times he was a captive, because Mars and Saturn, rulers of the MC and the ASC, by their presence besieged the cusp of the 12th, which is the house of prisons, and they were both in the 12th; for this same reason, he has hitherto had little success in his undertakings and actions and dignities; and he will scarcely be more fortunate in the future; it is clear that there will be perpetual difficulties on account of the Sun and the Moon being opposed from the 1st and 7th houses. He should be on his guard against a violent death on account of the Moon in the 7th in the antiscion of Mars and Saturn.

Can nativities be given in the northern part of the Earth that more accurately agree with the temperament, character, intelligence and accidents of fortune? Therefore, that which I formerly disclosed and postulated solely by reason, is now proved to be very true by experience; namely, that in the northern part as in the southern part of the Earth, the natures of the Signs and the rulerships and natures of the Planets are the same and invariable, which, nevertheless, it is pleasing to confirm here with the three following reasons.

[1] Mars can only be said to rule the 7th because part of Scorpio is in that house.

[2] Mars and Saturn in early Pisces are not in trine to the ASC and the Sun in Aries. The sign they are in is semi-sextile the ASC and the Sun sign.

First. Because the Sun in both hemispheres is found to be hot and dry in whatever Sign it is located; the Moon, cold and moist; Saturn, cold and dry; etc. Therefore, since these (qualities) are not received from the Signs of the Zodiac, it must necessarily be concluded that these are their own proper natures, which, through the motions of the Planets in their own orbits, even changed by the eccentricity, when they pass from the northern part of the World to the southern part, it would be silly to think (that they are changed). For what would their own proper natures be under the equator?

Second. If the natures of the Signs were otherwise in the southern part than in the northern, the nature of the triplicities would collapse. For if Sagittarius among the southerners was a water Sign, then Aries and Leo would also be water Signs, contrary to the experiences of northerners in the temperaments of the air and of natives (of those Signs).

Third. If an astrologer living in the southern part should erect the figures of many northern natives, he would find by experience that Mercury in Virgo and in the 1st house would produce an intellect that was very excellent and with more aptitude for mathematics than in any other Sign, other things being equal; and if he would judge otherwise, he would stray away from the truth; but we observe the same thing in the northern part; therefore, the Planetary nature of the Sign Virgo is not other in the southern part than in the northern one; and in both cases it is Mercurial.

Truly with regard to these southern figures, the reader must be warned that in the *Rudolphine Tables*[1] abbreviated by me, I have said incidentally how they should be erected. But here it is pleasing to explain another and shorter method, with the following sent in advance.

First. The right ascensions of opposite points are distant everywhere by 180 degrees from each other.

---

[1] *Tabulae rudolphinae ad meridianum Uraniburgi supputatae a Joanne Baptista Morino...* (Paris: J. Le Brun, 1650). These were Morin's version of Kepler's *Rudolphine Tables.*

Second. The oblique ascensions and descensions of points of the *Caelum* have in the southern part of the Earth, through their right ascensions and ascensional differences, (values) only absolutely contrary, to these that are observed in the northern part.

Third. The oblique ascensions of opposite points in the same latitude of the place, or in the same place on Earth, differ among themselves in the sum of the ascensional difference of those same points, and the ascensional difference of these is the same.

Fourth. The oblique ascension and descension of the same degree of the ecliptic or of a point of the *Caelum* in the same latitude of the place differ in two ways in the ascensional difference of that degree.

Fifth. The northern ascension and the southern ascension of the same degree in equal latitudes of the place, or in places on Earth that are diametrically opposed, differ in two ways from the ascensional difference of that degree.

Sixth. The northern ascension of any degree and its southern descension in places of equal latitude are identical; and the same is true of the northern descension and the southern ascension.

Seventh. The oblique ascension of a point of the ecliptic in the northern part, and the oblique ascension of the opposite point in the southern part in equal latitudes differ by a semi-circle; and the same is true of the northern descension and the southern descension.

Eighth. As in the northern part of the Earth, the degree of the cusps of the ecliptic, or the first degrees of the houses, correspond in their own oblique ascensions, and those opposed in their own oblique descensions, according to the Tables constructed by Regiomontanus; but on the contrary, in the southern part the degrees of the eastern cusps of the 11th, 12th, 1st, 2nd, and 3rd ought to correspond to their own oblique descensions, and those opposite (cusps) to their own oblique ascensions by those same Tables. And the reason is because the part of the *Caelum* that ascends for us, descends for the southerners, and vice versa. And therefore, because for the northerners it is an ascension, for the southerners it is a descension; and vice versa. And the above said is very evidently plain on a celestial globe.

Ninth. The right ascension of the Sun, and the given hours converted into degrees of the equator make everywhere the right ascension of the MC at the given time.

With these things understood, now for the erection of a celestial figure, this will be the general method in the southern part of the World.

First. For the given time in the southern part, converted into degrees of the equator and the right ascension of the place of the Sun, taken at that time and properly corrected and equated, makes the right ascension of the MC, and the degrees of the ecliptic corresponding to it are taken.

Second. If Tables of Houses corresponding to the latitude of the place for which the figure is to be erected are lacking, to the right ascension of the MC 30 degrees are added for the oblique ascension of the house, or the cusp of the 11th; and to that 30 more degrees for the oblique ascension of the 12th; and to that 30 more degrees for the oblique ascension of the ASC; etc.; and this is done in the erection of a figure in the northern part for the 5 eastern houses, the 11th, 12th, 1st, 2nd, and 3rd.

Third. Let the elevation of the pole, north as well as south, be found above the circles of position of those same individual houses; and let there be found from Regiomontanus's Tables the degrees of the ecliptic corresponding to the ascensions of those houses as it is given for the northern part; for the degrees of those same cusps will be the degrees of the cusps of the oriental or ascending houses in the southern part, although in that part their oblique ascensions differ from the oblique ascensions of the same degrees in the northern part. This, moreover, will be nothing else than to construct a northern figure for the southern part.[1]

[1] But this is wrong! And it disagrees with his own definitions given above. The proper way to use the house tables calculated for the northern hemisphere is sim-

Let it be proposed as an example the figure of Francisco Gomez Cortez erected for Pernambuco in the year 1627 on the 5th of October at 18:02:24, at which moment the Sun arises there; and to that time let there be added 3:04 for the 46 degrees difference in meridians from Uraniborg,[1] the place of origin of Kepler's Ephemerides; and they make 21:06:24. From which, subtracting 0:12 for the equation of time from our Table, and there remain 20:54:24 for the mean time at Uraniborg.

The place of the Sun at that time from Kepler is 10 degrees 38′. the right ascension of which is 189° 46′ and hours 18:02:24, and they make 270° 36′, of which the sum is 100° 22′ for the right ascension of the MC, to which corresponds 9° 31′ Cancer. To these 100° 22′ add 30°; they make 130° 22′ for the northern oblique ascension of the 11th house, which has a north pole elevated 4° 02′; and therefore the corresponding degree of the ecliptic for that house or cusp will be 9° 14′ Leo, neglecting the seconds.[2] To these same 130° 22′ add 30°; they make 160° 22′ for the northern (oblique) ascension of the 12th house, which, from Regiomontanus's Table of the rational houses has a northern pole elevated 6° 57′; and the degree of the ecliptic corresponding to that cusp will be 9° 47′ Virgo. Therefore, in the figure for the southern part (of the World), the MC will be 9° 21′ Cancer, the 11th house will be 9° 14′ Leo; the 12th house will be 9° 47′ Virgo; and so on with the other houses 1, 2, and 3. Moreover, the opposite houses

---

ply to add 180° to the RAMC, take the cusps from the house tables and reverse the signs of the zodiac. It is surprising that Morin did not realize this.

[1] The actual difference in longitude is 12E42 + 34W59 = 47° 41′ or 3:10:44, but Morin's figures were close enough.

[2] The Polar Elevation is calculated by the formula tan P.E. = tan Lat. X cos 60° for Houses 11 and 3 or from tan P.E. = tan Lat. X cos 30° for Houses 12 and 2. For North Latitude 8°, the Poles are 4° 01′ and 6° 56′, very close to the values Morin gives. To find the cusp of the 11th house from the tables, add 30° to the RAMC and subtract 90° from the sum; then for that value of the RAMC find the ASC for the Polar Elevation; and that will be the value of the 11th cusp. For Morin's example 100° 22′ + 30° - 90° = 40° 22′; and with that value of RAMC, we find for Latitude 4° 01′ North the ASC 9° 14′ Leo; and that is the value of the cusp of the Regiomontanus 11th house.

will have the opposite degrees of the ecliptic. And the southern figure will be erected by this method, by means of the southern descensions of their own oriental or rising cusps in the southern part of the World.

But the southern oblique ascension of each of these houses 11, 12, 1, 2, and 3 is found thus by the directions of the ascending part of the *Caelum*.

Let the southern oblique ascension of the 11th house, or 9° 14′ Leo,[1] be found; its right ascension has the value 131° 41′. And the north declination is 18° 07′. And the ascensional difference under the pole 4° 02′ is 1° 18′; the double of which, 2° 36′, added to the northern oblique ascension of the 11th house, namely 130° 22′ makes the required oblique ascension 132° 58′, which also will be had if to the right ascension of 9° 14′ Leo is added the simple ascensional difference of 1° 18′. Moreover, if the declination had been south, the ascensional difference or its double would have had to be subtracted. And in short it should similarly be done for the southern oblique ascensions of the other houses, 12, 1, 2, and 3. As all these things are plain from the nine notes above or from a celestial globe.

But from this it is sufficiently made known that in a southern figure the directions of the Significators in the ascending or descending part of charts must all be done in accordance with the Regiomontanus Tables or with those of Argol, as in the northern figure (above). Therefore, in the figure of Felipe Bandeyra de Mello, and (in the case of) the homicide committed by him on the evening of a drunken party in the year 1635, it is deduced that the given time was truly later by around 13 hours, which done, the direction of the ASC on the day of the party was in sinister sextile to Mars, ruler of the ASC, of the Sun in the 1st, and of the 8th house; and on that day, the Sun was by transit partilely on the radical place of Mars; moreover the Moon, which occupied the 7th in the radix transited through the radical place of the Sun. But let what has been said so far about the southern figures suffice.

[1] Here, as elsewhere from time to time, the Latin text by mistake has the symbol ☊ instead of the symbol ♌.

Chapter 2.

At the Beginning of the World the Zodiac was Divided by the Sun into Parts Conformable to the Individual Planets by their Elemental and also by their Influential Nature.

Since four primarily contrary natures are found separately in the Zodiac; but none of these are inherent in the *Caelum*, which is very homogeneous, but only from the Sun's determining them, as was said in Book 14, Chapter 5, therefore the Zodiac itself will also be divided by that same Sun into the elemental natures of all the Planets; for anyone of these is from anyone of the four contrary (qualities); indeed, the Sun and Mars are hot and dry and therefore fiery, and Mars is the more intense; but Jupiter, because in it too heat dominates, is more inclined to a fiery nature than to another, but less than the Sun. But the Moon is of a water nature, Saturn of an earth nature, Venus of an air nature; and finally Mercury, because in it dryness prevails with some little bit of cold, must also be reduced to an earth nature. Wherefore, from the parts of the Zodiac, determined as stated above, the differing natures of all the Planets are poured out upon these inferior things; namely, those natures that are inherent in the very bodies of the Planets, as it was said in Book 14, Chapter 5, about the Sun in Aries at the beginning of the World. If in fact the qualities of the elements are inherent in the Planets, and they are also more perfect and more efficacious than the elements themselves, as is plain from the heat of the Sun, which the heat of a ball of red hot iron of ten times the apparent diameter of the Sun would not equal, circling around the Earth at only a thousand miles.

And because the nature or the complete virtue of the Planets, on account of their mixture and substantial form consists of elemental qualities and influence, from whatever rising Sign, the emptiness of Planets is observed to produce the native's temperament, character, intelligence, etc; qualities both elemental and influential proper to any Planet; it certainly follows that from that same Sun, the Zodiac at the beginning of the World was simultaneously divided by determination into the natures of the Planets, both elemental and influential; And therefore both natures in the Planets are inseparable, so in the parts of the Zodiac, or the Signs, they will be inseparable; and consequently there are given in the Zodiac places or Signs conformable to both the elemental and influential virtue of each Planet. And that not only allows homogeneity to the *Caelum* and an eminential indifference, determinable to any kind of nature, but it can also be proved by reason thus. For since it is proved by experience that with a Planet posited in whatever place of the Zodiac, it produces influxes on these sublunar things according to the nature of the Planet and its place or Sign; if a Planet and a Sign coincide both in their elemental and influential nature, a simple influx will arise from that, from which the nature of both the Sign and the Planet can be easily detected; but if they do not coincide, an influence mixed from different natures will arise; and yet an understanding of that mixture is not given, or a previous notice of a simple (influx); or there will therefore be no understanding of the influx of the Planets and the Signs, contrary to experience; or, there will be in the Zodiac parts coinciding both in their elemental and influential nature with the individual Planets, by which the simple influxes of the Planets may be known in advance, since it is always necessary that each one of the Planets be posited under some one of the 12 Signs of the Zodiac.

Chapter 3.

In which the Influential Natures of the Signs are Disclosed and the Domiciles of the Planets are Established.

Having therefore explained those things above, since as in the Signs so in the Planets but more or less, they share the same elementary nature, for which see Book 12, Section 2, Chapter 1, and then Book 13, Section 1, Chapter 2. Therefore, if a part of the Zodiac is assigned to any particular Planet, agreeing more with that one according to its intrinsic elemental nature, it also agrees more with that same one according to its influential nature, since both natures, as in the Planets, are thus said to be inseparable, and Signs in the Zodiac are given to the virtue of each Planet, with both elemental and influential agreement; and therefore that part of the Zodiac will rightly be called the domicile of that Planet; namely one in which there is nothing opposing, but just as if (it were) in another self, and consequently with doubled powers, it is going to act simply in accordance with its own predominant intrinsic nature.[1] And therefore, since the Sun is of a fiery nature, it will have a fiery Sign for its domicile. But because the Sun is not a Planet in which an acuteness of a fiery nature greatly flourishes, Aries, in which such a nature greatly flourishes, is not a suitable domicile for it; but neither is Sagittarius, which shares that same nature least of all, because the Sun is not a Planet in which the fiery nature flourishes least of all; therefore, in the case of the Sun, although it is flaming, its fiery nature only flourishes moderately, on account of the abundance of airy and etheric moistness, by which that stupendous light of the whole World is nourished, and it may also flourish moderately in Leo, Leo will [therefore] be the natural domicile of the Sun. Moreover, Aries suits Mars, which of all the Planets is the one most sharing the acuteness of fire; and Sagittarius suits Jupiter, previously said to be fiery, but the least fiery of all.

But for the Moon, the most watery of Planets, the domicile will be Cancer, the most watery of the Signs; the domicile of Saturn, the most earthy, will be Capricorn, the most earthy Sign; Libra, the most airy Sign, will be the domicile of Venus, the most airy Planet; and finally, for Mercury, somewhat inclined to an earthy nature, the domicile will be the Sign Virgo, the last in virtue of the earth Signs.

And these are the domiciles that most agree with the 7 Plan-

---

[1] The planetary domiciles were assigned defmitively by the Alexandrian astrologers in the 2nd century B.C. by the simple expedient of moving step-by-step, in the clockwise direction from Cancer and in the counter-clockwise direction from Leo, with the planets in the order of the speed of their motion, viz. Mercury, Venus, Mars, Jupiter, and Saturn. But Morin has devised an alternative method of assignment based upon matching the natures of the planets with the natures of the signs. However, at the end of the present chapter he gives a table illustrating the ancient method of assignment.

ets, according to the intrinsic nature predominating in them, that is the elemental and at the same time the influential nature; and they must therefore be said to be their *primary* domiciles, although many (astrologers) would assign Aquarius for Saturn and Scorpio for Mars as their primary domiciles, for the sake of tempering them, which, however, is not to be considered here, but only that any Planet must be located in a Sign similar to itself by the force of the above said determination.

But since the Sun and the Moon are of only one sex and sect, and are therefore of only one formal nature—that is, the Sun is masculine, diurnal, and fiery, but the Moon is feminine, nocturnal, and watery; therefore, a single domicile agrees with each of these and is sufficient to exercise the total virtue of its nature in a jointly natural manner; namely, Leo, a fiery, masculine, and diurnal Sign for the Sun; but Cancer, a watery, feminine, and nocturnal Sign for the Moon, even as those lights are between them opposite in their natures.

But in the case of anyone of the rest of the Planets, because they are strong with a duplex sex and sect, their nature is therefore duplex and opposite, as is said in Book 13, Section 2, Chapter 2. Therefore, a single domicile cannot suffice for it for exercising the total virtue of its nature naturally; for even if any Sign, viewed as a material object should eminently contain all the opposite natures; nevertheless, viewed formally, or as a Sign, it should exist as one (comprised) of opposite natures, namely of that to which its was determined by the Sun at the beginning of the World. As, therefore, with the lights on account of their single nature, a single domicile in the Zodiac is suitable; accordingly, with the rest of the Planets, on account of their dual nature, two domiciles will have to be allowed, but both of them agreeing with the opposite natures of each Planet, in accordance with its degree of exertion, as much as can be done, as was already observed in the distribution of the principal domiciles because of the reasoning set forth there.

Therefore, because Jupiter is strong in its opposite natures, that is fiery formally and at the same time eminently, and consequently only eminently watery to the same degree of exertion, it is moreover the least formally fiery of the Planets; and therefore Sagittarius, the least fiery of the Signs was allowed for it as its principal domicile; also, Pisces, the least watery of the Signs will fit it for its least principal domicile, namely the one in which it is going to act more efficaciously with its own and eminently watery nature, and its own and eminently feminine sex, and its own nocturnal sect. And so, for Mercury, of the Planets the least formally earthy, Gemini, the least airy of the Signs, is suitable for its least principal domicile. But for Saturn, formally the most earthy, Libra would be suitable for its least principal domicile, because it is the most airy Sign; but because for Venus, formally the most airy (of the Planets) it is most suitable for its principal domicile; therefore, Aquarius, coming second to Libra, or posited in its sinister trine, and therefore second in virtue in the airy triplicity, will be the secondary or least principal domicile of Saturn itself. By the same reasoning, Cancer might suit Mars, the most fiery (of the Planets), as its least principal domicile, but because it is the principal domicile of the Moon; therefore, Scorpio, succeeding to Cancer, will be the secondary domicile of Mars. Finally, Capricorn would suit Venus, the most airy (of the Planets), for its least principal domicile, but because it is the principal domicile of Saturn, Taurus, succeeding Capricorn, will be the secondary domicile of Venus.

Nevertheless, it must be noted that a Planet in its own principal domicile acts elementarily more efficaciously, and also influentially, if they both agree in their sex; otherwise, it will emit its influx more efficaciously from its least principal one, but the one of the same sex; thus, Saturn will chill more strongly from Capricorn, but it will have a stronger influx from Aquarius; so, Venus more strongly moistens from Libra, but it has a stronger influx from Taurus; moreover, Mars pours out its elemental and influential strengths very much more strongly from Aries; and the reasoning is the same for the rest (of the Planets and Signs).

Besides, it must be noted that the determination of the Signs to the natures of the Planets was not by the location of their own rulers over them; for example, because the Sun at the beginning of the World was not in Leo but in Aries; and because from Saturn, Jupiter, Mars, Venus, and Mercury, each one was allotted two domiciles, but in both of which it could not be at the same time. Therefore, (that determination) was made more conformably only by the Sun, as the king and chorus leader of all the Planets, only until now so exposed.

So, therefore, having depended upon these causes – not fictitious ones, but those with a natural foundation and experience – the 12 Signs of the Zodiac and the 7 Planets are distributed according to their nature. Whence, it is plain that the division of the Zodiac into both elementary and Planetary natures that was handed down to us by the ancients only cabalistically and without legitimate reasons, is not an invention of the human intellect, both because it is not established among the first writers of astrology about its invention or about its author; and then because the life of no one even of the first men had been able to supply in detecting that by experience and establishing it; but the talents of many men came together with regard to that same invention of so much time and difficulty, it is alien to their nature and cooperation. And so, it must be said that that division, even as the division of the houses of the celestial figure, was produced by that universal knowledge that God the Best and Greatest infused into Adam at the beginning of the World, through which, when he bestowed true and appropriate names on all things, as Sacred Scripture relates, he must have stated that which was very complete and very clear in the *Caelum* and on Earth.

But from what has been said above, it is proper to define the domicile of a Planet thus—namely, that it is a Sign of the Zodiac with an elemental or influential nature or both greatly related or conformable to that Planet through determination.

Besides, therefore, the *Caelum* divided determinatively into parts with the diverse forces of the Planets, both to supply the virtue of the Planets lying hidden under the Earth, and because the proper accidents of any space or house of the celestial figure are latent in any Planet by which they are excited or moved forward, and by whose nature they are apprehended; and they are not indiscriminately from any Planet, and therefore they ought to be solely from that one that is determined to the accidents of that space, as will be shown below in its own place. Moreover, a Planet can only be determined by body or by rulership or by aspect; and consequently, since it often happens that a space or house of the figure is devoid of the body or an effective aspect of a Planet, it was necessary that that part of the *Caelum* that occupies the space, even if it is of itself essentially neither good nor bad, but it was determined to the nature of some other Planet; namely so that accidents can be produced from the nature of the space itself, or rather accidents that are determined to some nature of the Planets. But then the wisdom of God is greatly commended, who, by the proper motions of the Planets continuously wandering to the north and the south, and by the diurnal motion of the movers, wished to cause their encounters and their absences, lest by the primary rulers of the World, the Planets, heaped up in one place in the *Caelum*,—as in my own nativity—the places of the Earth deprived of their aspects, then also placed vertically too much were known—the latter by excess, but the former by the lack of influxes from the Planets, but it will reinforce those, the former are moderated by the disposition in the *Caelum* of the virtue of the Planets, which otherwise gathered together into a single place of the *Caelum* would be more irresistible.

Furthermore, this very ancient division of the Signs squares marvelously well with the Tychonic System, in which the Sun and the Moon are placed to revolve solely around the Earth, free from itself in turn and from the other Planets. But Saturn, Jupiter, Mars, Venus, and Mercury primarily revolved about the Sun, to which they are bound, and which they comply with as their own chorus master; secondarily, moreover, around the Moon and the Earth. For thus, the domiciles of the Sun and the Moon, that is Leo and Cancer, are just like the centers of the domiciles of the rest of the 5 Planets, whose domiciles surround the domiciles of the lights on both sides, in the same order as in the system itself, their bodies surrounding the body of the Sun; namely, both domiciles of Mercury closely surround the domiciles of the Sun and the Moon; then, both the domiciles of Venus; then, both of Mars; and then both of Jupiter; so that finally both of Saturn that are at the greatest distance from Leo and Cancer; as is plain in the list placed below, from which the truth of the system of Tycho is confirmed, and the true system of the World is deduced—the true system of the World first became known to astrologers by reasoning, and then to astronomers by observation.

♑	♐	♏	♎	♍	♌	♋	♊	♉	♈	♓	♒
♄	♃	♂	♀	☿	☉	☽	☿	♀	♂	♃	♄

Besides, this is also worthy of note, that both domiciles of Mercury are in semi-sextile aspect to the domiciles of the Sun and the Moon; both domiciles of Venus in sextile; both of Mars in square; both of Jupiter in trine; and both of Saturn in opposition; that is, the individual Planets from their own masculine domiciles aspect the domicile of the Sun with a fortunate ray, and also from their own feminine domiciles aspect the domicile of the Moon with a fortunate ray, with the exception of Saturn, which in its own domiciles is opposite the domiciles of the lights.

But on the contrary, the masculine domiciles of the Planets are in bad aspect to the domicile of the Moon, and the feminine ones are in bad aspect to the domicile of the Sun, which certainly also greatly suits the dignity of the lights, and then the sex and the nature of all the Planets.

But perhaps someone might inquire why, having based the division of the Signs on the elemental natures, according to Book 14, Chapter 5, the domicile of the Sun is not Aries, and the Moon's domicile Pisces, since Aries with the Sun and Pisces with the Moon agree in their elemental nature; the Sun was posited in Aries at the beginning of the World, and the rest of the Planets could have their own domiciles of the same elemental nature and arranged in the same manner with respect to Aries and Pisces, as above with respect to Leo and Cancer, which is shown in the following table.

♍	♌	♋	♊	♉	♈	♓	♒	♑	♐	♏	♎
♄	♃	♂	♀	☿	☉	☽	☿	♀	♂	♃	♄

A twofold reason can be offered. First, because from what was said previously, the domiciles of the Planets are based upon the greatest elemental commensurability of Sign and Planet, which is not given between the Sun and Aries, but (rather) between Mars and Aries, with which the greatest acuteness of the fiery nature agrees; and also the greatest watery nature is not given between the Moon and Pisces, the Sign that is least of the water Signs; and not (either) among the other Planets and the other Signs. Second, because the rulership of the Planets should have been the same in the northern part of the World and in the southern part; if indeed the Sun ruled the northern part and the Moon the southern part, and each of the others, Saturn, Jupiter, Mars, Venus, and Mercury, would have had its rulership both in the north and in the south; but there would have been the greatest difference and disparity between the two, and the south inferior and obedient to the north; that, therefore, was not in harmony with the decree of the most wise God on the good fortune and preeminence of the northern part of the World.

You will object. The light—that is, the Sun according to us—was created on the first day, but the rest of the Planets were only made on the fourth day; therefore, the Sun at the beginning of its own creation did not determine the Signs to the natures of the Planets, which were not yet in existence.

I reply. That if the light was created on the first day, the globe or the set of all the Planets were not yet distinguished among themselves, as we have said in a similar (discussion) about the terrestrial globe in Book 2, Chapter 8, there would appear to be no difficulty that the Sun, which was most powerful in virtue and magnitude in that globe—since the Sun according to Hansberger's hypothesis in his *Uranometria*[1] is at least seven times greater than all the rest of the Planets together, of which it was going to be the king—it also on the first day of creation determined the Signs to the natures of the 7 principal Planets.

Chapter 4.

The Exiles of the Planets.

The Signs opposite the *domiciles* of the Planets were called their *exiles* by the ancients, then also their *detriments*. And consequently, since the Sign Aquarius is opposed to Leo, which is the domicile of the Sun, Aquarius is said to be the *exile* of the Sun. similarly, since Cancer and Leo are opposed to the Signs Capricorn and Aquarius, which are the domiciles of Saturn, Cancer and Leo will be the *exiles*, so determined of Saturn, and thus with the rest.

Thus, moreover, they seem to me to be rightly named for three reasons. First, because just as among men the place of exile is distant from that of the nativity or the place of habitation, so the exile of a Planet is distant by the whole opposition of the *Caelum* from any one of its domiciles, which we have said above to be of the same nature as the Planet. Second. Since a Planet in exile is situated in a Sign partly contrary to its own nature and in the domicile of a Planet elementally or influentially *unfriendly*, which is plain from the Sun in Aquarius, the domicile of Saturn, or from, Saturn in Leo, the domicile of the Sun, and thus with the rest (of the Planets). Third. Because the exile of a Planet corrupts its own domicile with an opposite and malefic aspect.

Therefore, from these causes, a Planet in exile is said to assume either a listlessness of virtue or a certain malignity; not because it is changed in itself, but because its proper influx is overthrown with respect to us, as will be explained in its own proper place. Whence, not unhelpfully, the Planet located in its own exile

[1] Possibly a reference to Philip van Lansberge (1561-1632), *Tabulae motwm coelestivm perpetuae.* (Middelburg, 1632).

or *detriment* is said to be in *exile* with respect to itself, but in *detriment* with respect to us.

A Table in which is Shown the Domiciles, Exiles, and Enemies of the Individual Planets, and then the Opposite Signs.					
Venus	Mercury	Moon	Sun	Mercury	Venus
Taurus	Gemini	Cancer	Leo	Virgo	Libra
Scorpio	Sagittarius	Capricorn	Aquarius	Pisces	Aries
Mars	Jupiter	Saturn	Saturn	Jupiter	Mars

Leo is the domicile of the Sun, Aquarius its *exile*, and Saturn is its *enemy*; Leo, moreover, and Aquarius are opposite Signs; and the scheme is the same in the rest of the columns. Vice versa, moreover, Aquarius is the *domicile* of Saturn, Leo its *exile*, and the Sun its *enemy*.

Chapter 5.

The Exaltations and Falls of the Planets.

Ptolemy discusses these in *Quadripartite*, Book 1, and Cardan in his *Commentary*. But the causes or reasons for these that they offer are equally groundless,[1] as are those that they offer for the domiciles; from which it follows namely that the *exaltations* are different in the southern part of the World from what they are in the northern part, which is also asserted by Campanella, and they add many other absurdities that have given Pico Mirandola

[1] It is now known from the decipherment of clay tablets found in Iraq that the *exaltations* of the planets actually go back to the Babylonians, who called them the "secret houses" of the planets but gave no reasons for their selection. Firmicus was aware of their origin, for he says in *Mathesis* ii. 3 "For this reason, the Babylonians wanted those signs in which the individual (planets) are exalted to be their *domiciles,* saying that in fact Saturn's *domicile is* Libra, Jupiter's Cancer,

and others an opportune and just occasion for scoffing at astrology. But to set forth and disprove their individual reasons would be a mere waste of time, which should not be spent on worthless things, especially since they are sufficiently overthrown in similar fashion by those things that were stated by us in Chapter 1 on the immutability of the domiciles. And so, since experience confirms the *exaltations* no less than the *domiciles* of the Planets, it only remains for us here to inquire into their foundation, or their truer causes, and to present our opinion about these.

I say, therefore, that the cardinal Signs are not rashly said to be mobile and cardinal too; since changes more frequently happen from them; indeed, they are the ones that are greater than the rest. And the reason is that since those Signs are the sources of the primary qualities in the *Caelum*, as we said in Book 14, and consequently for changes—indeed, they are suited to and inclined towards greater changes than the others, but especially the equinoctial Signs of the cardinals are primary, as was shown in that same Book 14. Moreover, this was noticed in astrological observations in the four cardinal Signs; then, in those that are contiguous to the primary cardinal Signs, the virtues of the Planets are so exalted or helped that they burst out suddenly in great effects, and violent ones as it were, or ones over and above their proper virtues, which does not happen to these Planets when they also enter their own domiciles or pass through them. For these reasons, therefore, the above said Signs were said by the ancients to be the exaltations of the Planets, and not moreover (as Pico, *Against the Astrologers*, Book 6 Chapter 14, says from [a passage in] Pliny) because the apogees of the Planets were once in those Signs in which they are said to be exalted; since Mars's apogee was never in Capricorn, nor Venus's in Pisces, as is established in the *Rudolphine Tables*.

Mars's Capricorn, the Sun's Aries, the Moon's Taurus, Venus's Pisces, and Mercury's Virgo." This should have given later astrologers a clue as to their origin, but instead they followed the lead of Ptolemy and invented various theoretical reasons for the selection of the exaltation signs. And like Ptolemy, Morin accepts the traditional exaltation signs, but not knowing their origin, he fills four columns of his text with what seemed to him to be appropriate reasons for those choices.

Furthermore, that is not at all a matter of indifference, namely as any Planet might be exalted in any one of those Signs, but as all the rest are done according to reason, so also should any Planet be reasonably allotted its own Sign in which it is exalted; not to be sure because of an affinity or nature per se, for the fiery Jupiter is exalted in Cancer, a water Sign; and the earthy Saturn is exalted in Libra, an air Sign; and not from friendship or enmity with the rulers of the Signs of exaltation; for Saturn is exalted in the domicile of its enemy Venus; however, Venus (is exalted) in the domicile of its friend Jupiter. And not by similarity of sect or sex; for Jupiter, according to Book 13, Section 2, Chapters 1 & 2, is masculine and diurnal, and yet it is exalted in Cancer, a feminine and nocturnal Sign; and only Mercury is excepted, which happens to be exalted in Virgo, its own domicile; but all the Planets are allotted their own exaltations in the Zodiac by an analogy of their own virtue to the virtue of the Signs in which they are individually exalted. So that for that Planet which of itself is of (some) major virtue, there ought rightly to be a place in the Zodiac for it (where it is) more effective, so that from the conformable similarity of virtue of the Planet and the place, the Planet may operate more efficaciously; whence, a Planet in such a place is said to be exalted in its powers; and such a place is deservedly called the exaltation of the virtue of the Planet. And in fact, even as a little catapult cannot produce a great effect corresponding to itself or to the ball with a big ball as a missile, nor even a huge catapult with a little ball, but both ought to be proportioned to the effect of the catapult and the ball, so the Planets, from the places in the Zodiac proportioned by their degree of virtue, produce notable effects; but from those that neither in virtue nor in the degree of virtue are related or proportioned, they act either against their own nature or in a weakened manner.

But from what was said above, it is deduced that since this dignity of the Planets does not accrue to them from a similarity of nature, it seems to be unsuitably said to be an *essential* dignity.

Since, therefore, the Planets are allotted domiciles in the Zodiac from a similarity of nature, so the exaltations are allotted according to a proportion of virtue; therefore, for the Sun, having surpassed all the Planets in virtue, it should have Aries for its exaltation, which is the first and most efficacious of the Signs; but the rest of the cardinal Signs ought to be allotted to the three superior Planets; that is, for Saturn, the highest and most powerful of those, Libra; for Jupiter, Cancer; and for Mars, Capricorn; Cancer is inferior in virtue, as has been shown elsewhere. But the Signs that are adjacent to the equinoctial (signs) are suitable for the three inferior (Planets); that is, for Venus, Pisces; for Mercury, Virgo; for the Moon, Taurus, which is also adjacent to Aries, and is midway between the northern cardinal Signs, one of which, namely Cancer, the Moon itself rules; whence, that location for the lowest of the Planets and the one closest to us seems most apt in the proportion of its virtue. For, as the Moon is more powerful than Venus and Mercury, so Taurus as a site prevails over Virgo and Pisces; but from these, Cardan's opinion is rejected in his *Book on the Judgment of Nativities*, Chapter 27, where he wants Mercury to be exalted in Gemini. And let these (comments) on the exaltations of the Planets suffice, which exaltations, it is plain, are Signs of the Zodiac, proportioned by virtue of acting for the Planets and conformable to the individual Planets on account of the above said cause.

But the *fall* or *dejection* of each Planet is the Sign diametrically opposed to its exaltation. For every opposition among the celestial things, either of the Signs or of the Planets, is primarily and per se a cause of contrariety with respect to the Earth, always involving some malignance; and that is done not only by reason of nature, which in opposite things is always partly contrary, but principally by reason of its mode of acting, which happens through the same line, in which the ends, since they are established as acting on an intermediate point, restrain whatever action (there is from) their opposed points, not with dispersed (forces) or reflected on the other (point), but united on the same line, and through that it attacks with forcible powers, whereby in the battle the powers of both are as it were violently commingled. Therefore, on account of this contrariety of the opposition, a sharing of malignity, it is conformable to reason that Planets in opposite Signs have themselves in a contrary mode; and consequently, if any Sign was the *domicile* or *exaltation* of a Planet, its *exile* or *fall* is in the opposite Sign, in which it acts lazily and as if below its own strength.

Table of the Exaltations and Falls of the Planets.			
☉	☽	♃	☿
♈	♉	♋	♍
♎	♏	♑	♓
♄		♂	♀

Libra is the exaltation of Saturn; and Aries is its fall or dejection; but in turn Aries is the exaltation of the Sun, and Libra is its dejection. And so with the other columns.

Furthermore, from the domiciles and exaltations of the Planets placed above, much more clearly is shown the excellence, dignity, and vigor of the northern part of the World over the southern part, which we have already shown from the nature of the Signs in Book 14, Section 1, Chapters 5 & 9. And in fact the domiciles and exaltations of the Sun and the Moon are in the northern part of the World, along with the domiciles and exaltation of Mercury. And therefore, even if the Sun, Moon, and Mercury are located in the southern part of the World, their virtue and influence always flourishes, however, in the northern part. Add to these (facts) that the first motion of the lights was to the northern part—namely, with the Sun posited in Aries at the beginning of the World, and the Moon in Taurus, so that it might rule the night, by increasing rather than by decreasing. Whence, it is not surprising if the principal monarchies, all sciences and religions, have their origin in the northern part of the Earth; in which CHRIST also wished to be born and to hand down the spiritual and truly divine law for establishing the Kingdom of the Heavens, which would be made known to the whole World. Moreover, in the southern part, Saturn, Mars, and Venus rule by domicile and exaltation, but Mercury is exiled and dejected. Therefore, the inhabitants of the southern Lands are irreverent, idolaters, lustful, wild, and they have remained set apart from the sciences; and if Jupiter with its own rulership in that part (of the World) had not weakened its malignity, the life of the southerners would have been animal-like rather than human, especially from their lack of the sciences and the recognition of the true GOD; and these things shall only be said as far as the stars incline some men to the higher sciences, and from those to the recognition and worship of GOD, who by his own creatures is very recognizable by his natural light; but they do not incline others in any direction, whence it follows that they remain atheists or irreligious.[1] Furthermore, the southern part of the Earth abounded very much in gold, silver, and in other riches, as is obvious from the mines of the Peruvian kingdom, on account of the rulership of Saturn and Jupiter in the southern part of the *Caelum*, which among the Planets is greatly though to be in command of riches, whom Venus also aids no little in gems, large pearls, and spices, on account of her domicile in Libra, an equinoctial Sign, and the exaltation of Saturn, and then her exaltation in Pisces, the domicile of Jupiter.

But for this consideration, the 4 cardinal points or the mobile Signs are principally noted, which are devoted principally to actions and changes; for the equinoctial Signs belong to the rulership of Mars and Venus, but by exaltation to the Sun and Saturn; but the solstitial Signs to the Moon and Saturn from their rulership, but to Jupiter and Mars from their exaltation. Therefore, Aries belongs to the Sun and Mars, but Cancer to the Moon and Jupiter, which is greatly in accord with the northern peoples. But Libra belongs to Venus and Saturn, and Capricorn to Saturn and Mars, which agrees well with the southerners; and consequently, the northerners are made the most powerful by the Sun, Moon, Jupiter, and

---

[1] In Morin's day, the southern parts of the world were mostly inhabited by wild tribesmen and by what appeared to Europeans to be primitive civilizations, such as those in Peru and the East Indies. And the southerners either followed animist religions or non-Christian religions.

Mars, but the southerners by Venus, Saturn, and Mars, which is most worthy of note, as being in agreement with their effects.

Chapter 6.

The Triplicities of the Planets, or the Trigons and the Trigon Rulers According to the Opinions of the Ancients.

Nothing in the whole of astrology has so agitated my understanding as that the greater part of the old astrologers, but especially the Arabs, on all the sublunar effects have especially judged from the *trigons* and their rulers, but not from the exaltations or their rulers; nevertheless, since the Arabs, the Greeks, and the Latins disagree very much among themselves about the rulers of the *trigons*; due to that, they have offered to the haters of astrology no small opportunity for impugning and deriding it..

But so that this doctrine may be made more clear, it must be applied from Book 14, Section 1, Chapter 5, that there are four *triplicities* of Signs in the Zodiac, that is a *fire triplicity* of Aries, Leo, and Sagittarius; an *earth triplicity* from Taurus, Virgo, and Capricorn; an *air triplicity* from Gemini, Libra, and Aquarius; and a *water triplicity* from Cancer, Scorpio, and Pisces. And all astrologers agree with this; and the Signs of the same *triplicity*, are among themselves of the same nature or temperament; which is contrary to Cardan's *Commentary* on Book 1, chapter 16, of the *Quadripartite*, as was shown by us in Book 14, Section 1, Chapter 5.

But as for that which pertains to the rulers of the triplicities, Ptolemy in the *Quadripartite*, Book 1, Chapter 16, gives the rulership of the *fire trigon* to the Sun by day and to Jupiter by night; the *water triplicity* to Mars both by day and by night, and yet to which he associates the Moon by day and Venus by night; the *air triplicity* to Saturn by day and to Mercury by night; and finally the *earth triplicity* to Venus by day and to the Moon by night. Moreover, Cardan will have it in his *Commenary* that Ptolemy had the sexes and the sects right in this distribution of the Signs and the Planets.

But truly those suffer from many defects. First, because he assigns three rulers to the *water trigon*, but only two to the rest. Second, because in the *water trigon* he excludes the Moon from the principal rulership, even though it is conformable by sex and by sect, and in that same *trigon* it is the most powerful by domicile—indeed, as ruler of a cardinal Sign; but he admits Mars, which is in its dejection in Cancer and contrary by sex according to Ptolemy himself; then too by its sect, namely because the reason why Ptolemy made it of the nocturnal sect is absurd, as (is shown) in Book 13, Section 3, Chapter 2, because in the *fire trigon* he rejects Mars, which is in its domicile and more powerful than the rest (of the Planets)—indeed, the one that rules the equinoctial Sign—and is similar in sex and sect, then too it is very much more fiery than the others; and yet he wants the *fire trigon* to be mixed with the south-west wind because of Mars's domicile, which rouses up the south-west or western winds, in which he contradicts himself. Fourth, because he wants that same trigon to be northerly, on account of the southern Sign Sagittarius, which Jupiter rules, since Jupiter's rulership in that trigon is less than the rulership of the Sun or Mars; for in that trigon, the Sun is allotted a domicile and an exaltation, but Mars is allotted a domicile in a cardinal and primary Sign. It is therefore established from what was said above that that distribution is not consistent and not natural but only on a false foundation of sect and an artificial one of sex, as is demonstrated from (the situation) with Mars.

Moreover, the Arabs, along with Julius Firmicus, John of Spain, and the rest of that faction, assign three rulers for each trigon.[1] That is, in the fire trigon, (they assign) the Sun by day, Jupiter by night, and Saturn as a partner both by day and by night,

[1] Unknown to Morin, the triplicity rulers given by these authorities are the standard ones of Greek astrology and presumably go back to the Alexandrian inventors of horoscopic astrology. They are mentioned by Dorotheus, *Pentateuch,* i. 2. (See the translation of the Arabic version by Pingree, *Carmen Astrologicum* (Leipzig: B. G. Teubner, 1976), which also gives the Greek citation by Hephaestio of Thebes, *Apotelesmatics,* i. 6.). But the oldest authorities give no reasons for the choice of rulers.

which is surely absolutely ridiculous, since Saturn is by nature contrary to that trigon and in it is greatly debilitated. In the water trigon, Venus by day, Mars by night, and the Moon always; for the foundation of the Arabs is also similarity of sex and sect, as above; and therefore in the case of Mars they follow Ptolemy's error, or he follows theirs. In the air trigon, Saturn by day, Mercury by night, and Jupiter always, which is again most absurd, since in this trigon Jupiter has neither domicile nor exaltation, but on the contrary is allotted an exile. Finally, in the earth trigon, Venus by day, the Moon by night, and Mars always, on account of a false opinion about its sect, having excluded Mercury that is of a common nature, sex, and sect—as they will have it—which in this trigon is the strongest of all.[1] Moreover, Cardan, the most absurd of all, assigns 5 rulers in his *Book on the Judgments of Nativities*, Chapter 27, namely Venus and Mercury by day, the Moon and Mars by night, and Saturn both by day and by night. But the famous astrologer Schöner differs somewhat with the Arabs only in the fire and earth trigons; for in the fire trigon, he assigns Mars by day and night, or always; and in the earth trigon, he assigns the Moon by day, Venus by night, and Saturn always.

Therefore, Ptolemy makes the diurnal *trigonocrators* to be those Planets that rule the fixed Signs of the trigons, because according to Cardan in his *Commentary*, those Signs are pure, sincere, and most powerful. Schöner chooses those that are exalted in the trigons themselves, on account of the unexpected changes that result from the exaltations. But the Arabs preserve no order here; whence, it is plain how much confusion there has been among astrologers hitherto with regard to these rulers of the trigons, which I subjoin below with their authorities for the sake of easier comprehension.

[1] Dorotheus adds 'and in Virgo is also a share for Mercury' (Pingree's translation). The Greek original has: 'Taurus, Virgo, and also Capricorn Venus rules by day, and by night the shining Moon, and third after these the god starting wars, and now in Virgo Mercury receives an offshoot'.

			Ptolemy			The Arabs			Schöner		
			D	N	P	D	N	P	D	N	P
♈	♌	♐	☉	♃		☉	♃	♄	☉	♃	♂
♋	♏	♓	☽	♀	♂	♀	♂	☽	♀	♂	☽
♎	♒	♊	♄	☿		♄	☿	♃	♄	☿	♃
♑	♉	♍	♀	☽		♀	☽	♂	☽	♀	♄

(Where D indicates the Day ruler, N the night ruler, and P the Partner.)

Chapter 7.

The Trigons and the Trigonocrators According to our Opinion.

Before we establish anything about this matter, by which the errors that have been introduced with regard to the *rulers of the trigons* may be expelled, it seems to be necessary to supply here from the practice or observations of astrologers what if a great conjunction or a solar eclipse occurs in any particular Sign of the Zodiac, there is made about either a judgment principally from the nature and state of the Planet that rules the place of the eclipse or the conjunction; and similarly if in any nativity Aries was in the ASC, the judgment will be made about the accidents pertaining to the ASC or the MC, from the nature and state of Mars, which is the ruler of Aries; but not primarily and per se from the nature and state of a Planet that in those places is lacking in rulership; and much less even from the nature and state of a Planet that was allotted its exile in those places. And the reason for this rule is because, as will be explained more fully elsewhere, these Signs and their rulers are determined to the subjects of the houses in which they are and which they rule; and the effects of the Signs are changed in accordance with the different state of their own rulers, to which, therefore, attention must be paid for a particular judgment and not indiscriminately to any Planet; for example, to Saturn for the effects of the Aries, Leo, and Sagittarius (*trigon*) according to the Arabs. For otherwise, there would be no certain foundation of astrology, and consequently no certitude, which is inconsistent with the truth of that practice.

Nevertheless, since not only do the Signs of the same *trigon* agree with themselves in their nature, as we have said above in contradiction of Cardan, but also the rulers of those Signs of the Planet agree among themselves, either in their principal or predominating nature, which namely is inherent in them both elementally and influentially, or in the less principal, which is only inherent in them influentially. Therefore, on account of that consensus, whatever happens in any Sign or from any Sign, pertains in a way to the whole *trigon* of that Sign and to the Planets that are rulers of those Signs; whence it happens that both the latter and the former are set in motion to act or to influence together. And no one should marvel at this, if indeed it does seem very marvelous that on the same guitar or on different musical instruments when any string is touched, by its own motion another string is not touched but having the same sound it also moves, but if it does not have the same sound, it does not move, the reason for this effect must be referred solely to the identity of the nature of the sound, as is learnedly proved by the Reverend Father Marin Mersenne (1588-1648) in his *Harmonics*,[1] Book 4, Proposition 27.

Moreover, it is shown thus singly that Planets which rule the Signs of the same trigon agree among themselves in their principal or less principal nature. For Mars, the Sun, and Jupiter rule the fire Signs Aries, Leo, and Sagittarius, of which Planets the Sun is totally of the nature of fire, but Mars and Jupiter are principally of that same nature, as was shown above in Chapter 3; and therefore

[1] Possibly a reference to Father Marin Mersenne, *Harmonicorum libri xii...* (Paris: G.Baudry, 1648), which contained reprints of two earlier books, one of which was *Harmonicorum instrumentorum libri IV* (Paris: G. Baudry, 1636); but Morin may have cited the earlier edition of that book.

they agree in a fiery nature. The Moon, Mars, and Jupiter rule the water Signs Cancer, Scorpio, and Pisces, of which the Moon is totally of a watery nature, but Mars and Jupiter are of that same nature but less principally, (as shown) in that same 3rd Chapter. Venus, Saturn, and Mercury rule the air Signs; all of those (Planets) are of an airy nature—Venus indeed principally, but Saturn and Mercury less principally. Finally, Saturn, Venus, and Mercury, with the same earthy nature among themselves, rule the earth Signs Capricorn, Taurus, and Virgo; Saturn, indeed, and Mercury principally, and Venus less principally, (as shown) in that same 3rd Chapter. So that consequently, in the Signs of the Zodiac making up the *trigons* and their rulers the greatest consensus is brought forth, and it is not fictitious but entirely natural, so that that thing either should not nor cannot be conceived otherwise, unless confusion and falsity are introduced here and there.

And here it comes to be noted incidentally that Jupiter and Saturn are thus formally determined to a fiery and watery nature, in such a way that they are not determined by any formal or intrinsic reason to an airy or earthy (nature). But on the contrary, Saturn, Venus, and Mercury are so formally determined to an airy and earthy nature, that they may not be determined by any formal reason to a fiery or watery (nature); whence, it is evident which Planets in the individual trigons can (do) more and should be particularly looked at. And how absurd it was for the Arabs[1] (to say that) Saturn was a ruler for the *fire trigon*, Venus for the *water trigon*, Jupiter for the *air trigon*, and the Moon for the *earth trigon*!

But from these things said in advance and understood, I now say that to each trigon three rulers or *trigonocrators* are assigned, namely those Planets that exercise dominion over the individual Signs of that *trigon*; and consequently the rulers of the *fire trigon* or the *trigonocrators* are Mars, the Sun, and Jupiter; of the *water trigon*, the Moon, Mars, and Jupiter; of the *air trigon*, Venus, Saturn, and Mercury; and of the *earth trigon*, Saturn, Venus, and Mer-

[1] But the Arabs were merely repeating the assignments of the Alexandrian astrologers, who unfortunately did not explain their rationale.

cury; and the reasons that are evident from what was said previously need not be repeated here superfluously because they have already been sufficiently explained by us. The whole difficulty, therefore, consists of determining which of the Planets in whichever trigon, other things being equal, should be preferred to another for the rulership, or which will be the first ruler, which the second, and which the third; about which the Arabs are so much occupied; or which will rule by day, which by night, and which at both times but less importantly according to Ptolemy and the others.

Moreover, these prerogatives of rulership (can be determined) by three self-consistent reasons. First. That a Planet ruler of a cardinal Sign, as the principal (ruler) of the whole *trigon*, rules principally or primarily by day; the ruler of the fixed Sign principally by night; and the ruler of the common Sign by day and by night less principally or secondarily. Besides, this order would plainly oppose the nature, sex, and sect of the lights; for the Sun in its whole nature is fiery, masculine, and diurnal; consequently, it would be absurd for it to rule principally in the *fire trigon* by night and not by day, which *trigon* is also masculine and diurnal. But the Moon in her whole nature is watery, feminine, and nocturnal; and therefore (it would be) absurd for her to rule principally by day and not by night. This order must therefore be rejected, which those absurd (assignments) are the consequence of.

Secondly, that a Planet ruler of the fixed Sign rules by day, the ruler of the mobile or cardinal Sign by night, and the ruler of the common Sign rules at both times, which method by reason of the diurnal rulership agrees with Ptolemy; but in this he seems to go wrong because Jupiter and Mercury never rule principally, but always and solely less chiefly according to that order;

Thirdly, that the Planet which in the *trigon* was more powerful than the rest of the Planets, namely by domicile and exaltation, short of debility, is put in charge primarily by day, and that one must be specially noticed in judging by triplicities; but the one that was the ruler of the cardinal Sign also rules primarily by night, and finally the rest (of the Planets) secondarily by day and by night. So that here they are put according to our opinion. Where note that this is very much more powerful, that the diurnal trigonocrators are among themselves in contrary domiciles; that is, the Sun and Saturn between themselves; and Jupiter and Mercury between themselves; and the same thing is (true) of the nocturnal ones; namely, Mars and Venus[1] between themselves; and the Moon and Saturn between themselves. And the same thing (is true) of the partners; namely, Jupiter and Mercury between themselves; and Mars and Venus between themselves, in the same order.

				D	N	P
East	♈	♌	♐	☉	♂	♃
North	♋	♏	♓	♃	☽	♂
West	♎	♒	♋	♄	♀	☿
South	♑	♉	♍	☿	♄	♀

In which the Sun and the Moon are especially optimally disposed; but the Moon much more reasonably than in Ptolemy, the Arabs, and Schöner.

In addition, moreover, the one that is more powerful in the *trigon* always precedes the one that is weaker, as is plain in the *fire trigon* from Jupiter, which is only the ruler of the common Sign; and therefore it is put last as the partner of the diurnal and nocturnal rulers. Similarly in the water (trigon), Mars, even though it is the ruler of the fixed Sign, nevertheless because it is dejected in Cancer, it is put in the last place. In the air (*trigon*), Mercury follows the reasoning of the above said Jupiter. And in the earth (*trigon*), Venus (follows) the reasoning of (the above said) Mars. And there is no Planet that does not sometimes rule principally ei-

[1] The Latin text has the symbol for Mercury rather than the symbol for Venus.

ther by day or by night. Therefore, this order, besides that it agrees the most with nature and reason, is also the most self consistent; and to sum it up, it is the most perfect (order) of all that could be thought up; in which besides it is discerned that every *trigonocrator* is at least allotted a domicile in its own triplicity, but not by the Arabs, who most absurdly assign Saturn to the *fire trigon* by day and by night, because in that *trigon* it is exiled and dejected. And therefore, about a Planet's being in any particular Sign, in which trigon it does not have a domicile, it is rightly said to be *peregrine*, that is because it is *peregrine* in that alien *trigon* due to its own nature, and where it is lacking in any dignity unless it is *exalted* in the Sign that it occupies, for there it would not be said to be *peregrine*, for the rulers of the trigons are established rather by reason of their domicile than by their *exaltation*—that is, the *trigonocrators* ought to agree with the *trigons* in their nature per se; moreover, they agree by reason of their *domicile* as is plain, but not by reason of their *exaltation*; otherwise, Mars exalted in Capricorn would be of an earthy nature, which nevertheless is inherent in it neither principally nor less principally; and therefore from those places where the *trigonocrators* themselves are best placed.

Chapter 8.

To What Regions of the World the Trigons Pertain; and Consequently, Which Regions of the World the Trigon Rulers Principally Rule.

Ptolemy and the Arabs differ among themselves about this, for the former in *Quadripartite*, Book 1, Chapter 16, the *fire trigon* is attributed most strongly to the North, on account of Jupiter that rules Sagittarius, a Southern Sign. And so all the same it receives a mixture of the West or the Afric direction on account of Mars, which nevertheless he expels from any rulership of that *trigon*—from which it is sufficiently plain how poorly these things hang together. For that which he says—that Jupiter rouses up the northern winds, and Mars the western ones—would it not then follow therefore that the *fire trigon*, in which it is less powerful, is northern. For by chance it would happen on account of another *trigon*, in which it would be more powerful, such as the *water trigon*. But conformably he attributes the *water trigon* to the West with a mixture of the South; the *earth trigon* to the South with a mixture of the East; and the *air trigon* to the East with a mixture of the North; but of the Planets he gives Jupiter the command over the North, Mars over the West, Venus over the South, and Saturn over the East; he says, on account of its familiarity with the Sun. But the Arabs will have the *fire trigon* to be East, over which Jupiter presides; they attribute the *water trigon* to the North, over which Mars presides; the *air trigon* to the West, over which Saturn presides; and the *earth trigon* to the South, over which Venus presides; but here again no reason is apprehended in the rulers of the *trigons*; and no order is consistent for them. And in fact in the fire trigon, Jupiter is the ruler of the common Sign without any misfortune (elsewhere in the triplicity); in the water trigon, Mars is the ruler of the fixed Sign with a dejection or depression (in Cancer); in the air trigon, Saturn is the ruler of the fixed Sign with an exaltation (in Libra); and in the earth trigon, Venus is the ruler of the fixed Sign with a fall or depression (in Virgo); and it must not be said that in this matter the Arabs looked at the sex and sect of the trigons and the Planets, since Mars by sex and by sect is of itself opposed to the *water trigon*, as was already said above. Since, therefore, those things that are arranged by nature are self-consistent and in conformity to reason, it seems that it must be said that Ptolemy and the Arabs here too deviate from the truth; and those things that they have predicted from the trigons and their rulers have either occurred fortuitously or from other causes. Therefore, in order to resolve this difficulty, Nature itself must again be consulted. Moreover, it will indicate to us that the four cardinal Signs, Aries, Cancer, Libra, and Capricorn, the primary (signs) of the *trigons* are distributed to the four *regions* or corners of the World by their own location; and there is no difficulty with Cancer in the north and Capricorn in the south, but only with Aries and Libra—which one of these claims the east for itself, since both of them begin from the equator or the middle of the World. But the east should be (assigned) to Aries, namely the more noble of the cardinals. This is proved: First, because the active quality of heat predominates in Aries, but in Libra the passive quality of moistness; and the active quality is more noble than the passive. Second, because Aries is subject to the rulership of a masculine Planet, but Libra of a feminine one. Third, because Aries is in the nobler and commanding part of the World, namely the northern part, as was shown previously; but Libra is in the less noble and obedient part. Fourth, because the east is dry, like Aries, and the west is moist, like Libra. From these causes, therefore, Aries pertain to the east and Libra to the west. Therefore, the *fire trigon* is eastern, the *water trigon* northern, the *air trigon* western, and the *earth trigon* southern. And this entirely agrees with our division of the Zodiac (as shown) in Book 14, Section 5, Chapter 5, where we have said that the active qualities, heat and cold, are dominant in the northern part of the World because of Aries and Cancer in the east, namely, and the north; but the passive qualities in the south because of Libra and[1] Capricorn in the west and the south. And consequently, the *trigonocrators* that we have put above rule over those regions of the World in which their *trigons* fall. And from this, the reason is now plain why Jupiter excites the northern winds—that is, because it is the principal and most powerful ruler of the northern trigon—the Sun is the ruler of the eastern trigon, Mercury of the southern one, and Saturn of the western one.

You will object. The same part of the Earth is simultaneously eastern and western; and there is no place on the sphere of the Earth that is particularly assigned to the east or the west. Therefore, the *fire trigon* does not rule the east, and the *air trigon* the west.

I reply that there is of course no part that is simply and absolutely eastern or western, but only as compared to each other, as Germany is east of France but west of Hungary; and it can also be

[1] The Latin text has *in* by mistake for *&*.

said that Germany is north of Italy and south of Denmark. And consequently the division of the Zodiac into two parts, northern and southern and then into 4 trigons for the 4 corners of the World, insofar as they are referred to the Earth are indeed universal, so that nothing can be concluded from them as to particular parts of the Earth; for example, if an eclipse is made in the northern half of the Zodiac, it will primarily pertain to the northern peoples, but from that it cannot be particularly stated to which of them. Similarly, if an eclipse is made in the *fire trigon*, its effect will be allotted to those 4 places on Earth that will be east with respect to other places, and perhaps it will signify actively for the easterners and passively for the westerners, as when the King of Spain subjected western America to his rule. But it cannot be solely defined from those (considerations), which are the eastern places and which are the western ones. And since the east contains the space of the *Caelum* and the Earth, from the rising of the Sun in the beginning of Cancer to the rising of the Sun in the beginning of Capricorn, if the eclipse occurs in Aries or in Leo, it will certainly be said that the eastern place that is signified by it forms the northern part (of the Earth); but this signification is still more general than one that can designate it as a particular location. But a celestial figure erected for some particular place at the time of mid-eclipse, if it has its degree of the ecliptic in the eastern part of the figure, it will show by its eastern place that a part of the Earth is signified that is between its place in the figure and the 90th degree to the east; moreover, the distance of the place of the eclipse from the meridian will more particularly designate that place according to its terrestrial longitude, but not according to its latitude. Therefore, other things will still have to be considered, which will be discussed in Book 20, Section 1, Chapters 4 & 5. And more precise conjectures must be elicited from them. Moreover, if the eclipse occurs in Sagittarius, the eastern place will be signified in the southern part (of the Earth). And if the ruler of the eclipse was in the fire trigon, it will be more certain that the signification of the place is eastern; (but) if it is in another trigon, there will be a signification of a place, or of many places, that is mixed from the two trigons; as, if the eclipse was in the fire trigon and its ruler in the water trigon, the place will be signified between the east and the north; but if the ruler was in the air trigon, which rules the west, since that place cannot be both east and west with respect to it, at least two places will necessarily be signified, one of which will be east of the other.

Furthermore, the things said above will be understood (to refer) as well to dispositions of the air, such as winds, as to changes in kingdoms. Moreover, in particular natal figures, if a fire Sign was in the 9th house, it will Signify a journey to the east; if an earth Sign, to the south; if both, to both regions. And if the rulers of the Signs were both in a water Sign, the journey will still be made principally to the north. And the reasoning is the same with the rest (of the Signs). And these things are plain in my nativity, where Sagittarius and Capricorn are in the 9th. And their rulers are conjoined in Pisces and in the 12th house. And by my own choice, I traveled into Provence to the south, to Paris to the north, and to Hungary to the east with respect to Villefranche, the place of my birth; and that was led by my own inclination impelled by the stars.

Chapter 9.

Some Things that should be Particularly Noted about these Trigons and their Rulers.

The rulers and regions of the triplicities having been defined by us as above, now some things about this follow that must be carefully noted.

First, that in the *fire trigon* the Sun is the most powerful of all—that is by its domicile and exaltation. In the *water trigon*, Jupiter is the most powerful by the same reason; in the *air trigon*, Saturn; and in the *earth trigon*, Mercury. Since indeed those Planets also experience no debility in those trigons; and therefore, in judging by triplicities, special account must be taken of these. And these 4 Planets have their own domiciles opposite: namely, the Sun and Saturn between themselves, then Jupiter and Mercury between themselves; whence it is plain that these are most appropriate especially for great changes in sublunar things, but very much in the air. Moreover, Mars, because it rules Aries and Scorpio, a fire and a water Sign, and is exalted in Capricorn, an earth Sign, is strongly disposed to rains, lightning flashes, thunder, lightning & thunderbolts, for fire, earth, and water concur in these; besides which, because Mars itself is principally of a fiery nature, and less principally of a watery one.

Second. Because the northern equinoctial Sign, namely Aries, pertains to the Sun and Mars, and that very much corresponds to northerners, who in sovereignty, glory, and arms are superior to the southerners. The southern equinox pertains to Venus and Saturn, which squares with the southerners, who are lustful, ugly, idle, and servile.[1] The northern solstice pertains to the Moon and Jupiter, which very much suits the northern peoples on account of their fame, religion, justice, and the mutability, for which they are well-known. But the southern solstice pertains to Saturn and Mars, whence impiety and moral depravity are familiar to the southern peoples. And consequently, the northern nations are principally affected and ruled by Jupiter and Mars; but the southern ones principally by Mercury, Saturn, and Mars, which must be understood in general and is very worthy of note.

Third. Because the particular predominance of the trigonocrators ought to be defined by the following rules.

1. The one in the trigon should be preferred to one that is absent.

2. The one that is above the Earth should be preferred to one that is beneath the Earth.

3. A diurnal (Planet) should be preferred by day if it is above the Earth, and a nocturnal (Planet) by night.

[1] Nearly all the "southerners" in Morin's day were tribesmen in South America, South Africa, Borneo, Celebes, New Guinea, and Australia; the inhabitants of Sumatra and Java were exceptions; but Morin's characterization of the differences between the majority of "northerners" and "southerners" was mainly true at the time in which he wrote.

4. A diurnal (Planet) has a secondary or less principal power by night, and a nocturnal (Planet) by day—(in both cases) if they are above the Earth.

5. With the diurnal and nocturnal (Planets) posited under the Earth, the diurnal ones will be preferred by day and the nocturnal ones by night.

6. With two Planets conjoined in the same Sign of their own *trigon*, the ruler of that Sign should be preferred instead of the *trigon* rulership of that Sign.

7. In the place of an eclipse or in the place of any significator, let the ruler of the Sign of the eclipse or of the significator be preferred, especially if it is above the Earth and in the *trigon* and aspecting that place.

8. The partner of the rulership, or the one that rules both by day and by night, will rule primarily when it is above the Earth, but that one is under the Earth that either attains the rulership either by day or by night.

But of (all) these rules, only this one is fundamental—that the one that is stronger must always be preferred to one that is weaker. Furthermore, what should be felt about the doctrine of the Arabs, from those *trigonocrators*, in the case of universal constitutions, as well as in the natal charts of men, here and there in a particular mode for those judging, we shall set forth in its own place; here it is incidentally sufficient to warn that it was entirely erroneous.

Chapter 10.

The Faces or Personalities or the Almugea of the Planets.

This dignity of the Planets is badly counted by Ptolemy, *Quadripartite*, Book 1, Chapter 10,[1] among the essential dignities, as will be shown below. And it is only a property of the 5 lesser Planets, or those that are secondary with respect to the primary

[1] These positions of the Planets are discussed in Quadripartite, Book 1, Chapter 23, not in Chapter 1.

Planets, the Sun and the Moon.

Moreover, it is said that each Planet has its own *face* or bears its own *person* with respect to the Sun and the Moon, when it is just as much distant from the Sun and vespertine or occidental to it, or from the Moon and matutine to it, as the domicile of the Planet following Leo, the domicile of the Sun, is distant from the beginning of Leo; or, as much as the domicile of the Planet preceding Cancer, the domicile of the Moon, is distant from the beginning of Cancer. For example, if Venus was occidental to the Sun and distant from it by 60 degrees, which is as much as the beginnings of Leo and Libra are distant from each other, Venus is said to have its own *face* with respect to the Sun; or, (it is said) by the Arabs to be in *almugea*[1] with the Sun. But if (the Planet is) oriental or matutine and is distant from the Moon by 60 degrees, which is as much as the beginnings of Taurus and Cancer are distant from each other, it is said to be in *almugea* with the Moon. And the reasoning is the same with the rest (of the Planets).

Having stated these things in advance, I say first. This dignity is not an essential one. For the essential dignities of the Planets are immutable, and they do not pass from one part of the Zodiac to another, as was shown above in connection with the domiciles, exaltations, and trigons; but this dignity can occur for a Planet in individual Signs of the Zodiac, due to simple orientality or occidentality with respect to the Sun and the Moon. therefore, it is not an essential dignity.

I say secondly, that with this dignity in place, I have destroyed the simple orientality of a Planet with respect to the Sun, when however Ptolemy himself and all the astrologers deservedly attribute great powers to Planets oriental to the Sun. For, about Mars in *almugea* with the Sun, that is occidental to the Sun, and with that same Mars oriental to the Sun, which one would Ptolemy say

[1] The Latin text has *Almugara* in error for *Almugea. Almugea* is the common Latin form of the Arabic word *al-muwâjaha* 'facing', which is a translation of the original Greek term *idioprosôpia* 'own face' that appears in both Ptolemy's *Tetrabiblos* and Vettius Valens's *Anthology*.

would prevail or be inferior? Besides, why have Ptolemy and the others not made the *almugea* of the Sun oriental and of the Moon occidental? For that would also have seemed to be more reasonable from Ptolemy's doctrine, which will have the Planets oriental to the Sun and occidental to the Moon to be strengthened.

Finally, there is no mention of the powers or effects of this dignity among the astrologers; and it is always with some aspect of a lesser Planet with a light with which its own force certainly coincides, so that it might be said to be from its own place; wherefore, I suspect that it has been taken from some of the fictions of the Arabs.[1] And therefore I impose an end here to the simple dignities of the Planets.

Chapter 11.

The Thrones, Seats, or Chariots of the Planets.

This dignity of the Planets is not simple, but mixed or composite from many essential things; for in the place cited above, Ptolemy, along with the rest of the astrologers, will have it that a Planet is said to be in its own *seat*, which, in the Sign that it occupies is allotted many essential dignities, and they think that rightly. For the one that in any Sign has many essential dignities, that one itself obtains the greatest authority in the Sign; whence, not without reason when occupying that Sign it must be said to sit as it were on its own *seat*. Moreover, since we only admit three essential dignities, namely domicile, exaltation, and trigon, it is plain when and where a Planet may be said to be on its own *chariot*. Indeed, it may have dignities of that sort in any house of the figure, such as the ASC, the MC, (the house) of the Sun, etc.; for if the ASC was in Aries, the Sun in the ASC will be at the same time strong by exaltation and trigon. And so with the rest.

And so, if the Sun is in Sagittarius it will simply be in its own trigon; but if it is in Aries or Leo, it will be in its own *seat*, because

[1] Not so! The Arabs got it from the Greeks, as Morin's citation from Ptolemy proves. See the preceding note.

in addition to (being in its) trigon, it has its domicile in Leo[1] and its exaltation in Aries; if Mars is in Capricorn, it will only be in its own exaltation; but if it is in Scorpio or in Aries, it will be in its own *throne*; and the reasoning is the same with the rest (of the Planets).

Chapter 12.

The Joys of the Planets.

The *joy* of a Planet is not its particular essential dignity, and it is neither a simple thing, nor a mixed one, and it is only proper for Saturn, Jupiter, Mars, Venus, and Mercury, each of which is allotted two domiciles in the Zodiac, of which that one was called the *joy* of the ruler that harmonized more with the ruler, either by reason of its principal nature, or by reason of its sex, or by reason of its more moderate effect or influx.

And indeed for the first mode, Saturn's *joy* will be Capricorn; this is indeed a cold Sign and with that it more harmonizes with the principal nature of Saturn, cold and dry (which is to it both elementarily and influentially, as was shown elsewhere), rather than to a hot and moist Sign; and so with the rest (of the Planets). In the second mode, Mars's *joy* will be Aries and not Scorpio, as astrologers have falsely supposed; for Mars is masculine in its sex, but Scorpio is feminine. Finally, in the third (mode), Aquarius will be the *joy* of Saturn, and Scorpio the *joy* of Mars, if indeed in Aquarius there is blended the cold and dry influx of Saturn, more than in Capricorn. And in Scorpio there is blended the hot and dry influx of Mars, more than in Aries. But because the third mode was only invented for our own sake, it is not natural to the Planets themselves, which the likeness of other physical causes, there they especially rejoice, where they find a greater similitude to nature, in addition to that, everything rejoices with something similar; therefore, the *joy* of a Planet will be properly defined in accordance with the two previous modes, which, where they agree in the same Sign,

[1] The Latin text has the symbol ☊ by error for the symbol ♌.

it will be the greatest *joy* of its ruler; otherwise, its nature as the first will have to be preferred to its sex. Therefore, from these causes the true *joy* of Saturn will be in Capricorn, of Jupiter in Sagittarius, of Mars in Aries, of Venus in Libra, and of Mercury in Virgo.

Chapter 13.

The Terms, Novenas, Decans, Dodecatemories, etc. of the Planets in the Individual Signs; Then, the Light and Smoky Degrees, the Pits, the Vacant Degrees, and the Monomoiriae.

Hitherto whole Signs of the Zodiac have been distributed to the Planets according to their commonly received essential dignities; and there is both the division of the Zodiac into 12 equal parts; then there is put above a natural distribution of these, or at least one depending upon a natural foundation, as is seen in Books 14 and 17. But as for the *terms*, *novenas*, *decans*, etc., the individual Signs are subdivided into diverse parts, which are again individually distributed to the individual Planets in accordance with the minor dignities mentioned above, which they also will have to be essential dignities that they have also introduced. But concerning these, this is my opinion.

The Devil, the worst enemy of men, having introduced blindness of mind into the human race through sin, little by little has diverted men from the true knowledge and worship of God, and he finally cast down the greater part of them into the pit of idolatry, so that not they not only paid the homage due to God alone to the Sun, the Moon, and the rest of the celestial bodies, but also to the vilest animals, and then to idols, the dead works of their own hands, and indeed to Demons themselves. And lest man, desirous by nature of knowing things, might recover the knowledge of the true God through the sciences, either those received from the tradition of Adam, or cultivated by the vivacity and inclination of intellect, but especially the celestial sciences, which above all the others are attested by God and His infinite goodness, wisdom, and providence;

the very bad Demons, either by their own inspiration or by a distorted natural light of men put under themselves polluted the celestial sciences among them with very many falsities, inventions, and superstitions—indeed, so that the truth, overwhelmed by their falsehoods, was not capable (of leading) them to the necessary acquaintance with God; but among some, overwhelmed by such deceit, they fell into contempt and derision, (which was) also another goal of the Devil.

From this situation, therefore, there came forth into astrology the *terms*, the *novenas*, the *bright and smoky degrees*, the *monomoiriae*,[1] etc., which are nothing more than the mere symbol of ineptitude, stupidity, and insanity of men, who were ignorant of the principles of this divine science, which the wiser astrologers have perpetually neglected. Moreover, the haters of astrology have made for themselves a very convenient opportunity to vilify, defame, and destroy the science.

But what is each of these dignities; and by what reasoning are the Signs divided among the individual Planets themselves; and it is indeed not pleasing to expound here these crazy things that are unworthy of our time; they may be left to stupid and ignorant people. But I do say this in a general way against their worthlessness. There is nothing occurring in the sublunary World about which from the above said dignities there cannot be at the same time true affirmation and denial; that is, there could be true (indications)

[1] These subdivisions of the signs have different origins. The *terms* were devised by the Alexandrians, but they left no explanation of the rationale behind their creation. The *novenas* or thirds of the *decans* are mentioned by Julius Firmicus Maternus, *Mathesis,* ii. 4, and were evidently part of Greek astrology; they passed to the Hindus and became an important part of their astrology; The *bright and smoky degrees* were part of a medieval elaboration that goes back to Firmicus, *Mathesis,* iv. 22, who called them *empty and full degrees;* They were evidently based upon a catalogue (now lost) of the longitudes of the fixed stars associated with the *decans.* The *monomoiriae* were a standard feature of Greek astrology, mentioned by Vettius Valens, *Anthology,* iv. 26, and elaborately set forth in tables by Paul of Alexandria, *Introduction,* Chapter 32; they were devised to designate a specific planetary ruler for each degree of the zodiac according to some arbitrary scheme.

from the *terms* and false ones from the *decans* or the *novenas*, etc., on account of the fact that the various divisions of the Signs and the distributions of the Planets are disagreeing with each other, as is seen among the authors. Add to these, that those divisions of the Signs and distributions of the Planets do not rest upon a natural foundation, and they are only fictions. And this is plainly proved because the division of each Sign into 30 degrees is not natural, but only devised for the convenience of calculation;[1] but the above said dignities are founded upon the hypothesis of that division; therefore, they are only fictitious. And this will be plainer from those tables of dignities. For among the Arabs,Saturn has its *terms* from 21 to 27 degrees in Taurus, its *decan* from 20 to 30 degrees, its *novena* (from zero) to 6 2/3 degrees, and its *dodecatemory* from 7 ½ to 10 degrees; and so with the others.

Nevertheless, all modern astrologers till now will indeed object to the *novenas*, *decans*, and all the rest being banished from the true science of astrology. And that I have wrongly rejected the terms, since they are universally approved and retained by Ptolemy and all astrologers.

But I reply that I not only marvel that philosophers, especially Christian ones, make use of these trifles of *novenas*, *decans*, *monomoiriae*, *pitted degrees*,[2] etc.; and have made them principles or foundations of their own judgments—thinking, with Julius Firmicus Maternus that there are great powers in them and great mysteries that must not be revealed to the multitude; but also that up to the present time they have retained them, although from Ptolemy alone their worthlessness can be most evidently proved, even though in *Quadripartite*, Book 3, Chapter 14, he will have the

[1] This is true. The Babylonians counted numbers to the base 60. They observed that there were 365 and a fraction days in a year, which was close to 6 X 60 = 360. So, when they invented the signs of the zodiac, they assigned 360 parts (or degrees) to the whole zodiac; and dividing that by 12, the number of signs, they got 30 degrees for each sign. And Morin is right: they did that arbitrarily for its convenience in calculating the positions of the Sun, Moon, and planets in the zodiac.

[2] *Pitted degrees* were a medieval term, perhaps an elaboration of the *bright and smoky degrees,* for which see the previous note.

anaereta not to kill when it runs to the *apheta* in directions if it is in the terms of a benefic Planet; and so he attributes no small force to the terms themselves.

For Ptolemy, in Book 1, chapters 18 & 19, expounds three kinds of terms, or a triple partition of the individual Signs, by those terms; that is, an Egyptian, Chaldean, and (one) of a certain old codex; of which he rejected the first two and followed the latter, in which Saturn, Jupiter, Mars, Venus, and Mercury are distributed to the individual Signs that are divided into 5 parts. For example, in Aries Jupiter has the first 6 degrees of that Sign for its terms according to the Chaldeans, Venus the 6 following, Mercury the 8 following, Mars the 5 following, and Saturn the last 5.[1] But in the Ptolemaic mode, Jupiter has the first 6, Venus the 8 following, Mercury 7, Mars 5, and Saturn the 4 last degrees; and so on for the individual Signs, with the Sun and Moon excluded. Moreover, Ptolemy offers some reasons for this diverse division and distribution, both for those modes that he rejected and for the one that he follows, but those (reasons) are in the truth of the thing merely inventions, equally lacking in a natural foundation like the novenas, the decans, etc., which are similarly divided and established; so that consequently Cardan frankly confessed in his *Commentary* that he found a great confusion in these various modes of terms; not content with which, he wanted also to devise an appropriate method for himself, in which each Sign is distributed to 7 Planets; and he gave both his reasons for it and a table in his *Book on the Judgments of Nativities*. And I once, adding inventions to inventions, thought up another mode of terms, also with more plausible reasons than (those given by) Ptolemy and Cardan; but what are they other than outstanding trifles? And so, both the terms and the rest (of these divisions) should be rejected from our astrology.[2]

[1] All of these numbers are wrong; and the sequence of planetary rulers is also wrong for the *Terms According to the Chaldeans,* for which Ptolemy, *Tetrabiblos* i. 21, gives Jupiter 8 degrees, Venus 7, Saturn 6, Mercury 5, and Mars 4. Actually, Morin has given (correctly, but with the wrong name) the *Terms According to the Egyptians,* for which see *Tetrabiblos* i. 20.

[2] But Placidus found the terms to be effective, thus disagreeing with Morin.

Moreover, this reason is offered by us as to why the terms have been used by Ptolemy and the rest of the astrologers hitherto. Certainly, Ptolemy in *Quadripartite*, Book 3, Chapter 10, wanted to have only 5 Significators to be directed in the natal figure for all the accidents of the native; namely, the ASC for health and travel; the Part of Fortune for finances; the Moon for the mind, morals, and association; the Sun for dignity and glory; as well as the MC for the rest of the actions of life and the procreation of children; but since the bodies and aspects of the Planets coming to those Significators would not satisfy all the accidents, either on account of the small number of Significators or the lack of promittors coming to them, they supposed that in addition to the bodies (of the Planets) and the aspects, there are still other promittors in the nature of things, and they could not conceive of any others than those terms, which they invented; and by the introduction of which, promittors were seldom lacking, from whose occurrence in the directions some reason for the effects or the accidents of the native might be found. And so, it is very frequent in Junctinus and the rest of the astrologers for a man to pass away by even a violent death from a direction of the ASC or of the *apheta* of a light to the terms of Saturn or Mars, or for a great dignity to come from a direction of the Sun to the terms of Jupiter or Venus, etc. But since it seemed very absurd to me to ascribe so great effects to such slim and controversial causes, which in the same way they were able to impute to *novenas*, *decans*, and *dodecatemoria*; finally, from a careful examination of directions and tireless study I have perceived those terms to be fictitious causes, and not only Significators that are directed, but also aspects that must be multiplied, from the nature of the thing; and so to find the true causes of all the native's accidents—but about these (we shall speak) more full in their own place, namely when the subject of directions is discussed. And about the essential dignities and debilities of the Planets, let what has been said already suffice; and let it be noted that every Planet that is located outside its own domicile, exaltation, or *trigon* is said by us to be peregrine; and consequently, peregrination is twofold—a simple kind without essential debility, such as the Sun in

Capricorn, but the other is mixed with an essential debility, such as the Sun in Aquarius, and this is a worse kind.

Chapter 14.

The Friendships and Enmities of the Planets among Themselves.

Having explained the essential dignities of the Planets above, and their elemental, influential, and analogical natures, it is an opportune time to add something here about their friendships and enmities among themselves; which, indeed, are handed down here and there by astrologers, but with absolutely no logical reasoning provided—indeed, occasionally contrary to reason, as when they assert Saturn to be a friend of the Sun and the Moon, which will be perceived below to be manifestly false. Besides, even so as between the elements fire and air are said to be friends, as well as earth and water, but fire and water are said to be enemies. So, among the Planets some are found to be contrary or inimical to others in their own effects. And it is no wonder that there are primary governors of the sublunar World differing among themselves in kind and powers of acting; which differences provide friendship or enmity. Moreover, since this friendship consists universally of some benefic concourse in sublunar effects, but especially in the generation of man, which is the most outstanding effect of the stars, while enmity consists of a malefic concourse; for that reason, it seems to us their friendship and enmity ought to be chosen from many categories, as follows.

First, therefore, the Planets that are similar in their elemental and vital qualities are mutual friends, such as the Sun and Jupiter in heat, likewise Jupiter and Venus; and then Venus and the Moon in humor.

Second. The Planets that are similar in benefic influences are mutual friends, such as the Sun and Jupiter for life and honors, Jupiter and Venus for good fortune, riches, children, and friends, and Venus and the Moon for spouses and lovers.

Third. Planets that are in fact not similar in their influences, but which by their mutual concourse produce a mixed benefice on something; these too are said to be friends in this (connection), such as Jupiter and Saturn for prudence, seriousness, and aptitude for doing great things; then, Saturn and Mercury for profundity of intellect; Mars and Mercury for diligence and activity and fraud.

Fourth. Those whose domiciles are placed in benefic aspect, such as Mars and the Sun, Jupiter and the Moon, and Saturn and Mercury.

But the (Planetary) enemies are said to be:

First. Those who have opposed domiciles; and so Saturn is an enemy of the Sun and the Moon; Jupiter is an enemy of Mercury; and Mars is an enemy of Venus. Or, those whose domiciles are square, such as the Sun and Mars; the Moon and Mars; and Saturn and Mars.

Second. Those contrary in their elemental qualities and intensely so, such as the Sun and Saturn in heat and cold; Saturn and the Moon in moistness and dryness; then Saturn and Venus; and also Mars and the Moon in active and passive qualities. For an intense contrariety makes for a violent concourse.

Third. Those that are contrary in their influences. Thus, Venus, the cause of love, peace, and leisure, is inimical to Mars, the cause of hate, wars, and hard labor; Saturn and Venus, for bodily beauty; and likewise, Saturn and the Sun. for honors, dignity, and fame, unless Saturn was determined in the figure to causing honors and was well disposed.

Fourth. Those that are similar in their elemental qualities, but with a ruinous excess, such as the Sun and Mars, on account of too much heat and dryness from the two of them; Saturn and the Moon, on account of the excessive cold from both; and Saturn and Mars, on account of the excessive dryness.

Fifth. Those similar in influential qualities that are malefic, such as Saturn and Mars, for dangers, depravity of morals, misfortunes, and violent death; the Moon and Mercury for inconstancy; Mars and Mercury, for fraud, impudence, and rashness; and the Sun and Mars, for haughtiness and arrogance.

From which it is plain that Saturn and Mars are enemies of the Sun and the Moon in almost everything. And besides that, two Planets can be said to be friends with respect to one (sort of) effect and enemies with respect to another; and consequently, the friendship and enmity of the Planets cannot be definitely declared in any nativity, unless notice is first taken as to whether both of them are determined to the same effect and with regard to what, such as life, honors, children, etc., and what sort of propensity both of them have for that effect, either by nature or by analogy.

It is also plain that Saturn is the worst of all the Planets, because its domiciles are only connected by opposition to the domiciles of the Sun and the Moon, and therefore it is most unfriendly to them.

Jupiter is the best of all, because its domiciles are only connected by trine with the domiciles of the Sun and the Moon; and consequently it is the most friendly to them.

Mars is partly a friend and partly an enemy both to the Sun and to theMoon, because Aries is square Cancer, and Scorpio is square[1] Leo; but Aries is trine Leo, and Scorpio is trine Cancer.

Venus is partly a friend and partly unfriendly, because Taurus is sextile Cancer and square Leo, and Libra is square Cancer and sextile Leo.

Finally, Mercury is only a friend of the lights, because Gemini is semi-sextile Cancer and sextile Leo; but Virgo is semi-sextile Leo and sextile Cancer.

And so, Jupiter, Mars, and Venus in their own diurnal domiciles are amicably joined to the domicile of the Sun, and in their nocturnal domiciles to the domiciles of the Moon. And it must be noted that the Planets that are rulers of the four cardinal Signs are plainly contrary in their elemental natures—namely, Mars and the Moon between themselves, and Venus and Saturn between themselves.

End of the Fifteenth Book.

---

[1] The Latin text has △ by mistake for □.

Index of Persons

Note: the characterization given for each person is not necessarily complete, but it represents the type of work that he did to which reference is made in the Preface or in the Translation or the footnotes

Bibliography

Campanella, Tommaso
Astrologicarum libri VII.
Frankfurt, 1630.

Cardan, Jerome
Clavdii Ptolemaei Pelusiensis
Libri Quatuor
De Astrorum Iudiciis cum expositione
Hieronymi Cardani. pp. 93-368
[Claudius Ptolemy of Pelusia's
Four Books on the Judgments of the Stars
with Jerome Cardan's Commentary]

Liber de Iudiciis Geniturarum. pp. 433-457
[A Book on the Judgments of Nativities]

[both works in vol. 5 of the omnibus edition of Cardan's
works published at Lyons in 1663.]
New York and London: Johnson Reprint, 1967. 10 vols. facs.
reprint

Dorotheus Sidonius
Carmen astrologicum.
[Astrological Poem]
[Arabic, Greek, and Latin text, with
an English translation of the Arabic]
Leipzig: B. G. Teubner, 1976. xx,444 pp. diagrs.

Firmicus Maternus, Julius
Matheseos libri VIII.
ed. by Kroll, Skutsch, and K. Ziegler
[Latin text, intro. and notes]
Leipzig: B. G. Teubner, 1968. 2 vols. reprint of 1913 ed.

Holden, James Herschel
A History of Horoscopic Astrology.
Tempe, Az.: A.F.A., Inc., 1996. paper xv,359 pp.
Tempe, Az.: A.F.A., Inc., 2006. paper xvii,375 pp.

Kepler, Johann
Tabulae RUDOLPHINAE...
[The Rudolphine Tables...]
[a complete set of tables of the motions
of the Sun, Moon, and Planets]
Ulm: Jonas Sauk, 1627.

Mersenne, Father Marin
Harmonicorum libri xii...
[Twelve Books of Harmonics...]
Paris: G. Baudry, 1648.

Morin, Jean Baptiste
Astrologia Gallica.
The Hague, Adrian Vlacq, 1661. folio xxxvi,784 pp.

Tabulae Rudolphinae ad meridianum
Uraniburgi supputatae a Joanne Baptita Morino...
[The Rudolphine Tables, Calculated by Jean
Baptiste Morin for the meridian of Uraniburg...]
Paris: J. LeBrun, 1650. 4to 117 pp. tables

Paul of Alexandria
Paulou Alexandreôs Eisagogika.
[Paul of Alexandria's Introduction]
[Greek text with Latin and German notes]
Leipzig: B. G. Teubner, 1958. xxvi,181 pp. diagrs.

Introduction
trans. from the Greek by James Herschel Holden
circulated privately xvii,102 pp. diagrs. tables

Pico della Mirandola, Giovanni, Count
In Astrologiam libri XII.
[Twelve Books Against Astrology]
Bologna: Benedictus Hectoris, 1496.

Pliny the Elder
Natural History.
trans. by H. Rackham, W.H.S. Jones, and D.E. Eicholz
Loeb Classical Library
Cambridge, Mass.: Harvard Univ. Press, and
London: William Heinemann, 1962. 10 vols. repr.

Ptolemy, Claudius
Tetrabiblos.
ed. & trans. by F.E. Robbins
Loeb Classical Library
London: William Heinemann, Ltd.
Cambridge, Mass.: Harvard Univ. Press, 1940. xxiv,466 pp.
diagrs. tables

Roger, Father Eugène
La Terre Saincte ou Description topographique…
des Saincts Lieux…et une rélation véritable de
Zaga Christ, prince d'Ethyopie, qui mourut
à Ruel prez Paris.
[The Holy Land or a Topographical Description…
of the Holy Places…and a True Account of
Zaga Christ, Prince of Ethiopia, who died at
Ruel, near Paris]
Paris: Antoine Bertier, 1646. 4to 440 pp.

Vettius Valens
Vetti Valentis Antiocheni Anthologiarum
Libri Novem./ edidit David Pingree
[Nine Books of Anthologies by Vettius
Valens of Antioch/ edited by David Pingree]

[Greek and Latin text with Latin intro. and notes]
Leipzig: B. G. Teubner, 1986. xxi,583 pp.

Jean-Baptiste Morin

Astrologia Gallica

Book Nineteen

The Elements of Astrology or the
Principles of Judgments

Translated from the Latin

By

James Herschel Holden, M.A.
Fellow of the American Federation of Astrologers

TABLE OF CONTENTS

Translator's Preface

Book 19 is one of the shortest books of the *Astrologia Gallica*, but it is an important book because it gives explicit definitions of astrological terms and many valuable rules for interpreting charts. It begins with the Definitions, then passes to Axioms and a Caution, and finally to 28 Theorems. Their main purpose seems to be to provide logical explanations of terms and their use in various configurations. Morin emphasizes that in interpreting a particular position or configuration in a chart both the characteristics of the influence and the characteristics of the native or the subject acted upon must be carefully considered in order to understand the action in a particular case. And he illustrates this by one of his favorite sayings, "The Sun hardens clay and melts wax," thus showing that the same celestial influence may have quite a different effect upon different subjects.

In discussing the Theorems, he sometimes states something that is a fallacy and then points out that it is contrary to an Axiom or Theorem previously stated, thus providing the proof of a Theorem by denying its opposite. After which he says, "Therefore," and cites the first word or words of the theorem.

Morin uses a number of words in a technical sense. I have rendered them by their most common English equivalent, even when their most common present-day meaning is not what he had in mind. An example is the Latin word *virtus*, which I have translated as 'virtue'. The Latin word's root meaning is 'strength', but it carries the implication of a particular kind of strength arising from the condition of its possessor. The English word 'virtue' now means mainly 'moral uprightness'. But to translate *virtus* as 'strength' is not adequate, for to Morin it referred to the characteristics of a planet as well as to its active force—'strength' does not carry that implication. So I have rendered it simply as 'virtue', but I have added a footnote to explain the term at its first occurrence.

The word *determinatio* 'determination' is another similar

case; it is a very important technical term in Morin's astrology. In classical Latin the word means 'boundary', 'conclusion', or 'end'. But Morin used it as a noun derived from the verb *determino*, whose secondary meaning was 'to fix or settle something'. Consequently, for him a 'determination' was the making of a particular signification, especially by the action of a celestial house on a planet that was in it or was its ruler. The usual sense of the word in English is 'maintenance of a fixed purpose to do something', although in legal circles it means 'a judicial decision' or 'the logical resolution of a question', which is somewhat like Morin's meaning.

Morin, like the older astrologers, also uses the Latin word *domus* 'house' to refer to a sign ruled by a particular Planet. So, like his younger English contemporary William Lilly, he speaks of Aries as being a 'house of Mars'. However, this usage is now obsolete. Modern astrologers only use the word 'house' to refer to a 'celestial house'. I have therefore translated *domus* as 'domicile' when it is used to refer to a sign rulership.

In the case of the Latin word *Caelum*, which means 'sky' or 'heavens', I have chosen to retain the Latin word in italics. Morin sometimes uses it to refer to the 'sky' in general, but more often he has in mind the orientation of the zodiac and the placement in it of the planets at a particular time, when it could be translated as 'celestial configuration', but *Caelum* is simpler.

James Herschel Holden
31 October 2006

ASTROLOGIA GALLICA

BOOK NINETEEN

PREFACE

A Principle is generally taken to be rightly defined as that thing which relates to another by reason of some original property. That is to say, because every Principle is in some way first, by that which it is said to be a Principle. And consequently, since for us this is the agenda of the Principles of Astrology, it is necessary that these things be first, and of the sort that Astrology can arise from them.

But now, every sort of natural science, by witness of Aristotle himself, takes its origin from the senses, or from experience, which in Book 10, Chapter 2, we have said to be three-fold—namely, intellectual, sensible, and intermediate or rational, which neither by sense alone, nor by reason alone, is had, but by the concourse of both. Therefore, since Astrology is a natural science, also one appointed to practice, even as Medicine; therefore, as it is founded on experience, so it will have to be founded on that experience. And consequently, to set forth Astrology scientifically, that which rational experience supplies us is going to be diligently noted, especially those things relating to the nativities of men, in which the force of the stars manifests itself more evidently. For, just as the science of Astronomy is born from the observations of the motions of the Planets and the Fixed Stars seen from the Earth in the Caelum, *so is Astrology begot from the phenomena, or the effects of the influences of those same bodies seen in the horoscopes of men being born here. And as denying that the location of the stars, or their places set forth by skilled astronomers in tables, can be related to the instruments by means of which those places are measured, so is denying that the Principles of Astrology must be related to the charts of their lives and their life or to their accidents. And just as fire is hot, or as the magnet attracts iron, by no reasoning, but only by sense or by sensible experience does it become known. So, the Sun does one thing in Aries and another in Taurus; then, one thing in trine to Mars and another in its opposition, as well as one thing in the 1st house of the chart and another in the 12th; the truth is that which has only become known by rational experience; and although that experience or those effects of the celestial bodies have their own causes or Principles in their bodies, which are their formal virtues,*[1] *yet because these are not known to us per se, but [only] through their effects, which are for us the first Principles of knowing their virtues, they will, therefore, be for us the first Principles of learning and teaching astrology itself.*

Besides, among mathematicians they are accustomed to expound three scientific kinds of Principles—namely, Definitions, Postulates, and Axioms, which are said to be the Theorems of science. We shall, therefore, try here to emulate them as far as the matter of Astrology allows.

DEFINITIONS.

There is no need here to define the terms of Astrology, which are the Planets, the Apects, the Antiscions, the Houses of the figure, the Domiciles of the Planets, Exile, Exaltation, Fall, and similar terms, which we have already expounded in their own places. But we shall only define the following items that relate to what we have proposed, which have not yet been discussed.

1. The celestial chart is the position of the stars in the *Caelum*, taken at some moment of time, with respect to some particular

[1] The word *virtue is* used as a technical term to represent the characteristic influence of a Planet.

point or place on the face of the Earth, just as that position is distributed into the parts of that whole mundane space, which we call the houses of the chart.

2. The ruler of a sign is the Planet of which that sign is its own domicile.

3. The ruler of a Planet is another Planet that is the ruler of the sign in which the first Planet is located.

4. The ruler of a house is the Planet that is the ruler of the sign occupying that house.

5. The ruler of a celestial chart is the Planet that in that chart excels the rest of the Planets by virtue of its own rulership of the principal places of the chart.

6. A significator is the cusp of some particular house, or a Planet signifying some effect by reason of its location or rulership in the chart.

7. To act *per se* is to produce an effect by its own virtue.

8. To determine *actively* is to apply an efficient cause, either universal or not specific, to some kind of an effect.

POSTULATES

First. A celestial figure can be erected from ephemerides or tables of the celestial motions for any moment of time for any place on Earth.

Second. A man provided with sense and reason can observe something in the natal horoscopes of men whether it is both the parts of the *Caelum* and the stars, then what they do in [the lives of] those men, since the country folk observe something about the Moon and a little about the Planets, and then about the Fixed Stars, having some rougher knowledge and without charts, in agriculture.

Astrological Axioms, whose Truth rational Experience makes known.

Axiom I.

A Planet does one thing in one house of a celestial figure and another kind of thing in another house. Which is also true of the Fixed Stars and the signs of the zodiac.

The truth of this axiom is based upon rational experience, or astrological observation, whether this is done at one time or at different times. For at the same moment of time, the same Planet is in all the houses of the celestial figure with respect to the whole Earth. As when the Sun is in the 1st house in Spain; it is at the same time in the 12th house in Hungary; in the 11th for the Syrians and the Persians; for the Indians near the Ganges, in the 10th; for the Chinese or the Japanese, in the 9th; etc., as astronomy teaches. Moreover, it is perceived by the Spanish to act upon those things being born, then upon the life of a man, his character, his intelligence; by the Hungarians, to act upon illnesses, enemies, imprisonment; by the Syrians and Persians, upon friends; by the Indians, upon actions and honors; by the Chinese, upon religion and the journeys of the native; and so on in the rest of the houses; if in fact for every nation, it judges about the essential things signified by each house, and by the Planet occupying that house; but these effects are diverse in kind. Therefore, the same Planet does something…, etc.

But at different times it is also established that however many times the Sun is found with the dawning light in the 1st house, whether this is at the same place on Earth, or in different places, the Sun itself acts upon the life, character, and intelligence of the native; if it is in the 12th, upon his illnesses and enemies, etc. Therefore, the Axiom is true, and it will be proved by similar experience with the Fixed Stars and the signs of the zodiac that are called twelfths.[1] And concerning these, there are Aphorisms contained here and there in the books of the astrologers. Therefore, the same thing [is true for another] Planet, etc.

---

[1] Morin often calls the signs *duodecatemoria* or *twelfths,* but I generally translate those words as *signs*.

Axiom II.

In the same house of the figure, the Sun does one thing per se, the Moon another, Saturn still another, etc. Which is also true of the Fixed Stars and the signs.

It is plain from experience, for the Sun, especially if it is alone in the 1st house, and in the solar sign Leo, makes the native *bilious,*[1] magnanimous, generous, and famous. Similarly, if the Moon is there in Cancer, it makes the native *phlegmatic,*[2] timid, and inconsistent. Similarly, with Saturn in Aquarius he will be *melancholy,*[3] serious, prudent, hard-working, and patient; and so with the rest of the Planet—not only in the 1st house, but also as observed in the other houses—concerning which matter there are aphorisms sparsely in the books of the astrologers, but confused and full of flaws, as is made manifest elsewhere. Therefore, in the same house of the figure, the Sun does one thing, the Moon another, etc.—at least per se and by their own virtue.

And the same thing must be said about the Fixed Stars and the signs. For Spica Virginis in the ASC or the 1st house bestows placid manners, the Heart of Scorpio[4] bestows fierce ones. Moreover Leo in the 1st or in another house acts like the Sun because it acts with the solar virtue, and it therefore does almost the same thing as the Sun. And similarly, Cancer does almost the same thing as the Moon; Aquarius almost the same thing as Saturn; and the rest of the signs, almost the same thing as their rulers, to the nature of which they were determined at the beginning of the World, as was explained by us in Book 14, section 1, Chapter 5, and which experience proves.

---

[1] One personality type of the Four Humors, also called *choleric.* A charismatic, vigorous person.

[2] Another type of the Four Humors. A *phlegmatic* person is compassionate and reliable.

[3] Still another type of the four Humors. A *melancholic* person is depressive and a perfectionist.

[4] Antares or a Scorpii.

Axiom III.

The same Planet does one thing by its own conjunction with another Planet, or in one house of the figure, and another thing by its own opposition, still another by its own trine, and yet another by its own square.

Experience also proves this, namely because if Saturn is opposed to or square the Sun, it renders the effects of the Sun inferior or more difficult than if it was posited in its trine or sextile. Similarly, if Saturn is in trine the ASC, not withstanding its own malefic nature, it would confer something good with regard to character, intelligence, and life; but if it was opposite or square the ASC, it would undoubtedly produce bad effects with regard to those same things. And the logic is the same for the rest of the Planets, connected both among themselves, as well as with other houses of the figure—as about this matter aphorisms and experience are found here and there among astrologers. Therefore, the same Planet…, etc.

Axiom IV.

The square of Saturn or Mars does one thing, and the square of Jupiter or Venus does another.[1]

It is plain from experience that the squares of Saturn and Mars are absolutely malefic; however, the squares of Jupiter and Venus are not, at least not per se; similarly, the trine of Jupiter or Venus is entirely benefic; but the trine[2] of Saturn or Mars is not entirely benefic, And the logic is the same for the rest of the aspects, which must at least be understood per se.

[1] The Latin text has 'the square of Jupiter or Mars', but plainly this is an error for 'Jupiter or Venus'.

[2] The Latin text has the square symbol, but this is an error for the trine symbol.

Axiom V.

The same Planet does one thing when it is the ruler of the 1st house, another kind of thing when it is the ruler of the 2nd house, and still another kind of thing when it is the ruler of the 3rd house, and so on with the rest of the houses.

This is also proved by experience. Because the ruler of the 1st house certainly acts upon the life, character, and intelligence of the native, even though it is not [present] by body in the 1st house. The ruler of the 2nd acts on riches, and so on with the rest. Concerning which, the books of the astrologers abound in experiences and aphorisms.

Axiom VI.

The same point of the Caelum, *if it is the place of the Sun, is powerful with the force or the solar influence with respect to the native, as long as he lives here. If it is the place of Saturn, it is powerful with the saturnine force, and so on with the rest of the Planets. Similarly, that same point of the* Caelum, *if it is the place of the ASC in any nativity, is powerful with the force relating to the life of the native; if it is in the MC, it is powerful with the force relating to his actions and profession; and so on with the rest of the houses. And the logic is the same with the rest of the aspects of the Planets.*

The truth of this Axiom is plain from the daily proofs of the directions of these places, and from the transits of the Planets through those places, during the life of the native. If indeed a transit of Venus, ruler of the 5th, through the ASC of a man who is by nature lustful, it stimulates him to lust whenever that transit is made; and Mars, ruler of the 7th transiting through the ASC, excites him to quarrels, lawsuits, murders, etc., especially in the case of men who are bilious by nature, which many times would not happen, unless there was a force in the place of the ASC inclining towards [that] character of the native, which is potent as long as he lives.

Axiom VII.

The same point of the Caelum that is the place of the Sun for one native, can be the place of Saturn, Jupiter, Mars, Venus, Mercury, or the Moon for another.

This is plain from the motion of the planets, which individually pass through the individual signs of the zodiac, when they run through them. Therefore, Saturn in the nativity of one man can be found in the same place in the zodiac that the Sun holds in the nativity of another man.

Axiom VIII.

Whatever is acting per se, acts only in accordance with its own force and nature.

For if it should happen that it acts in accordance with an alien force, it will not therefore be acting per se, contrary to the seventh hypothesis and Definition.

Axiom IX.

Whatever is being affected is affected in accordance with its own nature. Or whatever is received is received in the manner of the receiver.

For when the Sun heats, it hardens clay, it liquefies wax,[1] it stimulates the growth of a plant, it excites the senses of a brute animal. But in addition to the reason concerning the force of the intelligent heat, it awakens the nature of investigating. And similarly, the Sun is influencing the same thing in a brute animal and a man, and it affects each of these in accordance with its own nature. And finally, it does one thing in the case of a prince and another in the case of a countryman, even though it is done by entirely the same virtue.

---

[1] A favorite saying of Morin. See Origen (3rd cent.), *The First Principles,* I, 1,11.

Axiom X.

The same thing remaining the same always does the same thing to the same thing. Which we have already discussed in Book , Chapter 15.[1]

It seems to us that this Axiom ought to be the principal one handed down scientifically for astrology, as will be more evidently plain below; and consequently, its truth will have to be explained a little more fully. Moreover, it can be proven not only by experience, but also by that most universal and metaphysical principle of principles—that it is impossible for the same thing both to be and not to be. For if the same thing does not always do the same thing to the same thing; it therefore does sometimes do something different. However, the diversity of effect can only be, either by virtue of the thing acting, which by its kind, intention, configuration, or application is diverse; or by the subject being acted upon, which in kind, disposition, or application is diverse. Which said, either the one acting will not be the same, or the one being acted upon will not be the same, contrary to the hypothesis. Therefore, the same remaining the same always does the same thing to the same thing. Furthermore, because for the truth of this principle, that the identity of both the thing acting and the thing being acted upon is not required, is proved from this—because otherwise the same globe to be made hot while acting on two homogenous globules of wax, equal in mass, and similarly applied, would produce in them different effects; or on the contrary, two globules of hot iron, equal, and similarly applied to the same globule of wax, would produce different effects on that, which will be rejected by the reason of experience.

But if the one acting, or the one being acted upon, or the application should admit any diversity, then already the same effect would not be produced, but it would only admit a difference, such as they admit, either the cause acting from the thing acting, or being acted upon by the thing being acted upon, or both of them by

[1] The Book number is missing.

both of them, or the application by the application. And this is the prime cause of all things, why to twins not being born at the same moment, it plainly occurs that the same things are not happening, although they are both human, engendered by the same father and the same mother, born in the same place; namely, because the constitution of the *Caelum*, which is their producing cause, does admit some amount of diversity, seeing that it is of no small moment; as if having put the interval between the nativities at only four minutes of the hour, during which the position of the *Caelum* is varied by one degree, Saturn was for one of them in the ASC, for the other in the 12th house; moreover, with Saturn, ruler of the ASC for the one, in the 1st degree of Capricorn. Also, why a countryman and a noble being born at the same moment in the same place, have accidents not of the same kind or the same magnitude, although from the constitution of the *Caelum*, both are the same; namely, because the subjects are not the same in disposition, for one arises from common stock, the other from a noble class, and also both are from parents strongly diverse in power. finally, why men different in their parents, class, and born at different times; or from the same parents but at different times, experience different accidents; namely, because the causes, both those acting and those experiencing, always admit some differences among themselves; moreover, the difference in sex also relates to this.

And so, in order that the truth of the Axiom may be better perceived, it will have to be understood thus: The same thing active in kind and disposition (under which its concourse and application are understood), and much more if it is also the same in number (such as the Sun, the Moon, Saturn, etc.), does the same thing in kind and in intention [when acting] upon a passive thing, that is the same in kind and disposition. Which explanation removes all the ambiguity and difficulty, as will be more plainly evident below.

WARNING.

Perhaps it will seem rash to many to want to expound demonstrations of judicial astrology for the eyes of philosophers, since this has hitherto not only been unheard of, but also impossible to believe. Nevertheless, having set forth the Axioms above, whose truth is plain by rational experience; such as, fire burns that is felt by experience; from which there can certainly be deduced many Theorems that comprise the whole science of astrology, at least universally. Therefore, let there be:

Theorem I.

The Individual Houses of the Celestial Figure differ among themselves in their Virtue or Property.

For the same Planet does one kind of thing in the 1st house of the natal figure, another thing in the 2nd, and still another thing in the 3rd; and so on with the rest of the houses, also at the same moment of time, according to the first Axiom. Therefore, since the diversity of effect cannot be sought from the diversity of the Planet, or from its state in the *Caelum*, which is the same at the same instant of time with respect to the whole Earth, nor from some specific diversity of the subject in the nativities of men, it will necessarily have to be sought from the diverse nature and property of the houses in which the Planet is found, and by which it is applied in diverse ways to the same kind of subject. Therefore, angular houses differ in virtue, which was shown [previously].

Theorem II.

The Individual Planets differ among themselves at least in their Influential Nature and Virtue.

For the Sun does one thing influentially in the 1st house, as was explained by us in Book 12, Section 3, chapter 5; the Moon does another thing; Saturn still another, etc., per Axiom 2; and the logic is the same with every other house, whatever the celestial state of those Planets is. Therefore, since the difference of effect cannot be sought from that house that is the same for the individual Planets, and not from their celestial state; and finally, it cannot be sought from a specific difference of subjects when men are put as subjects; but it will necessarily have to be sought from the different nature and influential virtue of the individual Planets. Therefore, the individual Planets differ among themselves in their influential nature; which had to be shown here, even though it was already shown elsewhere in Book 9, Section 3, Chapter 2.

Theorem III.

The Individual signs of the Zodiac differ among themselves in their Nature and Virtue—either elemental or influential or both.

For Leo in the 1st house makes the native to be of a bilious temperament and solar by its influence; Cancer there makes him phlegmatic and lunar by its influence, per Axiom 2. And although Aries and Leo makes natives of bilious temperament, yet Aries makes them martial by its influx and Leo makes them solar; Similarly, although Aries and Scorpio make them martial by their influx, yet Aries makes them bilious by temperament and Scorpio makes them phlegmatic. Moreover, Aries and Taurus make them different in temperament and influx; and so with the other signs. Therefore, since this diversity cannot be sought from the 1st house, which is the same for the individual signs, nor from the Planets occupying the signs, because the signs empty of Planets admit the same diversity of effects, nor finally from a specific difference of subject when men are put as the subjects, it remains that it should be sought from the diverse nature and virtue of the individual signs. Therefore, ...etc.

Theorem IV.

The aspects of each Planet are diverse in kind; they differ among themselves in Virtue or in the quantity of their Virtue.

For Saturn does one thing when it is opposite or square the Sun or the ASC, and another thing when it is in trine or sextile to the Sun or the ASC, per Axiom 3. That is, each Planet impedites and harms by its own aspects when they are the square or opposition. However, by the trine and the sextile it benefits and helps in accordance with its own nature, at least in the nativities of men. But the opposition ray is more harmful than that of the square, and that more than the quintile. And similarly, the trine is more beneficial than the sextile and that more than the semi-sextile. And since these effects are observed to be from the Planets connected among themselves by these aspects, or with the houses of the figure, whatever is the remaining celestial state of the aspecting Planets, must necessarily be attributed to those aspects. Therefore, the aspects of each Planets…, etc.

Theorem V.

Not all of the fixed Stars are of the same Nature and Virtue

For Spica Virginis does one thing in the 1st house, and the Heart of Scorpio[1] does another, per Axiom 2. And also to the same kind of subject; therefore, they are of diverse virtue.

Theorem VI.

The forces of the Celestial Bodies are mingled in turn in the Subject experiencing them, as in a man.

For the Sun does one thing in the 1st house with regard to temperament, the Moon does another, Saturn still another, etc., per Axiom 2. But the temperament arises from the concourse and mixture of diverse quantities. Consequently, if the Sun and Saturn were together in the 1st house, the temperament would neither be simply bilious from the Sun, nor simply melancholic from Saturn, but mixed by both from both Planets, and [therefore] something intermediate between the simply bilious solar temperament and the simply melancholic saturnian temperament. Therefore, the elemental forces of the Planets are mingled in a man with regard to his temperament. And by similar reasoning, it will be proved that their influential forces are mingled with regard to character, intelligence, etc., and the reasoning is the same for the other houses and Planets, and also for the fixed stars and the signs. Therefore the Theorem is established.

---

[1] Antares or α Scorpii.

SCHOLIUM

Hence in fact it is plain that it is not rightly said that the Sun is in this or in that sign, but rather that in this or in that sign, it produces this or that effect.

Theorem VIII.

The same Planet does the same thing in kind with the same Sign of the Zodiac, both elementally as well as influentially.

This Theorem can be looked at in two ways. First, universally, and according as a Planet and a sign are only looked at in the *Caelum*, pouring out their own forces from it universally and indiscriminately upon the Earth. And so the Theorem is true. For the same Planet with the same sign is the same remaining the same; it will, therefore, do the same thing in kind with regard to the same thing, per Axiom 9; that is, with regard to sublunar things seen universally; that is, it will pour out the same force on those sublunar things. Although it may not always produce the same effect on them, because the sublunar things are not perpetually of the same passive disposition seen universally, as is had in the explanation of Axiom 9.

Secondly, it can be looked at in a particular manner. Taking the same subject in kind and the same application to it in kind—as from the 1st house of the figure. For the same Planet in the same sign [acting] from the same house is the same remaining the same; it will, therefore, do the same thing of its kind on the same kind for a particular subject, according to Axiom 9. And it will do that both elementarily as well as influentially, for it always remains the same mixture, or the same concourse of virtues, both elementally and influentially.

Theorem VIII.

No Planet does the same thing in different Signs of the Zodiac, at least not both elementally and influentially.

For the individual signs of the Zodiac differ in virtue among themselves, per Theorem III. And consequently, the same Planet in different signs is not the same in virtue remaining the same; whence it will not do the same thing in each one, according to Axiom 9.

Theorem IX.

Two Planets do not do the same thing separately in the same sign of the Zodiac.

For individual Planets differ among themselves in virtue, per Theorem II. And consequently, two Planets separately in the same sign are not the same in virtue, remaining the same. Whence, they do not do the same thing, according to Axiom 9.

Theorem X.

The same Planet does the same thing in the same house of the figure.

For the same Planet seen separately is the same remaining the same; then too it is similarly affected by reason of its celestial state, that is by reason of the sign that it occupies, and by its connection with the other Planets. Therefore, both viewed separately and affected similarly, it will do the same thing in the same place, according to Axiom 9. Or rather, however it is affected, it will still always be said to do the same thing in general—namely, to the extent that it will affect the native by reason of the same kind of accident. If indeed the Planet is in the 1st house, it always acts upon the life, character, and intelligence of the native; in the 2nd house, on his wealth; in the 10th on his actions, profession, and dignities—giving, taking away, denying, perfecting, depriving, or in general making him fortunate or unfortunate, according to the celestial state of the Planet and its force and individual nature. Therefore, a Planet does the same thing…, etc.

Theorem XI.

No Planet does the same thing in different houses of the figure.

For the individual houses of the celestial figure differ among themselves in virtue, per Theorem I. And therefore the same Planet in different houses is not the same in virtue or in application; therefore, it will not do the same kind of thing, per Axiom 9; for although opposite houses may be thought to be of the same virtue in a way, on account of that same line of opposition, the direction of the ASC to Jupiter in the 2nd will affect health, but to an opposition of Jupiter from the 8th, it will rather occasion an illness or a danger to life. But it must be said otherwise about the malefic Planets, because both their body and their opposition is bad; and therefore, both death, or a very dangerous illness, or a danger to life happens equally from the direction of the ASC to Mars in the 2nd and to its opposition from the 8th. Nevertheless, because the opposition of the Planet is at least evil, but also the body of a malefic, whatever there is of good or evil in a Planet has an influx, as we have said elsewhere. And besides, a Planet in the 2nd or in the 8th does not project the same aspects to the rest of the houses. It is rightly said that from different houses even the opposite one will do different things.

Theorem XII.

Two Planets do not do the same thing separately from the same house of the figure.

For the individual Planets differ among themselves in virtue, per Theorem II. And therefore, posited separately in the same house, they are not the same in virtue, although they are the same in application; therefore, they do not do the same thing, per Axiom 9.

Theorem XIII.

No Planet alone does that which it does when connected to another body or aspect.

For the individual Planets differ among themselves in virtue, per Theorem II. And also their aspects differ, per Theorem IV. Therefore, a Planet seen solitarily is not the same in active virtue as it is when connected to the body or aspect of another Planet, especially as the forces of the Planets concurring by body or by aspect are produced in a subject receiving them, as in a man, per Theorem VI. Therefore, no Planet does the same thing by its virtue [alone],... etc.

Theorem XIV.

The same Planet does the same thing in the same manner when connected to the same other Planet or to the same cusp.

For connected in the same manner to the same Planet or cusp, it is the same remaining the same. Therefore, for this reason and per se it does the same thing, according to Axiom 9.

Theorem XV.

No Planet does the same thing in different ways when it is connected to a particular Planet or cusp, as when it is connected to another one.

For the Planets and the cusps differ among themselves in virtue, per Theorems I & II. Therefore a Planet conjoined to one [particular] Planet or cusp is not the same as when it is connected to another one. Therefore, it will not do the same thing, according to Axiom 9.

Theorem XVI.

No Planet does the same thing in a different way when it is connected to the same other Planet or cusp.

For the individual aspects differ among themselves in virtue, per Theorem IV. Therefore, a Planet connected in a different manner to the same other Planet or cusp is not the same; whence it will not do the same thing, per Axiom 9.

Theorem XVII.

Two Planets do not do the same thing separately due to the kind of their aspects.

For the individual Planets differ in virtue among themselves, per Theorem II., but the aspects follow the nature of the Planets from which they come forth; for the square of Saturn does one thing, and the square of Jupiter does another, per Axiom 4. Therefore, two Planets with the same kind of aspect are not more the same actively than those same two Planets that differ among themselves in virtue. Therefore, they do not do the same thing, per Axiom 9.

Theorem XVIII.

The Virtue of the houses of the celestial figure is not in itself productive of effects, but it is determinative of the Virtue of the celestial bodies to kinds of effects by the Virtue of each house or the property of the concurrent things.

This Theorem is understood about the primary houses. And it is proved thus: for the essence of those houses is materially only a mundane space, from [what is said in] Book 18, Section 3, Chapter 3. With which space no active virtue coincides per se; but its formal essence consists only in the relationship of the location of that space to the place on Earth in which a particular person is born. Moreover, the relationship is not active in itself; therefore, the virtue of the houses of the celestial figure are not active either partly from their material essence or partly from their formal essence, nor is it productive of an effect; therefore, [the effects] are produced by the [celestial] bodies alone; and since they do not have from themselves, but from the houses, that they do one thing in the 1st house and another thing in the 2nd, etc., per Theorem I; they will, therefore, only have this [effect] from those houses by active determination, in accordance with the property of each house, as was explained by us in Book 21, Section 3, Chapter 1.

Theorem XIX.

The influence of each Planet is absolutely universal in efficiently causing things per se.

For [according to] Axiom 1, a Planet in the 1st house acts upon the life, the temperament, the character, and the intelligence of the native; in the 2nd it acts upon his wealth; in the 3rd, upon his brothers and relations; etc. This action is, moreover, simultaneous in all the astronomical houses of the figure on the whole Earth; where, consequently it acts at the same time with respect to the different natives on all the classes of accidents that can happen to the natives. Therefore, its force, [which is] absolutely universal of itself, is in acting and causing.

And the same thing must be said about the Fixed Stars and the signs, not only with regard to man, but with regard to all other subjects. Therefore, ...etc.

Theorem XX.

The influence of each Planet is in itself unique and invariable throughout its motion in the signs.

This is proved, both because the influence and virtue of a Planet is formal, as was said in Book 12, Section 3, Chapter 2. And also because if that same Planet was multiplex, it would not have the same influence in each sign, nor the same influence in each house of the figure, etc., but having taken away even the rest of the things by which its effects can be varied in kind, the Planet itself would do different things by itself in the same sign; and this however is contrary to Axioms 1 & 2, etc. Besides, since the same Planet does one thing in Aries, and another thing in Taurus, if upon leaving Aries it was bereft of all its virtue, and when entering Taurus it donned a new virtue, it would follow that all the Planets in the same sign would don the same virtue; and consequently, they would do the same thing in the same sign, contrary to Axiom 2. Therefore, [the Planet's virtue] is not variable due to its motion through the signs. And therefore, the influence of each Planet..., etc.

Theorem XXI.

No Planet restrains the influence of another Planet from making its influx and acting on sublunar things, even though it can restrain its elemental force.

For if the Moon also ruling the body of Saturn would restrain its influence, then the Moon by itself would do influentially what it does conjoined to Saturn, contrary to Theorem XIII; therefore..., etc. However, that one Planet can restrain the elemental force of another is evidently plain in the case of eclipses of the Sun, especially total eclipses, in which the Moon by the opacity and density of its own body restrains the light and heat of the Sun, at least lest it flow towards the Earth.

Theorem XXII.

Each Planet can do something on any kind of body when this is naturally produced.

For if there is given any kind of generative body on which Saturn can do nothing, but the Moon can; and, at the moment of birth of that body, the Moon is conjoined to Saturn, it will not produce the same effects from them conjoined that the Moon alone would produce, per Theorem XIII. And therefore, Saturn will be the cause of the diversity—not indeed by hindering the force of the Moon from making an influx and acting, per Theorem XXI. Therefore, by imprinting the proper force on the effect, by which the virtue of the Moon similarly imprinted is extended, it is produced or altered by the mixture; for which reason it will have to be stated that Saturn can act on that body, contrary to the hypothesis.

It is also proved from the figure of the birth of every natural body, for any Planet in its ASC will affect that in various ways according to the nature of the thing acting and the thing being acted upon. Therefore..., etc.

Theorem XXIII.

No Planet can produce everything on any kind of body, such as plagues, sterilities, constitutions of the air, wars, etc.

For no Planet does the same thing alone that it does when connected to another Planet, per Theorem XIII. Therefore, it cannot do everything on every kind of body. And that is plain in nativities, namely because the same Planet is not the cause and the significator of all the accidents pertaining to the twelve houses of the figure. This is also demonstrated in another way thus: let there be an action on a man being born with the Moon conjunct Saturn; it will not produce the same effect as it would from the Moon conjunct Mars, per Theorem XV. But if it is supposed that the Moon is capable of doing everything to that man, it would be able to do alone what it does when conjoined to Saturn; and similarly, the same thing that it does when conjoined to Mars. And therefore [it would do] the same thing when conjoined to Saturn as it does when conjoined to Mars, contrary to Theorem XV. Therefore…, etc.

Theorem XXIV.

The virtue of two Planets cannot be the same on anything being born, at least not influentially.

For if it were supposed that the virtue of Saturn and Mars is the same on anything being born, the Moon will then have the same effect conjoined to Mars as she has when conjoined to Saturn, per Axiom 9. For the Moon with the virtue of Saturn will be the same with the virtue of Mars; but that is contrary to Theorem XV. Therefore..., etc.

Theorem XXV.

The same Planet with the same influential virtue does different things simultaneously on the same things being born just now.

For in the first place, the Planet affects the native by reason of the house of the figure in which it is posited, per Axiom 1. Then, by reason of the house or houses that it rules, per Axiom 4. And finally by reason of the houses or in those houses of the Planets that it aspects, per Axiom 3. Therefore…, etc.

Theorem XXVI.

No Planet does the same thing by its influential virtue on different kinds of subjects or even on those only differing in some way.

For everything is experienced in accordance with its proper

nature, or whatever is received is received according to the manner of the one receiving it, per Axiom 8. Therefore, since the natures of a Planet, of a brute animal & a man, and then of a dog & a hare, are different, the same Planet will therefore do different things at least influentially on those individuals, also too on the son of a prince and the son of a countryman, as well as on a boy and a girl, being born at the same time in the same place, although they are being affected by the same virtue. Therefore, no Planet..., etc.

Theorem XXVII.

Two Planets separately do not produce per se the same effect on the same subject that receives it, at least not influentially.

This is proved first because the individual Planets have natures and forces of acting proper to themselves, at least influentially, per Theorem II., and anyone of them acts in accordance with its own force and nature, per Axiom 7. Therefore, on the same subject Saturn will produce a saturnian effect, and Mars a martial effect, which differ in kind.

Second, let it be supposed that Saturn and Mars will have the same effect separately on the same subject; the virtue of both of them will therefore be the same with regard to that subject; for if it were different, it would not do the same thing, but something different, per Axiom 9. And therefore the Moon will be able to do the same thing on the subject when it is conjunct Mars as when it is conjunct Saturn, per Axiom 9. But this is contrary to Theorem XV. Therefore..., etc.

Theorem XXVIII.

A Planet outside of its own domicile does something by reason of the house of the figure in which it is posited, and another thing by reason of its rulership of another house.

Otherwise, it does the same thing by reason of both. And because Mars rules the two signs Aries and Scorpio, which cannot be in the same house of the figure, and the reason is proper for both signs; therefore, either Mars remaining the same will do different things in each house, contrary to Axiom 9, or it will do the same things as the ruler of different houses, contrary to Axiom 4. Therefore the Planet…, etc.

Moreover, in the case of the Sun, which has only one sign, it is proved thus: the Sun does the same thing by reason of the house that it is in and by reason of the other house that it rules. Therefore, the property and determinative force of the houses will be the same, contrary to Theorem I. therefore, a Planet that is outside its own domicile…, etc.

End of Book 19.

INDEX OF PERSONS

BIBLIOGRAPHY

Astrologia Gallica.
[French Astrology]
The Hague: A. Vlacq, 1661. folio. Pref., 784 pp.
Astrologia Gallica: Book Fourteen
trans. by James Herschel Holden
Tempe, Az.: A.F.A., Inc., 2006.

Astrologia Gallica: Book 18.
trans. by Pepita Sanchis Llacer and
Anthony Louis LaBruzza
Tempe, Az.: A.F.A., Inc., 2003.

The Morinus system of Horoscope Interpretation.
[Astrologia Gallica:Book Twenty One]
trans. from the Latin by Richard S. Baldwin
Washington, D.C.: A.F.A., Inc., 1974.

CPSIA information can be obtained
at www.ICGtesting.com
Printed in the USA
BVHW070944230819
556546BV00001B/80/P